BUSINESS ECONOMICS IN A RAPIDLY-CHANGING WORLD

TAXING U.S. MULTINATIONAL CORPORATIONS

POLICY OPTIONS AND CONSIDERATIONS

Business Economics in a Rapidly-Changing World

Additional books in this series can be found on Nova's website under the Series tab.

Additional E-books in this series can be found on Nova's website under the E-book tab.

America in the 21st Century: Political and Economic Issues

Additional books in this series can be found on Nova's website under the Series tab.

Additional E-books in this series can be found on Nova's website under the E-book tab.

BUSINESS ECONOMICS IN A RAPIDLY-CHANGING WORLD

TAXING U.S. MULTINATIONAL CORPORATIONS

POLICY OPTIONS AND CONSIDERATIONS

ANGELIQUE GILDER
EDITOR

nova publishers
New York

For permission to use material from this book please contact us:
Telephone 631-231-7269; Fax 631-231-8175
Web Site: http://www.novapublishers.com

Library of Congress Cataloging-in-Publication Data

ISBN: 978-1-62618-145-8

Published by Nova Science Publishers, Inc. † New York

CONTENTS

PREFACE

In 2008, 12 percent of all federal revenues came from corporate income taxes. About half was paid by multinational corporations reporting income from foreign countries. How the federal government taxes U.S. multinational corporations has consequences for the U.S. economy overall as well as for the federal budget. Tax policies influence businesses' choices about how and where to invest, particularly as corporations assess whether it is more profitable to locate business operations in the United States or abroad. The tax laws also can create opportunities for tax avoidance by allowing multinational corporations to use accounting or other legal strategies to report income and expenses for their U.S. and foreign operations in ways that reduce their overall tax liability. This book examines policy options addressing particular concerns about the current system of taxation, with a focus on multinational corporations' investment strategies and reporting of income as well as U.S. revenues from corporate income taxes.

Chapter 1 – In 2008, 12 percent of all federal revenues came from corporate income taxes; about half was paid by multinational corporations reporting income from foreign countries. How the federal government taxes U.S. multinational corporations has consequences for the U.S. economy overall as well as for the federal budget. Tax policies influence businesses' choices about how and where to invest, particularly as corporations assess whether it is more profitable to locate business operations in the United States or abroad. The tax laws also can create opportunities for tax avoidance by allowing multinational corporations to use accounting or other legal strategies to report income and expenses for their U.S. and foreign operations in ways that reduce their overall tax liability. U.S tax revenues decline when firms move investments abroad or when they strategically allocate income and expenses to avoid paying taxes here. A country can take two general approaches to taxing the income of corporations that operate both domestically and abroad:

- Under a worldwide approach, the home country considers all of the income of its multinational corporations to be taxable, regardless of where that income is earned. But to avoid taxing income twice—in the home country and in the country where it is earned— a country would generally allow multinational corporations to claim a foreign tax credit against domestic tax liability for taxes paid elsewhere.
- Under a territorial approach, the home country taxes only the income earned within its borders.

No major developed country has adopted either approach entirely. Although many developed countries use a more territorial approach, the system in the United States leans toward a worldwide approach, but one that allows multinational corporations to defer or, in some cases, completely avoid paying U.S. taxes on some income they earn abroad. This study examines policy options that could move the United States closer to one system or the other, along with several approaches to addressing particular concerns about the current system of taxation. All would affect multinational corporations' investment strategies and reporting of income as well as U.S. revenues from corporate income taxes.

Chapter 2 – Among potential tax reforms under discussion by Congress is revising the tax treatment of foreign source income of U.S. multinational corporations. Some business leaders have been urging a movement toward a territorial tax, which would eliminate some U.S. income taxes on active foreign source income.

Under a territorial tax, only the country where the income is earned imposes a tax. Territorial proposals include the Grubert-Mutti proposal (included in President Bush's Advisory Panel on Tax Reform proposal in 2005) and, more recently, a draft Ways and Means Committee proposal and a Senate bill, S. 2091. The Fiscal Commission also proposed a territorial tax. Proposals have, however, also been made to increase the taxation of foreign source income, including S. 727, and proposals by President Obama.

Although the United States has a worldwide system that includes foreign earnings in U.S. taxable income, two provisions cause the current system to resemble a territorial tax in that very little tax is collected. Deferral delays paying taxes until income is repatriated (paid as a dividend by the foreign subsidiary to its U.S. parent). When income is repatriated, credits for foreign taxes paid offset the U.S. tax due. Under cross-crediting, unused foreign tax credits from high tax countries or on highly taxed income can be used to offset U.S. tax on income in low tax countries.

Some proponents of a territorial tax urge such a system on the grounds that the current system discourages repatriations. Economic evidence suggests that effect is small, in part because in normal circumstances a large share of income is retained for permanent reinvestment. Amounts held abroad may have increased, however, as firms lobbied for another repatriation holiday (similar to that adopted in 2004) that allowed firms to exempt most dividends from income on a one-time basis.

Opponents are concerned about encouraging investment abroad. A territorial tax is generally not viewed as efficient because it favors foreign investment, but that increased outflow of investment is likely to have a small effect relative to the U.S. economy. Artificial shifting of profits into tax havens or low tax countries is a current problem that could be worsened under some territorial tax designs, and proposals have included measures to address this problem.

Proposals also address the transitional issue of the treatment of the existing stock of unrepatriated earnings. The Ways and Means proposal would tax this stock of earnings, but at a lower rate, and use the revenues to offset losses from other parts of the plan, which would lead to a long-run revenue loss. S. 2091 has a similar approach. The Grubert-Mutti proposal does not have a specific transitional tax, but would raise revenue largely due to its disallowance of parent overhead expenses aimed at reducing profit shifting. The other two proposals also contain provisions to address profit shifting.

In addition there are complicated issues in the design of a territorial tax, such as how to treat branches and dividends of firms in which the corporation is only partially owned. A number of issues arise from the ending of foreign tax credits, with perhaps the most significant one being the increased tax on royalties, which are currently subject to tax, have low or no foreign taxes, and would lose the shield of excess credits.

The final section of the report briefly discusses some alternative options, including those in S. 727 and in the Administration proposals. It also discusses hybrid approaches that combine territorial and worldwide systems in a more efficient way, including eliminating the disincentive to repatriate.

One such approach is a minimum tax on foreign source income, which is proposed by the President in the context of current rules, but could be combined with a territorial system.

Chapter 3 – The House Ways and Means Committee has scheduled a public hearing for May 24, 2011 on the rules in certain foreign jurisdictions for taxing foreign income.

This document, prepared by the staff of the Joint Committee on Taxation, describes the U.S. international tax rules applicable to foreign income of resident taxpayers, provides a general overview of a territorial system of taxation, including a brief discussion of basic design considerations, and summarizes the rules of nine selected countries for the taxation of foreign income.

Chapter 4 – Advocates of cutting corporate tax rates frequently make their argument based on the higher statutory rate in the United States as compared with the rest of the world; they argue that cutting corporate taxes would induce large investment flows into the United States, which would create jobs or expand the taxable income base enough to raise revenue. President Barack Obama has supported a rate cut if the revenue loss can be offset with corporate base broadening. Others have urged on one hand, a revenue raising reform, and, on the other, setting deficit concerns aside.

Is the U.S. tax rate higher than the rest of the world, and what does that difference imply for tax policy? The answer depends, in part, on which tax rates are being compared. Although the U.S. statutory tax rate is higher, the average effective rate is about the same, and the marginal rate on new investment is only slightly higher. The statutory rate differential is relevant for international profit shifting; effective rates are more relevant for firms' investment levels. The 13.7 percentage point differential in statutory rates (a 39.2% rate for the United States compared with 25.5% in other countries), narrows to about 9 percentage points when tax rates in the rest of the world are weighted to reflect the size of countries' economies. (The OECD rates fell by slightly over1/2 of a percentage point between 2010 and 2012).

Regardless of tax differentials, could a U.S. rate cut lead to significant economic gains and revenue feedbacks? Because of the factors that constrain capital flows, estimates for a rate cut from 35% to 25% suggest a modest positive effect on wages and output: an eventual one-time increase of less than two-tenths of 1% of output. Most of this output gain is not an increase in national income because returns to capital imported from abroad belong to foreigners and the returns to U.S. investment abroad that comes back to the United States are already owned by U.S. firms.

The revenue cost of such a rate cut is estimated at between $1.2 trillion and $1.5 trillion over the next 10 years. Revenue feedback effects from increased investment inflows are estimated to reduce those revenue costs by 5%-6%. Reductions in profit shifting could have larger effects, but even if profit shifting disappeared entirely, it would not likely offset revenue losses. It seems unlikely that a rate cut to 25% would significantly reduce profit shifting given these transactions are relatively costless and largely constrained by laws, enforcement, and court decisions.

Both output gains and revenue offsets would be reduced if other countries responded to a U.S. rate cut by reducing their own taxes. Evidence suggests that the U.S. rate cut in the Tax Reform Act of 1986 triggered rate cuts in other countries.

It is difficult, although not impossible, to design a reform to lower the corporate tax rate by 10 percentage points that is revenue neutral in the long run. Standard tax expenditures do not appear adequate for this purpose. Eliminating one of the largest provisions, accelerated depreciation, gains much more revenue in the short run than in the long run, and a long-run revenue-neutral change would increase the cost of capital. Other revisions, such as restricting foreign tax credits and interest deductibility or increasing shareholder level taxes, may be required.

This report focuses on the global issues relating to tax rate differentials between the United States and other countries. It provides tax rate comparisons; discusses policy implications, including the effect of a corporate rate cut on revenue, output, and national welfare; and discusses the outlook for and consequences of a revenue neutral corporate tax reform.

Advocates of cutting corporate tax rates frequently make their argument based on the higher statutory rate observed in the United States as compared with the rest of the world. Sometimes the higher rate alone is used as an argument, and in other cases the arguments include claims that cutting corporate taxes would induce large investment flows into the United States, which would create jobs or expand the base enough to raise revenue.

President Barack Obama has supported a rate cut if the revenue loss can be offset with corporate base broadening, while the Citizens for Tax Justice has urged a revenue raising reform and business leaders have urged setting deficit concerns aside. House Majority Leader Eric Cantor has also proposed a 25% corporate rate in the context of tax reform and Ways and Means Chairman Dave Camp has proposed a 25% combined with a move to a territorial tax system.

Many issues arise regarding the corporate tax outside of the global perspective that are addressed in other reports. This report focuses on the global issue relating to tax rate differentials between the United States and other countries. The first section provides tax rate comparisons. The second section discusses policy implications, including the effect of a corporate rate cut on revenue, output, and national welfare; the possibility that a rate cut may induce reactions from other countries; and the outlook for and consequences of a revenue-neutral corporate tax reform.

In: Taxing U.S. Multinational Corporations
Editor: Angelique Gilder
ISBN: 978-1-62618-145-8

Chapter 1

OPTIONS FOR TAXING U.S. MULTINATIONAL CORPORATIONS*

Congressional Budget Office

NOTES

Unless otherwise indicated, the years referred to in this report are federal fiscal years, which run from October 1 to September 30.

Numbers in the text and in tables may not add up to totals because of rounding.

SUMMARY

In 2008, 12 percent of all federal revenues came from corporate income taxes; about half was paid by multinational corporations reporting income from foreign countries.[1] How the federal government taxes U.S. multinational corporations has consequences for the U.S. economy overall as well as for the federal budget. Tax policies influence businesses' choices about how and where to invest, particularly as corporations assess whether it is more profitable to locate business operations in the United States or abroad. The tax laws also can create opportunities for tax avoidance by allowing multinational corporations to use accounting or other legal strategies to report income and expenses for their U.S. and foreign operations in ways that reduce their overall tax liability. U.S tax revenues decline when firms move investments abroad or when they strategically allocate income and expenses to avoid paying taxes here. A country can take two general approaches to taxing the income of corporations that operate both domestically and abroad:

- Under a *worldwide* approach, the home country considers all of the income of its multinational corporations to be taxable, regardless of where that income is earned. But to avoid taxing income twice—in the home country and in the country where it is

* Jennifer Gravelle wrote this report which was released by the Congressional Budget Office, dated January 2013.

earned— a country would generally allow multinational corporations to claim a *foreign tax credit* against domestic tax liability for taxes paid elsewhere.

- Under a *territorial* approach, the home country taxes only the income earned within its borders.

No major developed country has adopted either approach entirely. Although many developed countries use a more territorial approach, the system in the United States leans toward a worldwide approach, but one that allows multinational corporations to defer or, in some cases, completely avoid paying U.S. taxes on some income they earn abroad. This study examines policy options that could move the United States closer to one system or the other, along with several approaches to addressing particular concerns about the current system of taxation. All would affect multinational corporations' investment strategies and reporting of income as well as U.S. revenues from corporate income taxes.

Current Federal Tax Treatment of U.S. Multinational Corporations

The U.S. government taxes both the domestic and the foreign income of businesses that are incorporated in the United States and that operate abroad. Often, such corporations also must pay income taxes to their foreign host countries. At the national level, the top corporate tax rate in the United States (the statutory tax rate on income in the highest bracket) is 35 percent. When combined with state and local corporate taxes, that rate rises to 39 percent—higher than that in any of the other 34 member countries of the Organisation for Economic Co-operation and Development (OECD). Weighted by gross domestic product (GDP), the average statutory rate among OECD countries in 2011, excluding the United States, was about 19 percent. Although the U.S. system is generally more worldwide than territorial, two important features of its tax system depart from the worldwide approach. First, a purely worldwide tax system would ensure that firms faced the same tax rate no matter where they operated. If the United States were to have such a system, it would not limit the credit granted to firms for the total taxes paid abroad, regardless of whether those taxes exceeded the domestic liability on the income. Under the U.S. system, however, the largest credit a corporation may take is one that matches the amount the firm would pay in U.S. taxes on the same income. Thus, U.S. corporations that operate in countries that tax at a higher rate than the United States does must pay the foreign tax rate on that income. Second, companies can defer U.S. taxes on income earned abroad by their subsidiaries until that income is remitted (or "repatriated") to the U.S. parent company, thus allowing some foreign income to escape U.S. taxation—at least temporarily. Those features of the U.S. tax system affect U.S. multinationals' decisions about whether and how to invest at home and abroad. The current tax system provides incentives for U.S. firms to locate their production facilities in countries with low taxes as a way to reduce their tax liability at home. Those responses to the tax system reduce economic efficiency because the firms are not allocating resources to their most productive use. Those responses also reduce the income of shareholders and employees in the United States and they lead to a loss of federal tax revenue. In addition, those investment decisions may initially result in more unemployment in this country. Over time, however, as the economy adjusts, other jobs are created and total employment would not be significantly affected. But as a result of such decisions, in the long run, total compensation for U.S. workers is lower, and employment may be concentrated in different industries and regions.

The current system also creates incentives to shift reported income to low-tax countries without changing actual investment decisions. Such profit shifting erodes the corporate tax base and leads to wasted resources for tax planning.

Policy Options

The options presented in this report are targeted at several areas of concern about the effects of the U.S. tax system on the flow of investment outside the United States and the reporting of U.S. corporate profits. Some options are broad, designed generally to address the flows of U.S. investment to other countries. Other options are narrower, addressing tax avoidance by U.S. firms that strategically allocate reported income and expenses between their U.S. and foreign operations. Some options would result in a more efficient allocation of resources among countries and also would impede the ability of corporations to avoid paying U.S. taxes; others would achieve just one of those two goals and could in fact make it more difficult to achieve the other.

A Worldwide System

Options that would move the United States closer to a purely worldwide tax system— by eliminating or curtailing deferral of U.S. taxes on income earned abroad—would dampen incentives to shift investment or reported income on the basis of concerns about tax liability. As a result, those options would generally lead to more economically efficient business investment and increase corporate tax revenues from firms that remained incorporated in the United States. But moving closer to a purely worldwide system also would strengthen the incentive for U.S. firms to incorporate, or register, abroad or to be acquired by or merge with foreign companies. Such a response probably would not increase the efficiency of investment decisions, and it would reduce the corporate tax base. On balance, however, eliminating deferral would boost both efficiency and tax revenues. In fact, eliminating deferral entirely would boost U.S. tax revenues by more than $100 billion over a 10-year period, according to an estimate by the staff of the Joint Committee on Taxation (JCT); that would be the largest revenue increase attributable to any of the options discussed in this report.

A Territorial System

Alternatively, the United States could move toward a territorial system—for example, by exempting some income earned abroad from U.S. taxation or by taxing domestic income only but using a formula that considered the location of a company's activities to determine the sources of its income. Such policies could result in a less efficient allocation of resources among countries by increasing incentives to shift business operations and reported income to countries with lower tax rates. Nonetheless, some options for moving toward a territorial tax would increase U.S. tax revenues by restricting the ability of multinationals to shield some income from U.S. taxation and by preventing them from deducting costs incurred abroad from income earned in the United States.

Other Options

Some options would restrict corporations' ability to use excess foreign tax credits, which are generated by income earned in countries where taxes are higher than they are in the United States. Under current law, a business can use those credits to offset U.S. taxes on income that is repatriated from low-tax countries, effectively decreasing the U.S. taxes they pay on foreign income and increasing their incentive to invest abroad. Thus, restricting the use of excess credits could increase federal tax revenues and reduce the incentive to invest abroad. Such a restriction, however, might push some firms to take greater advantage of provisions that allow deferral of taxes on income that is earned—and retained—abroad. The net effects of such a restriction on investment and repatriation of income are unclear, but it could increase U.S. tax revenues.

Other options would produce more incremental changes, generally limiting opportunities for corporations to shift reported income abroad and thus increasing the amount they must pay in U.S. taxes. Those options would treat entities and recognize income in a more consistent way across jurisdictions. One disadvantage is that such options also would strengthen incentives for shifting investments instead of just shifting reported income. However, such options are fairly narrow, and the overall effect on the location of businesses' investments would probably be small.

Two Basic Approaches to Taxing Multinational Corporations

Multinational corporations are businesses that incorporate and operate in one country (in this report called the home country) but that also maintain operations of various kinds in other countries (called host countries). Multinational corporations operate abroad for many reasons, including favorable tax laws, but they also do so to gain access to foreign markets, to employ a less costly labor force, and to obtain materials that are less expensive than those available at home.

There are two basic approaches to taxing the income of multinational corporations: the *worldwide approach* and the *territorial approach.* Under the first system, multinational corporations are taxed by the home country on their worldwide income without regard to where it is earned. Countries that adopt such an approach generally also provide for credits or deductions for taxes paid to host countries. At the other end of the spectrum, under the territorial approach, the home country taxes only the income that is earned within its borders, and it imposes no tax liability for any income earned abroad.

Each approach has different implications for the tax rates multinational firms face on income earned in foreign countries. If a country adopted a worldwide tax system with no limits on the size of its foreign tax credit (even if the foreign taxes exceeded domestic tax liability on the income), then all corporations' income—whether earned at home or from investments abroad—would be taxed at the home country's rate. Under a territorial system, by contrast, multinational corporations' tax liability would depend on the rate set by the host country, and the only way to ensure that all of a country's multinational corporations faced the same tax rate—regardless of the source of their income— would be to have a universal, territorial tax system under which all countries treated multinational firms the same way—that is, having the same tax base and rate structure.

How a home country taxes foreign-earned income can affect businesses in a significant way: Because many other countries in which such firms operate also tax income earned within their borders, business managers must decide whether investing abroad would he worthwhile, given the prospect of paying additional U.S. taxes on that same income.

Different countries take different approaches to and have different systems for taxing income earned abroad. No major developed country has adopted either a completely worldwide or a completely territorial tax system. Instead, many have developed what are essentially hybrid systems that incorporate significant aspects of both approaches. The U.S. tax system leans toward a worldwide approach; it imposes taxes on multinational corporations' foreign income but allows those businesses to claim deductions or credits for the taxes they pay abroad. Multinational corporations also can defer or, in some cases, completely avoid paying U.S. taxes on some income earned abroad. Deferral and some other mechanisms make the U.S. system territorial in some respects.

In contrast, most member countries of the Organisation for Economic Co-operation and Development take a largely territorial approach by exempting certain foreign-earned income from taxation (by means of what is often called an exemption system). Some of those countries also have "anti-abuse" rules that govern the type and source of foreign income that can be exempted from taxation, reducing the ability of firms to take unfair advantage of a territorial tax system by shifting the location of income.[2] France, for example, disallows exemptions for income earned in countries whose corporate income tax rates are at least 50 percent below its own. Germany taxes income earned in any foreign country where the tax rate is less than 25 percent, and it taxes all foreign income from certain types of business activities. Under Italy's anti-abuse rules, a "blacklist" prevents income earned by Italian multinational corporations in some countries from receiving an exemption from taxation at home. Strong anti-abuse rules can result in systems that effectively tax foreign income in a way that is much closer to a worldwide approach.

Federal Tax Treatment of U.S. Multinational Corporations

The amount of taxes that U.S. multinational corporations pay depends on several factors. As is the case for domestic corporations, multinationals are assessed corporate income taxes on earnings that exceed their expenses. Although those expenses can include taxes, current law generally provides for a system of credits for taxes paid to foreign governments that allows those companies some relief from what would amount to double taxation of that income.

The U.S. system allows multinational corporations to combine credits for taxes paid to more than one foreign country; in 2008, those credits amounted to about $100 billion. Moreover, payment of U.S. taxes on foreign income can be deferred until the income is repatriated to the United States. Because of such deferral, the corporation's total tax liability is effectively reduced if the taxes paid to another country are less than the amount the United States would levy on the same income.

Table 1. Progressive Structure of U.S. Corporate Income Tax Rates, 2012 (Percent)

Income Range (Dollars)		Statutory Corporate Tax Rate	Excess Tax	Total Rate
Over	But Not Over			
0	50,000	15	0	15
50,000	75,000	25	0	25
75,000	100,000	34	0	34
100,000	335,000	34	5 [a]	39
335,000	10,000,000	34	0	34
10,000,000	15,000,000	35	0	35
15,000,000	18,333,333	35	3 [b]	38
18,333,333	—	35	0	35

Source: Internal Revenue Service.

[a] The excess tax offsets the benefit of rates below 34 percent for income in the range between zero and $75,000.

[b] The excess tax offsets the benefit of rates below 35 percent for income below $10 million.

The Federal Corporate Income Tax

The U.S. corporate tax system defines income broadly to include revenues from sales, interest, dividends, capital gains, royalties, and rents. To compute taxable income, corporations subtract business expenses (including the costs of goods sold, depreciation, advertising expenses, and interest payments) from their total income. Although corporations are allowed to deduct the interest they pay to bondholders, they cannot deduct dividends paid to shareholders; such dividends are subject to the individual income tax as well.

In general, corporations' federal income tax liability is computed according to a progressive structure starting at 15 percent for the first $50,000 of taxable income and rising to 35 percent on income above $10 million (see Table 1). Income between $100,000 and $335,000 is subject to an additional tax of 5 percent (raising the effective rate from 34 percent to 39 percent), and an additional 3 percent tax is assessed on income between $15 million and $18.3 million (raising the effective rate from 35 percent to 38 percent). For corporations with income in those ranges, such "excess taxes" effectively offset the benefit of the three lower tax rates. Although the excess taxes yield a higher tax rate over some income ranges, most corporations' income is taxed at the 35 percent rate (the statutory rate that applies to income in the highest tax bracket). It is often noted that the top rate set by U.S. law— 35 percent (or 39 percent, on average, once state and local corporate taxes are included)—is among the highest for developed countries. However, other features of the U.S. tax code, such as credits and preferential rates, effectively lower the tax rates. (The appendix describes U.S. corporate tax rates and compares them with those of other countries.)

U.S. Rules for Taxation of Income Earned Abroad

Two important features affect the U.S. tax treatment of foreign income. First, the foreign tax credit is limited to the amount of U.S. taxes a corporation would pay here on its income from foreign sources; a corporation may not take a credit on its foreign income that is larger, in the aggregate, than its U.S. tax liability is for that income. Second, payment of U.S. taxes on income earned—and kept—abroad can be deferred until the income is returned to a U.S. parent corporation. That feature adds a territorial aspect to the U.S. tax system in that foreign income receives preferential treatment. Other provisions and regulations (discussed later in this report) also contribute to a partially territorial approach.[3]

Under the U.S. system, taxation of foreign income is affected by a corporation's structure. In some cases, multinationals operate abroad through branches that act as extensions of their U.S. parent companies; their foreign-earned income is considered the legal income of the U.S. parent company and thus is taxed as it is earned. In other cases, corporations establish subsidiaries that incorporate as separate entities abroad. For those businesses, the parent corporation owns shares in the subsidiary and receives income in the form of dividends, which are not subject to U.S. taxation until the money is returned to the U.S. parent. A common type of subsidiary, the controlled foreign corporation (CFC), is incorporated abroad and has a majority of its stock owned by U.S. shareholders.[4]

Limits on Foreign Tax Credits

When the corporate income tax was established in 1909, lawmakers allowed businesses to claim a deduction for taxes paid on income earned abroad. A tax deduction, however, only offsets a share of foreign taxes.[5] That tax deduction was later converted to a tax credit, with no limits on the amount received, ensuring that income from foreign operations would not be taxed twice. With an unlimited credit, businesses that operated in countries where tax rates were higher than those of the United States received a tax credit that exceeded the U.S. tax on their foreign income and thus could use the excess credit to offset the U.S. tax on their domestic income. By comparison, businesses operating in low-tax countries paid the full U.S. tax on their domestic income. An unconstrained credit also provided an implicit U.S. subsidy of foreign governments: A portion of the taxes paid to those governments was in effect paid by the U.S. government in the form of forgone revenues. In response to those concerns, in 1921, lawmakers capped the foreign tax credit. Under current law, the credit cannot exceed the amount of taxes that a company would pay under the U.S. tax code. That limit ensures that the United States does not subsidize other countries by extending credits in excess of what it collects in taxes. As an example, suppose a multinational corporation earns \$100 million in before-tax income in its domestic operations in the United States and an equal amount, currently subject to U.S. taxes, from the operation of its subsidiaries in other countries (see Table 2). Under U.S. tax law, the combined income is subject to a 35 percent rate—and the firm owes \$70 million in corporate income taxes (before allowing for credits). Suppose the other countries tax corporate income earned within their borders at a rate of 40 percent. The firm therefore would pay \$40 million in taxes to the foreign countries (40 percent on the \$100 million earned there). Under U.S. law, the firm can then claim a credit up to the amount it owes the United States on the same income—in this case, \$35 million (35 percent of the \$100 million). In this example, the firm pays \$75 million in taxes—\$35 million to the United States (after taking the credit) and \$40 million to the other countries—\$5 million more than it would if there was no limit on the amount of the credit. The credit that can be taken for paying foreign taxes has changed. Initially, there was an overall limit (as in the simple example above). From 1932 to 1976, the foreign tax credit was calculated separately for each country as a way to limit the ability of businesses to "cross credit" (that is, to use taxes paid to high-tax countries to reduce the U.S. tax on income from low-tax countries). Over time, the per-country limit has been replaced with separate limits for different categories (or "baskets") of income; the income from all countries is combined within each basket. Before 2007, businesses were required to calculate separate limits for nine different baskets. The American Jobs Creation Act of 2004 reduced that number, moving certain items, such as income from financial services, into a general-income category. There are now just two main categories—general income (largely, active income) and passive income.[6]

Deferral of Taxes on Foreign Income

Since the enactment of the corporate income tax in 1909, the United States has allowed firms to defer U.S. taxes on the income of foreign subsidiaries until that money is repatriated to the U.S. parent company. An early justification held that no income should be taxed before it is available for use by the taxpayer (just as taxes are deferred on capital gains realizations or pension income until those funds are received). Over time, concern over the ability of businesses to manipulate their foreign income led to proposals to restrict or eliminate deferral of taxes. Advocates defended deferral as a way to protect firms' ability to compete with foreign businesses in countries with lower tax rates or a territorial approach to taxation. Those competing concerns have led to a deferral system that is somewhat constrained by limits on its use. (Those limits are discussed later in this report in the section "Limits on Deferral.") Under current law, U.S. multinational corporations are taxed only on the income of subsidiaries that are incorporated abroad to the extent that the income from those operations is repatriated to the U.S. parent in the form of dividends. (Income earned by a branch, by contrast, is taxed as it is earned because branches are treated as legal extensions of the U.S. parent corporation.)

Table 2. Illustrative Effect of Limiting the Foreign Tax Credit on the Tax Liability of a U.S. Multinational Corporation

	No Limit on Tax Credit If There Were	**Foreign Income Is Subject to U.S. Taxes Tax Credit Limited to Amount Owed If Current Law:**
		Before-Tax Income (Millions of dollars)
U.S. Income	100	100
Repatriated Foreign Income	100	100
Total Income	200	200
	U.S. and Foreign Tax Liability and the Foreign Tax Credit	
U.S. Taxes Before Foreign Tax Credit		
Rate (Percent)	35	35
Liability (Millions of dollars)	70	70
Foreign Taxes		
Rate (Percent)	40	40
Liability (Millions of dollars)	40	40
Foreign Tax Credit (Millions of dollars)	40	35
	U.S. and Foreign Tax Liability After the Credit (Millions of dollars)	
U.S. Taxes	30	35
Foreign Taxes	40	40
Total Taxes	70	75

Source: Congressional Budget Office.

In the previous example (shown in Table 2), the limit on the foreign tax credit reduced the appeal of investing in a high-tax country. By contrast, the ability to defer U.S. taxes on income that is not repatriated increases the appeal of investing in lower-tax countries. Consider again a U.S. parent company that earns $200 million in before-tax income (see Table 3). Suppose $100 million of that income is earned from a wholly owned subsidiary in a host country with a tax rate of 15 percent. The multinational corporation in this instance reinvests half of the dividends in its foreign subsidiary and repatriates the rest to the U.S. parent. Without deferral, all foreign earnings would be subject to U.S. taxes. However, under the current rules, the multinational does not pay U.S. taxes on the $50 million of the foreign earnings that remain abroad. Only the $50 million paid to the U.S. parent company is taxed at 20 percent, the amount by which the U.S. tax rate exceeds the foreign tax rate. Thus, deferral reduces the company's U.S. tax liability by $10 million. If the multinational repatriates the income in some future year, it will owe U.S. taxes on that income. The firm still benefits, however, by deferring tax liability—and having the use of that money—until that future time.

Table 3. Illustrative Effect of Deferral on the Tax Liability of a U.S. Multinational Corporation

	If There Were No Deferral	Current Law: Deferral
	Before-Tax Income (Millions of dollars)	
U.S. Income	100	100
Foreign Income Before Foreign Taxes		
Taxable income repatriated to the parent company	50	50
Income reinvested abroad	50	50
Total Income	200	200
Income Subject to U.S. Taxes	200	150
	U.S. and Foreign Tax Liability and the Foreign Tax Credit	
U.S. Taxes Before Foreign Tax Credit		
Rate (Percent)	35	35
Liability (Millions of dollars)	70	52.5
Foreign Taxes		
Rate (Percent)	15	15
Liability (Millions of dollars)	15	15
Foreign Tax Credit (Millions of dollars)	15	7.5 a
	U.S. and Foreign Tax Liability After the Credit (Millions of dollars)	
U.S. Taxes	55	45
Foreign Taxes	15	15
Total Taxes	70	60

Source: Congressional Budget Office.
a. Credit is allowed for foreign taxes attributable to the repatriated foreign income.

Using Excess Credits to Shelter Income Repatriated from Low-Tax Countries

Because a firm's foreign tax credit is limited to its U.S. tax liability, income that is repatriated from a country with a higher tax rate than the U.S. rate generates "excess credits" (that is, potential credits from foreign tax liabilities that cannot be used because they exceed the amount owed to the United States). A firm that repatriates income from a country with a lower tax rate would receive a credit that was not enough to offset the entire U.S. tax owed on that income, and the firm would face a residual tax in the United States. U.S. tax law, however, allows firms to combine the income and credits from high- and low-tax-rate countries on income tax returns.

The excess credits attributed to the taxes paid on income earned in a high-tax country can be cross credited and applied to the income repatriated from the low-tax country, effectively offsetting some or all of the U.S. tax liability on income from the low-tax host country. Suppose a firm repatriates $100 million from a country with a 40 percent tax rate and $20 million from a country with a 10 percent tax rate (see Table 4). Without cross crediting, the firm could claim a credit of $35 million on its income from the high-tax country, the amount it owes under U.S. tax law on $100 million of earnings. The firm also could claim another credit for $2 million—the amount owed to the low-tax country on the $20 million repatriated from that country. However, under current law, that firm has excess credits of $5 million—the difference between the potential credit ($40 million) and the allowed credit ($35 million) from the taxes paid to the country with the higher tax rate. The U.S. firm can still apply the excess credit of $5 million against the amount due in U.S. taxes on income earned in the low-tax country.

The advantages of cross crediting increase as fewer restrictions are placed on the foreign tax credit.[7] The current system's smaller number of baskets eases the way for firms to use cross crediting, and thereby increases the use of that mechanism.[8]

Combining Deferral and Excess Credits

Corporations can increase their after-tax income by retaining some earnings abroad in low-tax countries and using excess credits from high-tax countries to shelter income repatriated from low-tax countries. Such actions allow them to avoid paying the U.S. taxes that would have been due on some of their income from low-tax countries. Consider again a firm that initially earns $100 million in the United States and $100 million in a country with a 15 percent tax rate. If the company does not defer any income, it would have a U.S. tax liability of $70 million, less a foreign tax credit of $15 million, and thus would owe $55 million in U.S. taxes; its total tax payments would amount to $70 million (see the first column in Table 3 on page 7). Deferral, by itself, would reduce those taxes by $10 million (see the second column in Table 3).

Alternatively, the firm could rearrange its investments and use the combination of deferral and cross crediting to reduce its total tax liabilities even more—and eliminate its U.S. tax liability. For example, say the firm moves its domestic and foreign investments to two foreign countries—one with a rate that is higher (40 percent) and the other with a rate that is lower (10 percent) than the U.S. tax rate (the example shown in Table 4).[9] If it repatriates $100 million from the country with the higher tax rate and $20 million from the country with the low tax rate, the company can use cross crediting to take the full credit of $40 million—the amount paid to the high-tax country—to eliminate the domestic tax due on income it repatriates from the low-tax country. Thus, by moving investments overseas, retaining some earnings abroad, and using cross crediting, the company could reduce its net U.S. tax liability from $55 million to zero and its total tax payments from $70 million to $50 million.

Deductions for Expenses

Another feature of the tax code that can affect the use of excess credits is the treatment of certain expenses incurred by the parent firm in the course of its general business activities.

Such expenses include interest on loans, spending on research and development, and overhead.

The foreign tax credit is limited to the U.S. tax liability on repatriated income, net of those expenses incurred in earning the income. Deducting the expenses reduces the allowable credit for firms affected by that limit. However, the lower limit could be used to generate additional excess credits from high-tax countries to shield income repatriated from low-tax countries from U.S. tax liability, thus encouraging some firms to allocate more expenses to their foreign earnings.

Table 4. Illustrative Effect of Cross Crediting Under the Foreign Tax Credit on the Tax Liability of a U.S. Multinational Corporation

	High-Tax Country	Low-Tax Country	Total
	Before-Tax Income (Millions of dollars)		
Foreign Income	100	100	200
Taxable Foreign Income Repatriated to the Parent Company	100	20	120
	U.S. and Foreign Tax Liability Before the Foreign Tax Credit		
U.S. Taxes Rate (Percent)	35	35	35
Liability (Millions of dollars)	35	7	42
Foreign Taxes Rate (Percent)	40	10	n.a.
Liability (Millions of dollars)	40	10	50
	U.S. and Foreign Tax Liability After the Foreign Tax Credit, with No Cros		
	(Millions of dollars)		
Foreign Tax Credita Potentialb	40	2	42
Allowedc	35	2	37
U.S. Taxes	0	5	5
Foreign Taxes	40	10	50
Total Taxes	40	15	55
	U.S. and Foreign Tax Liability After the Foreign Tax Credit, with Cross		
	(Millions of dollars)		
Foreign Tax Credita Potentialb	40	2	42
Allowedc	35	7	42
U.S. Taxes	0	0	0
Foreign Taxes	40	10	50
Total Taxes	40	10	50

Source: Congressional Budget Office. Note: n.a. = not applicable.

a Per-country credits are shown for illustration only and are not calculated separately for U.S. tax purposes.

b The potential credit is the foreign taxes paid on repatriated income.

c The allowed tax credit is the smaller of the potential credit or the U.S. tax liability due on repatriated foreign income.

Although deductions for expenses related to doing business abroad can reduce the foreign tax credit, those expenses can nevertheless be used in other ways to lower the company's U.S. tax liability. When determining that liability before tax credits, firms need not differentiate between domestic and foreign expenses; all foreign expenses can be deducted entirely against U.S. taxable income to reduce total U.S. tax liability.

Thus, expenses from foreign operations reduce U.S. tax liability, even before the application of the foreign tax credit. Moreover, the parent firm can take deductions for expenses it incurs for its foreign operations in the year that those expenses are incurred—even if the related foreign income is not repatriated until a later year.

Limits on Deferral

Income is taxed differently according to how it is earned (that is, whether it is passive or active income) and whether it is retained abroad or paid within the tax year to a U.S. parent company. Passive income is derived from businesses that a firm owns but for which the firm has minimal or no involvement in operations. For example, income from the sales of foreign property to related parties would be considered passive.[10] Passive income, often called subpart F income because of the portion of the tax code that specifies its treatment, is taxed as it is earned. Active income is generated by the firm in the management of its business, and it is taxed only when it is returned to the U.S. parent company.[11] For example, active dividends are taxed only when they are paid out to the U.S. parent. Additionally, some forms of income, such as interest, rents, and royalties, are taxed currently, regardless of whether they are earned passively or actively, because the money is paid immediately to the U.S. earner. Because government tax administrators cannot readily identify the source of passive income, it is easier to make financial arrangements to shift passive income to low-tax countries and escape U.S. taxation than it is to do the same with active income. If passive income was not taxed when earned, it would be possible for U.S. multinational corporations to defer paying taxes on all investment income, including that from U.S. businesses, by investing through foreign entities. That is not possible under subpart F because investment in U.S. property by U.S.-controlled foreign corporations is subject to tax. The subpart F rules limit the ability of businesses to shelter from U.S. taxation any passive income, including dividends from stock holdings. The separate limits on foreign tax credits for active and passive income reduce the impetus for corporations to use foreign tax credits related to active dividends that are subject to high foreign taxes as a way to shelter passive income associated with low-tax jurisdictions.

Impact of Foreign Tax Credits and Deferrals on Federal Revenues

In 2008—the latest year for which detailed data are available—12 percent of federal revenues came from corporate income taxes, and about half of that amount was from multinational corporations claiming credits for taxes paid to foreign governments (see Table 5). Although those 7,242 companies represented only four-tenths of one percent of all U.S. corporations, they earned about 70 percent of total taxable corporate income. In all, U.S. multinational corporations claimed about $100 billion in foreign tax credits on almost $700 billion in worldwide taxable income (including domestic income and foreign income repatriated to the United States). The credits reduced those corporations' income tax liability by about 40 percent.[12] Almost three-quarters of the foreign tax credits were claimed by corporations in the manufacturing sector, and those credits reduced their U.S. tax liability by 55 percent. Total foreign repatriated income is almost 60 percent of worldwide taxable income of the corporations claiming a foreign tax credit (comparing totals on Tables 5 and 6). About 10 percent of repatriated income came from the United Kingdom—a major U.S. trading partner (see Table 6)—and Canada accounted for another 8 percent. More than 9 percent was repatriated from countries often considered to be tax havens for U.S. corporate income because of their low tax rates: Bermuda, Luxembourg, the Cayman Islands, and the Bahamas (see Box 1 on page 13).

Table 5. Use of the Foreign Tax Credit, by U.S. Industry, 2008; (Billions of dollars)

Industry	Number of Returns	Worldwide Taxable Income[a]	U.S. Income Tax Before Credits	Credits		U.S. Income Tax After Credits[c]
				Foreign Tax	General Business[b]	
Manufacturing	1,268	384.0	134.4	73.5	4.4	56.1
Services	2,600	68.2	23.9	7.3	2.1	14.3
Mining	109	38.7	13.6	6.8	*	6.5
Information	253	52.4	18.3	4.8	0.8	12.5
Finance, Insurance, Real Estate, and Rental and Leasing	1,769	66.7	24.1	4.3	0.3	19.2
Wholesale and Retail Trade	570	73.1	25.6	2.9	0.6	22.0
Other	673	13.4	4.7	0.7	0.1	3.8
Total	7,242	696.4	244.6	100.4	8.4	134.4

Source: Congressional Budget Office based on data from the Internal Revenue Service.

Note: * = less than $50 million.

a Total income, consisting of domestic and repatriated foreign income that is subject to U.S. taxes.

b The general business credit combines many of the available business credits, such as the research and development credit and investment credits. Combining the credits provides a uniform method for determining limits on their amounts.

c Including additional credits that are not reported separately.

Measuring the impact of deferral is more challenging because multinational corporations are not required to report the amount of foreign income that is not repatriated.[13] The Bureau of Economic Analysis of the Department of Commerce has reported that earnings of U.S. foreign affiliates were, on net, about $900 billion in 2009 (that total does not include the foreign-branch income of U.S. parent companies).[14] Estimates of the cost of deferral use data on, or assumptions about, the distribution of U.S. corporate income among countries with different tax rates and assumptions about how corporations might respond to changes in tax policy. Some analysts estimate, on the basis of a review of the financial data from 880 companies, that as of May 2011, unrepatriated foreign income totaled $1.4 trillion.[15] JCT estimates that forgone revenues attributable to deferral totaled about $16 billion in fiscal year 2012 and that they will amount to a total of $87 billion from 2011 through 2015, making deferral of taxes on foreign income the largest corporate tax expenditure.[16]

EFFECTS OF THE FEDERAL TAX TREATMENT OF U.S. MULTINATIONAL CORPORATIONS

The current U.S. tax treatment of multinational corporations affects their behavior in ways that have an impact on U.S. tax revenues:

- The different treatment of foreign and domestic operations influences decisions about how much and where companies invest. Economic efficiency—the extent to which resources are allocated in a manner that maximizes their value—is reduced if firms forgo more productive investments because they are avoiding taxation.
- The current U.S. tax code encourages firms to artificially shift reported income abroad and between foreign counties.

- When firms choose to shift either their investments or their reported income abroad, U.S. revenues from corporate income taxes decline.

Location of Investment

The current U.S. tax system encourages firms to consider tax advantages as they choose whether to invest in the United States or in some foreign country:

- The limit on foreign tax credits encourages corporations to avoid investing in countries where tax rates are higher than they are in the United States,
- The ability to defer foreign income encourages firms to invest and retain earnings in low-tax foreign jurisdictions rather than in the United States to avoid paying higher taxes here, and
- The practice of cross crediting provides a further incentive for corporations to make foreign investments on the basis of their potential tax liabilities rather than their other business interests.

Table 6. Foreign Taxes Paid by and Foreign Taxable Income Repatriated to U.S. Parent Companies for Selected Countries, 2008

	Number of Returns[a]	Foreign Taxes Paid (Billions of dollars)	Foreign Taxable Income Repatriated	
			(Billions of dollars)	Percentage of Total
United Kingdom	1,142	10.3	39.3	9.5
Canada	2,430	11.0	32.8	7.9
Netherlands	709	7.8	21.5	5.2
Ireland	304	1.7	21.2	5.1
Switzerland	392	2.8	14.5	3.5
Japan	942	3.4	14.1	3.4
Bermuda	224	3.6	13.2	3.2
Luxembourg	202	2.6	10.9	2.6
Singapore	514	0.6	9.3	2.2
Cayman Islands (British)	227	1.3	8.8	2.1
Germany	645	2.1	8.7	2.1
China	590	1.1	8.0	1.9
France	638	2.4	7.5	1.8
Bahamas	116	2.1	6.3	1.5
Hong Kong	434	0.5	4.7	1.1
India	501	1.0	3.6	0.9
Italy	475	1.2	3.5	0.8
British Virgin Islands	82	0.2	1.1	0.3
Total for Selected Countries	**n.a.**	**55.6**	**228.8**	**55.4**
Memorandum:				
Total for All Countries[b]	7,242	121.2	413.3	100

Source: Congressional Budget Office analysis of data on foreign tax credits from the Internal Revenue Service.

Note: n.a. = not applicable.

a The number of returns for each country is the number on which that country is listed; a single return filed by a U.S. parent company can list more than one country.

b The total number of returns for all countries is the total filed by U.S. parent companies claiming a foreign tax credit.

A tax system that combines those three features yields a less efficient allocation of worldwide capital among domestic and foreign jurisdictions because companies can move capital from country to country in part to reduce their tax liabilities. Under the current U.S. tax system, a firm—faced with a choice between a project in the United States and a less productive investment in another country with lower taxes—might select the foreign investment because it yields a higher after-tax return.

The system also leads to an inefficient deployment of U.S. capital, thereby reducing the income of U.S. shareholders and employees. To the extent that firms are able to exploit market power (that is, to earn profits that are greater than the normal market return) in foreign jurisdictions, that profitability could benefit the U.S. economy. However, that benefit is unlikely to override the negative consequences (such as the loss of income to shareholders and employees) of inefficient allocation of U.S. capital.[17]

Box 1. Tax Havens

The term *tax haven* is often applied to countries that do not assess income taxes or that appear to set taxes purposely low to attract investment or income from foreign businesses or individuals. More formal definitions, however, have changed over time and vary among international organizations and governments. Factors other than tax rates are sometimes used to determine whether to call a particular country a tax haven.

The Organisation for Economic Co-operation and Development (OECD), for example, originally identified countries as tax havens if they levied minimal taxes or none at all and if they prevented exchanges of information with foreign tax authorities, exhibited a lack of transparency, and did not require corporations to establish substantial local business activity. In 2000, the OECD identified 35 such countries on the basis of those criteria.[1] Since then, the OECD has classified countries on the basis of their commitment—or lack of a commitment—to developing information exchanges with foreign tax authorities, and it assigns nations to what are known as the white, gray, and black lists.

As of May 2012, the OECD had listed three countries that had not substantially implemented information exchanges (Nauru, Niue, and Guatemala); none were black-listed as uncooperative tax havens. On the basis of its current criteria, the OECD does not designate as tax havens many countries that have low tax rates and that do not require corporations to have domestic business operations.

The Government Accountability Office has identified 50 countries as tax havens.[2] That list includes countries that had been identified by the OECD in the past as tax havens and others that also have had low tax rates for businesses or that offer financial privacy and that, as a result, are considered tax havens by other sources.[3]

1. Organisation for Economic Co-operation and Development, Towards Global Tax Co-operation: Report to the 2000 Ministerial Council Meeting and Recommendations by the Committee on Fiscal Affairs, Progress in Identifying and Eliminating Harmful Tax Practices (2000), www.oecd.org/document/43/ 0,3746,en_2649_33745_36153067_1_1_1_1,00.html..
2. Government Accountability Office, International Taxation: Large U.S. Corporations and Federal Contractors with Subsidiaries in Jurisdictions Listed as Tax Havens or Financial Privacy Jurisdictions, GAO-09-157 (December 2008), http://go.usa.gov/f1K.

3. See Dhammika Dharmapala and James R. Hines Jr., Which Countries Become Tax Havens? Working Paper 12802 (National Bureau of Economic Research, December 2006), www.nber.org/papers/w12802; and James R. Hines Jr. and Eric M. Rice, Fiscal Paradise: Foreign Tax Havens and American Business, Working Paper 3477 (National Bureau of Economic Research, April 1994), www.nber.org/papers/ w3477. Hines and Rice initially developed the criteria used by Dharmapala and Hines to identify 41 countries and territories as tax havens.

Concerns about tax-motivated decisions by U.S. multinationals to invest in foreign countries sometimes reflect the fear that the United States is losing jobs to other countries where tax rates are lower than they are here. However, the Congressional Budget Office anticipates that, apart from periods of general economic weakness— like the recent severe recession and slow recovery—jobs lost in that way tend to be replaced by others, perhaps in other industries, in other locations, and at different wages. Specifically, a shift of investment by U.S. multinationals to foreign markets can cause a loss of particular U.S. jobs (because a manufacturing plant is closed, for example, or a new one is not built). But over the long term, the economy as a whole generates enough jobs to compensate for those losses.

Still, the replacement jobs may be in different locations and for workers with different skills and experience. Moreover, unless that shift of investment is replaced by additional investment in the United States from other sources, less capital investment in this country will lead to lower overall wages and incomes for U.S. residents.

It bears emphasis that, although tax considerations matter, many other considerations, such as the quality of a country's labor force and infrastructure, its regulatory environment, and its legal and political institutions, play a role in decisions about where to invest.

The incentives to invest abroad would be different under a worldwide tax system with unlimited foreign tax credits: Firms would face the same tax rate regardless of where they invested because they would receive a credit for all taxes paid abroad whether or not those taxes exceeded the U.S. tax liability on that income. As a consequence, U.S. firms' investments, or capital, would no longer be inefficiently allocated because of tax considerations.[18] Departures from that system yield different tax rates for different investment locations, and economic efficiency is reduced to the extent that companies attempt to respond to those different rates.

Several researchers have tried to estimate how corporate taxes affect corporate investment behavior. One analysis showed that a 1 percentage-point increase in the U.S. tax rate relative to the tax rate in a foreign country increased U.S. multinational corporations' employment and sales in that foreign country by 1.6 percent and 2.9 percent, respectively. However, both the assets and the gross income of U.S. corporations in that country increased even more, suggesting that firms respond to differences in tax rates by shifting reported profits as well as by relocating business activities.[19]

Profit Shifting

Shifting investments to other countries can be quite costly, especially if the investment and the demand for skilled labor must be moved from a high-tax developed country to a low-tax jurisdiction that lacks an appropriate infrastructure or labor force and if goods that are produced abroad must be shipped to distant markets. Many of the tax advantages associated with relocating investment can be achieved—at a lower cost—by profit shifting, which allows businesses to maintain their actual investments in high-tax countries while reporting profits in low-tax jurisdictions.[20] Some profit-shifting methods are controversial, and government tax administrators and corporations find themselves at odds over the legality of such financial transactions between U.S. parent corporations and their foreign subsidiaries.

How do firms shift profits from one country to another? Some take advantage of the different tax treatment of entities and income in various jurisdictions, in some cases using rules that allow corporations to disregard, or ignore for tax purposes, income from certain subsidiaries. Another common way to reduce a company's tax burden is for a business to take advantage of transfer pricing— that is, how it sets prices on transfers of property, particularly intangible property (such as licenses to use intellectual property), among related businesses in different countries.

Differing Treatment of Entities and Income

U.S. parent corporations can—for tax purposes—transform their foreign subsidiaries into hybrid entities that shelter income from U.S. and foreign taxes. In a standard hybrid structure, a subsidiary of a CFC is treated as a corporation by the foreign jurisdiction but as what is known as a pass-through entity (for example, a branch of a CFC) under U.S. tax law. That arrangement allows the firm to take deductions in the foreign jurisdiction, but it also allows the income of the subsidiary to pass through to—that is, to be attributed to—the controlled foreign corporation. Thus, transactions between the two entities can be disregarded in calculating U.S. taxes, thereby avoiding U.S. taxes on such transactions. This feature of the U.S. tax system encourages companies to shift investments—and reported profits—abroad.

Such an intercompany transaction occurs, for example, when a subsidiary that is incorporated in a low-tax jurisdiction lends money to a subsidiary incorporated in a high-tax jurisdiction, effectively shifting income to the low-tax country in the form of interest payments. The borrowing subsidiary deducts, at the high tax rate, the interest payments made to the lending subsidiary. For U.S. tax purposes, however, the borrowing subsidiary can be treated as a *branch* of the lending subsidiary, and the income of the borrowing subsidiary is considered the legal income of the lending subsidiary. Therefore, the parent corporation can shield the passive income (the interest the borrowing entity has paid to the lending entity) from the taxation that normally would occur under the U.S. system. By allowing the company to disregard, for tax purposes, the passive income of the hybrid entity in the year it is earned, the tax code effectively defers the repatriation of the income and therefore the tax that will be owed on it.

Under "check-the-box" rules, a business can elect to treat a subsidiary as a separate corporation, a partnership, or a "disregarded entity" that is not treated as separate from its owner.[21] Those rules allow a corporation to remove a wholly owned subsidiary incorporated abroad from recognition by the U.S. tax system or to treat a partnership as a corporation for tax purposes. The rules were intended to simplify the classification of business entities by allowing multinational corporations to identify the status of an entity on its income tax forms.[22] But the rules also enhance the ability of U.S. parent companies to make use of differences in tax laws to generate tax credits on unrepatriated income or to shield passive income from U.S. taxation.[23]

A separate provision enacted in 2006 created the "look-through" rule, which instituted specific classifications of certain types of intercompany payments of CFCs. The look-through rule allows those intercompany payments to escape taxation, permitting much of what check-thebox rules also allow.[24] The provision originally was scheduled to expire at the end of 2008 but was extended through 2013. If the look-through rule is extended again, eliminating the check-the-box rules would not be sufficient to restrict the use of hybrid entities to avoid U.S. taxes.

Other features of the U.S. tax code also foster misalignments between deductions and income. U.S. corporations can deduct interest expenses from taxable income, regardless of the expenses' source. Therefore, a firm can claim the deduction for interest expenses related to foreign operations even if the income from those operations is never repatriated. That aspect of the U.S. tax code allows corporations to reduce the amount of income subject to U.S. taxation by deducting expenses for operations abroad without currently, or maybe ever, paying taxes on the income from those operations. This misalignment between deductions and taxation is attributable to the ability of firms to defer paying taxes on income earned abroad.

Transfer Pricing

U.S. firms also can shift income between countries through intercompany transfer pricing, a method of setting prices for the transfer of property, both real and intangible, between related parties, such as from a parent corporation to a subsidiary. Under Treasury regulations, that price should be determined by the "arm's length" standard—the price two unrelated parties would agree upon in the open market. However, for intellectual property of various kinds or for intangible assets, such as patents for production techniques, it is difficult to determine what an open-market price would be, and companies and tax authorities sometimes engage in costly disputes over the correct pricing. Companies have an incentive to underprice the transfer of assets to subsidiaries in low-tax countries and to overprice sales from affiliates in low-tax countries to those in high-tax countries.

A simple example of transfer pricing might involve a U.S. parent corporation's sale or lease of patent rights on a production innovation to a foreign subsidiary located in a low-tax jurisdiction.[25] Suppose the parent company developed the idea in the United States, where the research costs could be deducted from the company's taxable income at the U.S. corporate income tax rate. Then, suppose the patent right is sold by the parent company to a subsidiary in a low-tax country. Thereafter, the income from sales of the resulting product (net of production costs) is allocated to the patent holder in the low-tax country, and if production costs are low, most of the receipts will be attributable to that subsidiary. If the transfer price for the patent right is set below the open-market price, the parent company benefits by reducing its reported income in the United States while allocating most of the income generated from use of the patent to the patent-holding subsidiary in the lower-tax country. By reinvesting earnings in the low-tax subsidiary and not repatriating that income to the United States, the company avoids paying U.S. taxes associated with the U.S. invention.

Estimates of Profit Shifting

One study, noted earlier, showed that multinationals increased both real investment and reported profits in a country when its tax rate declined relative to the U.S. rate.[26] The analysis showed that a 1 percentage-point increase in the U.S. tax rate relative to the tax rate in a foreign country can increase U.S. multinational corporations' assets (including financial assets that may be unrelated to investment) and gross income (which are related to reported profits) in that country by 4.8 percent and 5.2 percent respectively, whereas employment and sales (which are indicators of real investments) in the host country increased much less. Those results suggest that profit shifting increases more than investment as a result of increases in the relative tax rate. Other studies present indirect evidence of profit shifting. Firms can relocate the legal home of their headquarters by merging with a foreign firm or by reincorporating abroad. If the firm relocates its legal headquarters to a low-tax jurisdiction, investments by the corporation are no longer subject to U.S. taxes even though the firm has made no changes to the location of capital. One report showed that an increase in the tax on repatriated income in the home country—assuming nothing else changes— increases the likelihood that a corporation will legally relocate, suggesting that the prospect of paying more in taxes can encourage firms to use accounting or other methods to change the location of the profits they report.[27] Some studies show that U.S. business income in low-tax countries is high relative to the actual presence of U.S. businesses in those countries.[28] Other research has shown disproportionately large ratios of profits earned by U.S. firms relative to GDP in low-tax countries.[29] Recent research has shown that firms' shares of income abroad are increasing but that their share of sales is not.[30] Those findings provide further evidence that firms are more likely to shift profits than to relocate investment in response to an increase in the U.S. tax rate relative to rates in other countries.

Budgetary Effects of Decisions About Location and Profit Shifting

Both the movement of investment abroad and the shifting of reported profits reduce income subject to U.S. corporate taxes. Several researchers have attempted to estimate how much tax revenue is lost to the U.S. Treasury through various accounting or other strategies that corporations use to reduce their tax liability on income earned from international transactions. The estimates vary widely—from a low of $10 billion to a high of $90 billion per year. The difference in those estimates is partly the result of what type of avoidance is analyzed, but the choice of research methodology also affects the outcome.[31] For example, some studies used data on differences in countries' rates of returns, but that method accounts only for profit shifting by U.S. multinationals. In contrast, regression analyses that estimate profit shifting encompass shifts by foreign firms to the United States and by U.S. firms to foreign countries. Those studies yielded the highest estimates of revenue losses. Other studies assess the impact of policy changes on revenue losses, but their results apply only to the specific activity affected by that change.

Policy Options

Among the avenues policymakers and analysts have suggested for changing—fundamentally or incrementally—the way the U.S. tax code treats multinational corporations are the following:

- Move significantly toward a purely worldwide system that limits or eliminates deferral,
- Move significantly toward a territorial system that exempts foreign income from domestic corporate taxation, or
- Prevent multinational corporations from avoiding taxes under the current system, for example, by restructuring the foreign tax credit or by treating entities and income consistently.

This report discusses some policy options in each of those categories.[32] Because the U.S. tax system affects multinationals' decisions about where to invest and how to report profits, those choices have consequences for economic efficiency and U.S. tax revenues—key criteria for evaluating trade-offs between tax policy options. This assessment of each policy option considers its potential effects on the following:

- Firms' decisions about where to invest,
- Firms' decisions about shifting profits from one country to another, and
- U.S. tax revenues.

Some options would dampen incentives to shift capital or profits abroad, thereby increasing economic efficiency and producing more tax revenue, others would bolster those incentives, and a third set could yield conflicting effects on efficiency and revenues (see Table 7). All of the options could be structured to boost U.S. corporate tax revenues, which could be used to reduce the deficit, pay for additional spending, finance reductions in corporate tax rates or other tax changes, or implement some combination of those actions. The economic and budgetary effects of the options would depend greatly on how they were structured. One important consideration in choosing among options involves firms' responses to different tax rates. For example, if multinational corporations are more likely to artificially shift reported profits than they are to adjust their investment behavior in response to lower tax rates abroad, options designed to limit such behavior may be preferable. Such options would restrict those corporations' ability to use various accounting methods to avoid paying taxes, and they might or might not impede efficient allocation of investments. Alternatively, if firms are more likely to adjust their investment behavior, tax policies that ensure economic efficiency could be more appropriate. However, it is difficult to distinguish between actual changes in investment behavior and those that are purely changes in accounting for profits. Although there is some evidence that firms' investment decisions are affected by changes in the U.S. corporate tax rate, research findings suggest that firms respond more by artificially shifting their reported profits abroad. The options presented here specifically address the taxation of foreign income earned by multinational corporations. Although this report does not discuss ways to change the treatment of U.S. corporations' domestic operations, the options presented could be combined with other, broader changes to the U.S. corporate tax system.

For example, changes in the taxation of multinational firms could be combined with a reduction in the corporate tax rate.

One proposal, presented in the 2010 report of the National Commission on Fiscal Responsibility and Reform (often called the Simpson– Bowles commission), would combine a territorial tax system with a reduction of the top corporate tax rate from 35 percent to a rate between 23 percent and 29 percent.[33] Although a territorial system would strengthen the incentive for firms to move operations and reported income abroad, the reduction in the corporate tax rate could offset those incentives and encourage firms to operate in and report their income in the United States.

Table 7. Policy Options for the Tax Treatment of U.S. Multinational Corporations

Policy	Description	Effect on Decisions About:		Change in U.S. Tax Revenue, 2012–2021 (Billions of dollars)
		Investment	Profit Shifting	
	Restructure the Foreign Tax Credit			
Determine Foreign Tax Credits on a Pooling Basis	Base the total foreign tax credit on the share of aggregate earnings repatriated from each country	Would increase incentives to invest in low-tax countries, although with little effect	Would increase incentives to keep profits abroad to avoid U.S. taxes on income from subsidiaries in low-tax countries and would reduce shifting of income	57[a]
Determine Foreign Tax Credits with a Per-Country Limit	Disallow cross crediting by limiting the amount of foreign tax credits allowed from each country	Would increase incentives to invest in low-tax countries, although with little effect	Would increase shifting of income from high-tax to low-tax countries	Potentially small increase
	Treat Entities and Income Consistently			
Eliminate Check-the-Box Rules	Allow income from foreign entities to be untaxed only if the entity's sole owner is legally organized or established within the same country	Would reduce incentives to invest abroad	Would reduce shifting of income from high-tax to low-tax countries	Increase
Defer Interest Deductions Related to Deferred Income	Defer the deduction of interest expenses so that the share of total foreign expenses that is allowed to be deducted is the ratio of repatriated income to total foreign income	Would indirectly increase incentives to invest abroad, although with little effect	Would reduce shifting of income	60[a]

Sources: Congressional Budget Office and the staff of the Joint Committee on Taxation.

a. The projected change in U.S. tax revenues for this option is for fiscal years 2013 to 2022. It includes the effects of interactions with other proposals in the President's fiscal year 2013 budget.

Other broad proposals involve combining reductions in the corporate tax rate with provisions that would move the tax system toward a more worldwide taxation structure. The President's fiscal year 2013 budget proposal, for example, called for reducing the top corporate tax rate from 35 percent to 28 percent and instituting a minimum tax on income retained in low-tax countries.[34] Reducing the corporate tax rate could dampen the incentive for multinational corporations to invest abroad or to change the location of reported income as a way to minimize their tax liability.

However, as long as some countries have low corporate income tax rates or none at all, such incentives will never be completely overcome by reducing U.S. tax rates.

Move More Toward a Worldwide Approach

Because the U.S. tax system taxes income earned abroad, it leans toward a worldwide approach. However, deferral of taxes on unrepatriated foreign income gives the tax system some characteristics of a territorial approach. Options that would eliminate or reduce the ability of multinational corporations to defer taxes on foreign income would move the U.S. tax system closer to a purely worldwide system. Some options would prevent U.S. firms from deferring U.S. taxes on foreign income; all income earned by those businesses would be taxed as it is earned.

Other options would maintain deferral but limit the types of income that could be deferred as a way to boost economic efficiency and increase revenues by removing incentives to shift income to low-tax jurisdictions or to invest in low-tax jurisdictions solely to avoid paying U.S. taxes.[35]

Eliminate Deferral

Under this option, all income earned by foreign subsidiaries of U.S. corporations—regardless of whether the income had been repatriated—would be subject to U.S. taxes. To prevent double taxation of foreign income, the foreign tax credit would remain in force, but, as under current law, that credit could not exceed the U.S. tax liability on foreign income. Because all income would be treated identically and taxed concurrently, however, the U.S. parent corporation's overhead expenses would no longer be allocated between domestic and foreign activities for determining the foreign tax credit.

Eliminating deferral would reduce the movement of capital and reported income to low-tax countries. Income earned abroad would generally be subject to the U.S. tax rate, thus reducing incentives to shift investment or reported income to countries with low taxes. With deferral, firms have an incentive to bring back only as much income from low-tax countries as can be sheltered by the excess credits generated from paying taxes in high-tax countries. Without deferral, the tax advantage of retaining income in a low-tax country would be diminished: All of a corporation's income would now be taxed currently at U.S. rates. Removing that advantage would reduce tax-based motivations to retain income in low-tax countries and encourage companies to redirect those resources to more efficient uses.

Although this option generally would dampen the incentive to shift investment and reported income to low-tax countries, in some circumstances, corporations might still find an advantage in doing so. Deferral might be eliminated, but the rules governing foreign tax credits would not change and the amount of the credit would still be limited to the U.S. tax liability on income earned abroad; firms investing in countries with tax rates above those in the United States would still be able to use cross crediting to avoid paying some tax. Thus, firms with excess foreign tax credits would still find it advantageous to shift investments or reported income from high-tax to low-tax countries. A variant of this option also would limit or eliminate cross crediting, further shrinking the incentive to shift investments to low-tax countries. Revenue gains resulting from eliminating deferral might be diminished if, in response, corporations shifted investment or reported income from low-tax to high-tax countries. A business that had transferred its income to a low-tax country solely to cut its tax liability, for example, would no longer benefit from retaining income in the low-tax country and might shift that income back to one or more high-tax countries. Such a response could offset the revenue gains to the United States. However, if the option was paired with limits on cross crediting, the tax incentives to shift investments or income to high-tax countries would be reduced. Eliminating deferral also could increase the incentive corporations have to incorporate, or register, abroad or to merge with overseas firms, thus reducing U.S. revenue gains in the future. However, the current tax system penalizes U.S. firms that "invert," or reincorporate abroad. A more worldwide system could encourage emerging businesses to choose foreign incorporation without fear of inversion penalties. (Under the current system, there seems to be little evidence that fledgling firms choose to start up abroad.)[36]

JCT estimates that eliminating deferral would raise, on net, about $50 billion between 2012 and 2016 and $114 billion over the 2012–2021 period.[37]

Eliminate Deferral for Certain Countries

This option would eliminate deferral of income earned in countries that are considered tax havens, giving corporations less incentive to invest in or shift income to those countries because all of the resulting income would be subject to U.S. taxation as it was earned. Those firms would still have an incentive to shift investment or reported income to other low-tax countries that are not considered tax havens. The net effects on investment and income-shifting are uncertain and have not been estimated. The effect on U.S. tax revenues also is not clear; it would depend on how firms responded to the new incentives for investment and income shifting. If the shift was from countries considered tax havens to high-tax countries, tax revenues attributable to repatriation could drop as firms relied more on cross crediting. Alternatively, if investment or income was moved to other low-tax countries and repatriated, U.S. tax revenues could rise.

Eliminate Deferral Related to Goods Produced Abroad

This option would eliminate deferral of income from the sale of goods produced abroad and imported to the United States, thus discouraging investment in foreign countries. The option would discourage the building of "runaway plants," which corporations use to shift production abroad while they either import the goods to the United States or export them to another country. In the absence of enforceable rules for tracing the path of goods from production to final consumers, U.S. multinational corporations can currently adjust the reported location of their sales, which may or may not require physical transfer of goods, to take advantage of deferral. For example, a firm might transfer goods or ownership of products to another country so that they could be imported back to the United States and the income from that sale would be deferrable. Because this option would target sales of goods abroad rather than transfers of reported income, it probably would have little effect on the shifting of income to low-tax countries. To the extent that this type of option is enforceable, U.S. tax revenues would probably increase because the option would limit the amount of income corporations could defer. However, the revenue gains could be minimal if the affected goods were produced in high-tax countries, where U.S. corporations can take larger foreign tax credits.

Move Toward a Territorial Approach

The United States could move formally toward a territorial system of taxation in any of several ways, one of which would be to exempt some or all income earned abroad from the U.S. corporate income tax.[38] Under one option, dividend income from investments abroad would be excluded from the U.S. tax base; in that case, by setting those dividends, multinational corporations would determine the amount of income earned abroad that would be excluded. Another option would require firms to use a formula, set by law, to distinguish foreign from domestic income. A formula approach is not necessarily limited to a purely territorial system; it could also be applied to a tax system, like the current one in the United States, that leans toward a worldwide system but has deferral.

Exempt Active Dividends Earned Abroad from U.S. Taxation

Exempting active foreign dividends from U.S. taxation would move the country toward a territorial tax system; active dividends from investments abroad would not be subject to domestic corporate taxes. All other forms of foreign income, including royalties, interest payments, and income from passive activities, would be taxed as they are under current law—as the income is earned.[39] Under this option, overhead expenses that are allocated to foreign operations (such as interest expenses generated by foreign subsidiaries' borrowing) would no longer be deductible because the income associated with those expenses would never be subject to U.S. taxation.

Exempting active foreign dividends would tend to increase investment in and reported income from low-tax countries. The option would make investment behavior by U.S. firms less efficient by increasing incentives to invest in low-tax countries.[40] Without a tax on repatriated dividends, U.S. multinational corporations would prefer to locate as much income as possible in the lowest-tax countries and would have more incentive to shift their reported income to such countries. Additionally, firms would have an incentive to characterize payments from foreign subsidiaries as active dividends because they would be exempt from U.S. taxation.

In general, countries with territorial (or exemption) tax systems collect less revenue, all else being equal, than they would with worldwide tax systems.[41] However, for two reasons, this option could raise revenues, despite the exemption of foreign dividends from taxable income: The option would restrict the ability of firms to deduct expenses associated with foreign operations, and it would more effectively tax income from royalties.[42] Other methods of exempting dividends could result in revenue losses.

All expenses now are deductible regardless of their source. Under this option, overhead expenses allocated to foreign operations would no longer be deductible and a corporation's taxable income would, according to JCT, increase enough to more than offset the Treasury's loss from not taxing active foreign income. If firms were allowed to continue to deduct all overhead expenses, including those associated with foreign operations, this option would probably result in a significant revenue loss.

This option also could result in added federal tax revenues because receipts from taxes on royalty income would probably rise once dividends were exempted. Current law subjects income from royalties to U.S. taxation. However, firms are able to use excess foreign tax credits generated by dividends from high-tax countries to cross credit against U.S. taxes on royalty income, allowing much of that income to escape U.S. taxation. Under this option, those dividends—once exempted from U.S. taxation— could not be used to generate excess foreign tax credits, thus increasing the likelihood that royalty income would become taxable.[43]

JCT has estimated that this option would increase revenues by about $32 billion from 2012 through 2016 and by $76 billion from 2012 through 2021.[44]

Apportion U.S. and Foreign Income by Formula

Another path to a territorial-type system would be to institute what is known as formula apportionment. Some observers consider this approach a simpler alternative to the current transfer-pricing rules, which require arm's-length pricing that is difficult to enforce. Under formula apportionment, before-tax income would be allocated to the United States and other countries according to a formula that accounted for the fraction of assets, sales, employment, and payroll a corporation had in each country, rather than relying on the taxpayer's reports of their income reflecting the transfer prices it had set.[45] The income allocated to the United States would then be subject to U.S. taxation.

Another type of formula apportionment would separately address the allocation of income from intangible assets, such as patents and trademarks, because that allocation is not readily observable. Such an approach would assign normal returns from an investment—that is, the return that would be expected to cover the cost of investment— to the country where the costs of producing the income are incurred and assign any remaining income (the income from intangible assets) on the basis of where the products are sold.[46]

With allocation on the basis of a formula, there would be fewer disputes between the tax authorities and taxpayers regarding the amounts that are reported as income. The formula would be statutory and based on actual business activity, so U.S. firms would find it more difficult to avoid taxes by moving reported income abroad. But because they would still have an incentive to locate real investment in countries with lower tax rates, this option would not reduce inefficiencies from decisions about where to locate investments.

In the United States, some states have already adopted formulas that determine taxable corporate income by the fraction of the corporation's sales, employment, or physical assets (or some weighted combination of each factor) within the state.[47] The European Union has proposed a similar form of formula apportionment under which taxable income would be determined using a weighted fraction of the share of sales, payroll, employment, and assets in a given country.[48]

Some important practical considerations could hamper the adoption of an apportionment system, however. For example, other countries might retaliate if the United States were to implement such a system without renegotiating its tax treaties and trade agreements.[49] Such concerns have led the European Union to limit its proposal for formula apportionment to its member countries.

Moreover, formula apportionment imposes an implicit tax on each factor used in the formula, which could reduce investment by discouraging companies from hiring workers or accumulating assets in high-tax countries (including the United States). As a result, those firms might shift their investments to low-tax countries, thus reducing U.S. tax revenues and increasing inefficiency. In addition, without coordination between countries, under this option some income could be taxed twice: Income would be treated as though derived from domestic sources and taxed in the United States, even though it was earned abroad and might be taxed by the host country as well.

Possible inefficiencies stemming from multinationals' incentives under the formula to change the location of investments would be mitigated by other factors that— both under current law and under the option—restrict movement in real activity. For example, firms might find it costly to transport materials or could find themselves constrained by the need to locate in a country where demand for their goods or services is high. Because capital is more mobile than customers, a formula that gave greater weight to the fraction of sales in a given country also would reduce the incentive to move production to a country that did not have a significant consumer market for the product.

This option would generally make it more difficult to shift reported income abroad because income would be allocated on the basis of relatively immobile factors, such as employment and sales. However, corporations could still take steps to minimize their taxes, especially if income was assigned in part according to the location of assets. For example, financial assets are relatively mobile and could be moved by firms trying to reduce their tax liability. The alternative approach, with separate allocations for income and intangible assets, would further constrain income shifting by allocating income on the basis of production costs and sales and reducing corporations' ability to strategically locate expenses and income in different countries. By using measures of actual business activity to allocate income between domestic and foreign sources instead of allowing firms to identify sources of income, this option would probably increase U.S. tax revenues. Because it would primarily impede corporations' efforts to shift reported profits as a way to avoid U.S. taxation, however, firms might respond by shifting their investments to low-tax countries, and the revenue gains from the option would be reduced.

Other Options

Two other types of options would address tax avoidance as it is permitted under the current system: restructuring the foreign tax credit and providing a system of more consistent treatment of various entities and income.

Restructure the Foreign Tax Credit

Although opportunities for cross crediting are limited because statutory corporate tax rates are generally higher in the United States than they are in other countries, some researchers still report significant use of cross crediting by U.S. multinational corporations.[50] Those results suggest that effective corporate tax rates, which reflect both the statutory rates and other features of the tax system, are lower in the United States than in some other countries (see the appendix for a discussion of effective rates). Concern over corporations' use of excess foreign tax credits to offset tax liabilities in low-tax countries has led to suggestions that the foreign tax credit should be restructured. Under one option, credits would be determined by "pooling"—limiting the total foreign tax credit according to the share of a firm's total foreign income that is repatriated to the U.S. parent company. Another option would limit the foreign tax credit that a corporation could claim for every country separately. Both options would affect repatriation of income by corporations that amass an excess of credits to shield repatriated income from taxation in the United States. The effects of such provisions on U.S. tax revenues would depend on firms' ability to adjust their repatriations or allocations of worldwide income. If modifications to the foreign tax credit were paired with an option that substantially reduced deferral or eliminated it altogether, those companies would be more likely to repatriate income, thus increasing U.S. tax receipts.

Determine Credits on a Pooling Basis. Under this option, foreign tax credits would be determined by pooling the firm's earnings from all foreign countries, and the total credit would be set according to the percentage of those aggregate earnings that are repatriated. In general, the option would reduce the foreign tax credit. As an example, consider a multinational corporation with gross earnings of $100 million from each of two subsidiaries—one in a country with a corporate tax rate of 12.5 percent and one in a country with a 40 percent tax rate (see Table 8). The firm pays a total of $52.5 million in foreign taxes. Suppose it repatriates all of its net earnings—$60 million—from the subsidiary in the high-tax country ($100 million in dividends minus the $40 million paid in taxes) but only $19.5 million from the subsidiary in the low-tax country ($22.3 million in dividends minus $2.8 million in taxes). In total, the firm pays $42.8 million in foreign taxes on the income repatriated to the United States. The foreign tax credit on the repatriated income also is $42.8 million—the top U.S. corporate rate of 35 percent applied to the repatriated gross income (that is, the income repatriated to the United States, including the foreign taxes that have been paid on that income, or $122.3 million). Thus, under current law the firm can take foreign tax credits equal to 82 percent of the total foreign taxes it paid ($42.8 million divided by $52.5 million). Under this scenario, the parent company has repatriated enough income from the subsidiary in the low-tax country to use up the excess credits from the subsidiary in the high-tax country. Under the option, credits would be assigned according to the amount of pooled foreign income, and the computation of foreign taxes paid would differ from that under current law in two key regards. First, the computation would start with the total amount of taxes paid to foreign entities ($52.5 million, in the example). Then, that total would be allocated among countries based on the share of total before-tax foreign earnings repatriated from each country.

In the example, the subsidiary in the low-tax country repatriated about 11 percent of the $200 million that the corporation earned through its operations in both foreign countries, and the subsidiary in the high-tax country repatriated 50 percent. The share of foreign taxes attributed to the low-tax subsidiary would be $5.9 million (11 percent of $52.5 million) and the share attributed to the high-tax subsidiary would be $26.3 million (50 percent of $52.5 million). The total would be $32.1 million and, under the pooling option, the foreign tax credit also would be $32.1 million. Thus, under the pooling option, the firm can take foreign tax credits only to the extent that those credits equal 61 percent of foreign taxes.

The foreign tax credit is smaller under the pooling option—in this example, it is reduced by $10.7 million—because the firm repatriated just 61 percent of its foreign income, and the credit would be limited to that share of the total foreign taxes the firm had paid. Under current law, the firm can claim a credit for more foreign taxes by repatriating more from high-tax countries than from low-tax countries. The pooling provision would reduce the amount of the credit because it would require a shared allocation.

The net effect on corporations' investment is not clear but probably would be small. Limiting the ability to cross credit could shift investment from high-tax to low-tax countries because corporations would not benefit as much from the larger tax credits. Firms also might respond to the higher taxes on repatriated income by increasing investment abroad and retaining more of the resulting earnings. The effects probably would be small, however, because the additional tax benefits would be insufficient to compensate for the barriers to moving investments abroad.

Nevertheless, determining foreign tax credits by pooling would have implications for the way firms allocate their income. As the example above shows, this option would restrict firms' ability to use excess credits from countries with high taxes to offset the U.S. corporate tax on income from countries with low taxes. It would thereby reduce the incentive to shift reported profits strategically between high-tax and low-tax countries to take advantage of cross crediting and deferral.

Table 8. Example of Pooling to Determine Credits (Millions of dollars)

	Low-Tax Country	High-Tax Country	Total
		Foreign Income	
Before-Tax Earnings	100.0	100.0	200.0
Foreign Tax Rate (Percent)	12.5	40.0	26.3 a
Foreign Taxes Paid on All Earnings	12.5	40.0	52.5
Repatriated Income	19.5	60.0	79.5
Repatriated Income Before Foreign Taxes			
Millions of dollars[b]	22.3	100.0	122.3
As a percentage of total before-tax earnings in both countries	11.1	50.0	61.1
		Taxes Under Current Law[c]	
U.S. Taxes Before Foreign Tax Credit	7.8	35.0	42.8
Foreign Taxes Paid on Repatriated Income[d]	2.8	40.0	42.8
Foreign Tax Credit with Cross Crediting	7.8	35.0	42.8
U.S. Taxes After Foreign Tax Credit	0	0	0
		Taxes Under a Pooling Option	
U.S. Taxes Before Foreign Tax Credit	7.8	35.0	42.8
Foreign Taxes Deemed Paid on Repatriated Income[e]	5.9	26.3	32.1
Foreign Tax Credit	5.9	26.3	32.1
U.S. Taxes After Foreign Tax Credit	1.9	8.7	10.7

Source: Congressional Budget Office.

a Amount is the average tax rate across the two countries.

b Repatriated income is "grossed up" to include the amount of taxes paid on that income to the foreign country; the value of the repatriated income is divided by one minus the tax rate of the country from which the income is repatriated.

c Per-country credits are shown for illustration only and are not calculated separately for U.S. tax purposes.

d Amount is the difference between grossed-up dividends and repatriated dividends.

e Amount is the product of total foreign taxes paid in both countries and grossed-up dividends in a particular country as a percentage of before-tax earnings in both countries.

Some income from subsidiaries in high-tax jurisdictions would be taxed at a substantially higher rate under the option than would be the case under current law. (In this example, the firm would pay the $40 million in taxes to the high-tax country, both under current law and with pooling, but the pooling option would require the firm to pay U.S. tax of $8.7 million in excess of the allowable foreign tax credit). That effect would be mitigated somewhat by the higher foreign tax credit imputed to the income repatriated from the lower-tax country ($5.9 million, compared with $2.8 million permitted under current law).

Corporations generally would no longer have an incentive to strategically choose individual subsidiaries from which to repatriate income because taxes would be proportionately assigned to each country and would not be linked to the individual subsidiary. In general, however, firms would still have an incentive to keep profits abroad to avoid paying U.S. taxes on income from subsidiaries in low-tax jurisdictions. Indeed, that incentive would be stronger because of the decline in the potential value of the foreign tax credit.

JCT estimates that adopting this option (the same as that proposed in the President's 2013 budget) would increase revenue by $25 billion between fiscal years 2013 and 2017 and by $57 billion between fiscal years 2013 and 2022.[51]

Determine Credits with a Per-Country Limit. Another option would disallow cross crediting by limiting the amount of credits allowed from each country. By requiring firms to compute a separate foreign tax credit for income earned in each country, a per-country limit, like that in effect in the United States between 1932 and 1976, would prevent firms from using repatriated income from a high-tax country to shield income from a low-tax country.

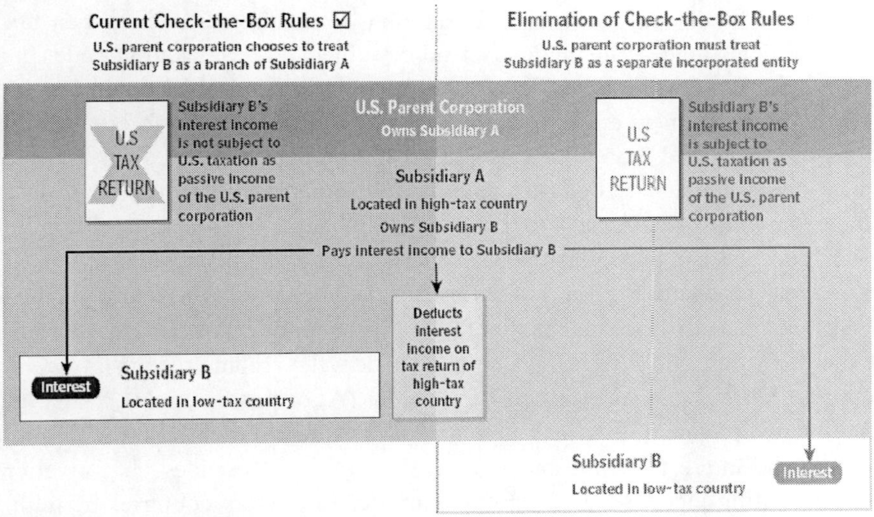

Source: Congressional Budget Office.

Figure 1. Effect of Check-the-Box Rules Under Current Law and If Eliminated.

By eliminating the ability of firms to cross credit by combining the income from high-tax and low-tax countries, this option would bolster the incentive to reinvest income in low-tax countries rather than repatriate it. Firms also would have an incentive to shift income from high-tax to low-tax countries. However, to the extent that income in low-tax countries is derived from passive activities, those firms could no longer shield the income from U.S. taxation through the use of excess foreign tax credits. It is not clear whether net repatriated income would decline as a result, but if repatriation responses were small, U.S. tax revenues would increase. A disadvantage of the option is its complexity. Firms would have to report the sources of income and calculate credits separately for each country instead of combining income from all countries under an aggregate credit as they do under current law. Large multinational corporations with multiple tiers of subsidiaries in different countries would face an especially large additional filing burden.

Treat Entities and Income Consistently

Another approach would be to incrementally change the taxation of U.S. multinational corporations by treating different forms of business entities and income more consistently than current law does. One option would repeal the check-the-box rules that allow U.S. multinationals to treat subsidiaries differently for U.S. tax purposes than they are treated by foreign jurisdictions. Another would preclude U.S. corporations from claiming interest deductions related to foreign income that stays abroad and out of reach of U.S. taxation. Both options generally would increase U.S. tax revenues because they would constrain the ability of firms to shift reported income from the United States to low-tax countries. However, they also could reduce economic efficiency if corporations responded by moving their investments to low-tax countries.

Eliminate Check-the-Box Rules

U.S. parent corporations currently can choose to shield the passive income of certain solely owned foreign subsidiaries from U.S. taxation by checking a box on their tax returns. (Under normal circumstances, the income would be subject to U.S. taxation under the subpart F rules that govern passive income.) Check-the-box rules allow multinational corporations to create and use hybrid business entities, which are treated differently by foreign tax authorities than they are by the United States. In a simple case, a parent company owns a Subsidiary A, which it has incorporated in a high-tax country. Subsidiary A wholly owns Subsidiary B, which is located in a low-tax country (see Figure 1). Subsidiary A borrows $100 million from Subsidiary B, and because Subsidiary B is a separate corporation, Subsidiary A is allowed to deduct its interest payments on the loan from its income on its tax return in the high-tax country. But Subsidiary B is treated as a branch of Subsidiary A for U.S. tax purposes under the check-the-box rules, and the U.S. tax code considers the income received by a branch (B, in this example) to be the legal income of the parent (A, in this example). Thus, under U.S. tax law, the interest payment, in effect, is treated as an internal transaction within Subsidiary A. As a result, the interest income received by Subsidiary B escapes U.S. taxation. Those rules facilitate shifting income from high-tax countries to low-tax countries by multinational corporations and encourage firms to shift investment and reported profits abroad to avoid paying U.S. taxes. By making interest payments to subsidiaries in low-tax countries and deducting those payments in high-tax countries, the firms effectively shift that income from subsidiaries in high-tax countries to subsidiaries in low-tax countries. Furthermore, those payments, which would be considered passive income and subject to U.S. taxation, are shielded from U.S. taxes by the check-boxrule that allows Subsidiary B to be treated as part of Subsidiary A. As a result, the interest payments are not considered income under current U.S. tax law. This option would require that income from foreign entities be excluded from taxable income only if that entity's sole owner is legally organized or established within the *same* country. That restriction would constrain U.S. parent corporations' ability to shift income from high-tax to low-tax countries through payments of passive income that currently escape taxation under subpart F. Passive income payments made between two entities could still be excluded from taxable income as long as both were in the same country. The advantages of investing abroad would decline under this option because firms would lose the ability to shield certain income from those investments. There would be no advantage to shifting income because payments would be taxed at the same time and at the same rates as the corresponding deductions. Moreover, U.S. tax revenues would increase because passive income from solely owned subsidiaries would not be shielded from U.S. taxation. (However, if the look-through rule provision was extended beyond 2013, eliminating check-the-box rules would not prevent firms from shielding intercompany payments from U.S. taxation.)

Defer Interest Deductions Related to Deferred Income

U.S. multinational corporations can deduct interest expenses from their taxable income. Those expenses are not allocated between foreign and U.S. sources for purposes of determining deductions against gross income that is subject to U.S. taxation. However, for determining the limit on the foreign tax credit, interest expenses are allocated to foreign and domestic sources in proportion to the ratio of foreign assets to total assets. This option would defer the deduction of interest expenses allocated to foreign income that is not currently subject to U.S. taxation. The proportion of all foreign-related deductions allowed would be the same as the ratio of taxable foreign income to total foreign income. The foreign tax credit would still be determined by allocating all expenses according to the share of a company's total assets in each country. In general, requiring interest deductions to be deferred until the associated income is repatriated would provide an incentive for corporations to accelerate repatriation. Still, increased repatriation could come from countries with higher taxes, and firms could still use cross crediting to shield income repatriated from low-tax countries under this option. By making it more costly for corporations to shift income abroad, this option might cause firms to respond by adjusting their investments to avoid an increase in tax liability. Nevertheless, the targeted nature of this option would probably produce little change in investment. The incentives to shift income would decline, because firms could no longer immediately claim deductions for expenses associated with foreign operations when taxes on the income earned from those activities was deferred. JCT estimates that adopting this option (which was proposed in the President's 2013 budget) would increase revenue by $28 billion between fiscal years 2013 and 2017 and by $60 billion between fiscal years 2013 and 2022.[52]

APPENDIX: CORPORATE TAX RATES

Corporate income tax rates are specified by the tax code. However, the actual tax rates that a firm faces differ from the rates in the tax code—the statutory tax rate— because of other provisions in the code that affect its tax liability. Both the statutory rates and those that the firm actually pays can be compared among countries to analyze the tax burdens firms face in different countries.

Statutory Corporate Income Tax Rates

Most developed countries—including all members of the Organisation for European Cooperation and Development (OECD)—tax corporate income, typically at the national and the subnational (state or province, for example) levels. Statutory tax rates on corporate income differ from one country to another. In 2011, the top rates among the 34 members of the OECD ranged from 12.5 percent in Ireland to 39.5 percent in Japan (see Figure A-1). Those rates combined the top national statutory corporate tax rate—that is, the tax rate that applies to income in the highest tax bracket—in each country with the average corporate tax rate set at the subnational level of government.[1] In 2011, the top U.S. federal statutory rate on business income that was subject to the corporate income tax was 35 percent, and the average top statutory rate imposed on that income by states was about 6 percent—for a combined top statutory rate of 39.1 percent (after accounting for the fact that state taxes are deductible from federal taxable income). Weighted by gross domestic product, the average combined tax rate for current OECD countries, excluding the United States, was 19.1 percent in 2011. (That average probably declined in 2012 because Japan cut its top corporate tax rate—at the national level—in April from 30 percent to 25.5 percent, making the statutory U.S. tax rate the highest among OECD member countries.)[2] Although the majority of OECD countries have a top corporate tax rate of at least 25 percent, some countries have rates that are so low (sometimes zero) that they are considered tax havens, attracting both investment by and reported income from multinational corporations (see Box 1 on page 13).

Average Tax Rates

Statutory rates may not represent the tax rate that multinational corporations actually face. Because of the graduated rate structure, deductions, credits, and other business tax provisions (such as favorable depreciation allowances and credits for certain activities), the average tax rates that corporations pay—the ratio of total taxes to aggregate income—are generally below the top statutory rates. For example, the average rate faced by U.S. domestic firms with no foreign operations between 2005 and 2009 was about 10 percentage points lower than the statutory rate.[3]

Effective Marginal Tax Rates

Another way to compare corporate tax rates among countries is to look at the effective marginal corporate tax rate—the rate of tax paid on an additional dollar of income. Like average tax rates, effective marginal tax rates take into account tax preferences as well as the statutory tax rate.

Corporations generally consider their marginal tax rates when they assess whether to make additional investments in ongoing projects. In contrast, average tax rates are more relevant when considering substantial investments, such as those required for building manufacturing plants abroad. As a result, average tax rates could carry more weight than marginal rates do in the calculations that determine whether a company will make a large new investment in a particular country.

Effective marginal tax rates depend on several factors, but two in particular—the treatment of depreciation and the treatment of financing—largely determine the differences between statutory rates and effective marginal tax rates. Consequently, an important component of the after-tax cost of using a capital asset is the rate at which it can be fully depreciated for tax purposes, which is specified in law for U.S. firms. (That rate may differ substantially from the rate at which the actual value of the asset decreases over time.)

Under U.S. tax law—unlike that in the other OECD countries—the rules for depreciation tend to favor investments in machinery over investments in industrial structures. Combining those depreciation rules with the relatively high U.S. statutory tax rates, the corporate income tax in the United States distorts, to a greater degree than occurs in most other OECD countries, the incentives for marginal investment that are associated with the choice between machinery and structures. Marginal tax rates in the United States are similar to those in other OECD countries for equity-financed investments in machinery, they are substantially above the average for equity-financed investments in industrial structures, and they are substantially below the average for debt-financed investments in machinery.[4] (Businesses finance investments either through equity—by selling ownership shares or stock—or through debt.)

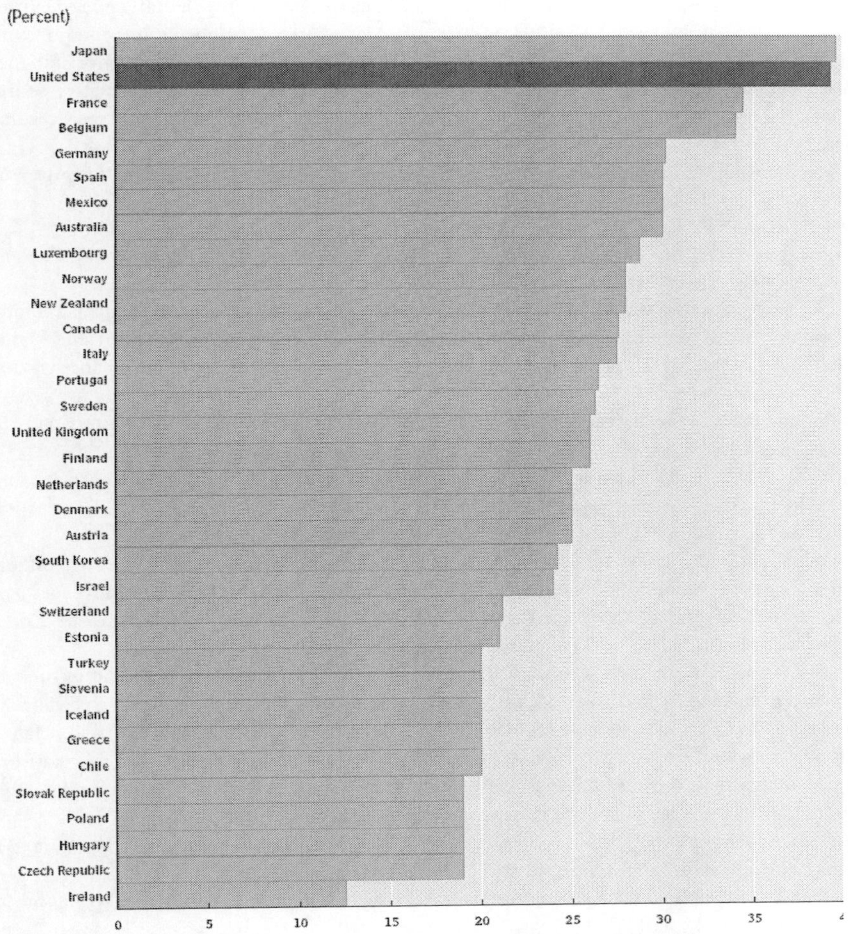

Source: Congressional Budget Office based on data from the Organisation for Economic Co-operation and Development (OECD).

Note: The combined corporate income tax rate is the rate charged at the national and subnational (state or province, for example) levels.

Figure A-1. Combined Corporate Income Tax Rate of OECD Countries, 2011.

End Notes

[1] That year is the most recent for which detailed data are available. Since then, receipts from corporate income taxes have accounted for a smaller share of federal revenues—ranging from 7 percent in 2009 to 10 percent in 2012.

[2] Such rules are sometimes called CFC rules because they apply to income from controlled foreign corporations. For a comparison of various national tax systems, see Joint Committee on Taxation, *Background and Selected Issues Related to the U.S. International Tax System and Systems That Exempt Foreign Business Income,* JCX-33-11 (May 20, 2011), http://go.usa.gov/gPrJ.

[3] See Edward Kleinbard, "Stateless Income's Challenge to Tax Policy," *Tax Notes* (September 5, 2011), pp. 1021–1042.

[4] Although each U.S. shareholder of a given CFC must own at least 10 percent of the stock, it is common for 100 percent of the stock in a CFC to be owned by a U.S. corporation.

[5] A deduction is an expense or an amount of money that reduces a taxpayer's taxable income, thus reducing the tax liability by the amount of the deduction multiplied by the applicable tax rate. A credit, by contrast, is a dollar-for-dollar reduction in the amount the taxpayer owes.

[6] Active and passive income are discussed in more detail later in this report. The tax code identifies two other categories for special treatment. The first consists of income from investments in countries with which the United States does not have diplomatic relations and from countries that support terrorism: Income in that category is not eligible for a tax credit. The other category consists of income that is sourced (that is, attributed) to foreign countries by treaty; corporations must compute the foreign tax credit separately for that income.

[7] See Kimberly Clausing, "Tax Holidays (and Other Escapes) in the American Jobs Creation Act," *National Tax Journal*, vol. 58, no. 3 (September 2005), pp. 331–346.

[8] See Harry Grubert and Rosanne Altshuler, "Corporate Taxes in a World Economy: Reforming the Taxation of Cross-Border Income," in John W. Diamond and George Zodrow, eds., *Fundamental Tax Reform: Issues, Choices and Implications* (MIT Press, 2008).

[9] Under both scenarios, the firm would face the same underlying tax rate on the new investments (before accounting for foreign tax credits, deferrals, and other adjustments). In the previous example (see Table 3), the firm faced an underlying tax rate of 25 percent ($35 million in U.S. taxes and $15 million in foreign taxes on $200 million of before-tax income). In this example (see Table 4), it also faces an underlying tax rate of 25 percent ($40 million in taxes in the high-tax country and $10 million in taxes in the low-tax country on $200 million of before-tax income).

[10] Specifically, if a U.S. CFC purchased foreign property and sold it to another foreign subsidiary that was controlled by that CFC—a related party—that income would be deemed passive.

[11] 26 U.S.C. §951 et seq. (2006 & Supp.).

[12] Some firms can take a deduction for foreign taxes *in lieu of* the credit. Such deductions are estimated to have resulted in forgone revenues of $0.2 billion in 2011 and are expected to reduce federal revenues by $1.2 billion over the 2011–2015 period. See Joint Committee on Taxation, *Estimates of Federal Tax Expenditures for Fiscal Years 2011–2015,* JCS-1-12 (January 17, 2012), http://go.usa.gov/flW.

[13] Information is available from several sources. For example, data on foreign and domestic income are available from financial statements and, with less detail, on the Internal Revenue Service's Schedule M3; data on distributions from CFCs are available on the information returns of those corporations; and repatriated income is reported on the tax form that corporations use to claim foreign tax credits. Still, comparisons involving repatriated income are difficult because the available data sources measure income differently and report income from different types of entities that are not easily linked.

[14] See Bureau of Economic Analysis, "U.S. Direct Investment Abroad: Financial and Operating Data for U.S. Multinational Companies" (November 19, 2012), http://go.usa.gov/fTf.

[15] Dane Mott and Amy Schmidt, "Accounting Issues: Show Us the Foreign Cash!" *North American Equity Research* (September 12, 2011).

[16] See Joint Committee on Taxation, *Estimates of Federal Tax Expenditures for Fiscal Years 2011–2015*, JCS-1-12 (January 17, 2012), http://go.usa.gov/flW. Tax expenditures are defined by the Congressional Budget and Impoundment Control Act of 1974 as "revenue losses attributable to provisions of the Federal tax laws which allow a special exclusion, exemption, or deduction from gross income or which provide a special credit, a preferential rate of tax, or a deferral of tax liability." Estimates of tax expenditures, unlike those for revenues, do not reflect any changes in taxpayers' behavior in response to changes in the tax code.

[17] In seeking to exploit market power, it is more likely that a corporation would use the many methods of manipulating returns on intangible assets, including licensing or franchising a brand name, that do not require a change in the location of an investment.

[18] That efficiency also could be achieved if every country had the same territorial tax system and thus identical effective tax rates on all foreign investments. Allowing unlimited credits also would amount to a U.S. subsidy for foreign governments.

[19] See Kimberly A. Clausing, "Multinational Firm Tax Avoidance and Tax Policy," *National Tax Journal*, vol. 62, no. 4 (December 2009), pp. 703–705.

[20] Profit shifting also imposes costs because it requires the use of resources for tax planning.

[21] Most corporate filers do not actually check a box; the classification form includes some automatic classifications that depend on the number of owners and their liability status. For example, an entity is automatically disregarded for taxation if it has a single owner without limited liability, and it is classified as a partnership by default if it has multiple owners, at least one of which does not have limited liability.

[22] Although those rules were enacted to simplify the process of classifying and structuring business arrangements, any gain is diminished by the use of such complicated hybrid tax strategies as the "Double Irish" and "Dutch Sandwich" approaches. See Jesse Drucker, "Google 2.4% Rate Shows How $60 Billion Lost to Tax Loopholes," *Bloomberg News* (October 21, 2010), www.bloomberg.com/news/2010-10-21/google-2-4-rate-showshow-60-billion-u-s-revenue-lost-to-tax-loopholes.html. Some observers assert that check-the-box rules add complexity by encouraging corporations to compute taxes under different scenarios to determine which entity status will yield the smallest tax liability. See American Bar Association Tax Section, Task Force on International Tax Reform, "Report of the Task Force on International Tax Reform," *Tax Lawyer,* vol. 59, no. 3 (2006), pp. 649–743.

[23] Similarly, foreign parent corporations can use differences between U.S. tax laws and those of other countries to shield income from taxation at home.

[24] For a comparison of check-the-box and look-through rules, see David R. Sicular, "The New Look-Through Rule: W(h)ither Subpart F?" *Tax Notes* (April 23, 2007), pp. 349–378.

[25] For a discussion of other ways to transfer income, see Joint Committee on Taxation, *Present Law and Background Related to Possible Income Shifting and Transfer Pricing*, JCX-37-10 (July 20, 2010), http://go.usa.gov/fiw.

[26] See Kimberly A. Clausing, "Multinational Firm Tax Avoidance and Tax Policy," *National Tax Journal*, vol. 62, no. 4 (December 2009), pp. 703–725.

[27] Johannes Voget, *Headquarter Relocations and International Taxation*, Working Paper 1008 (Oxford University Centre for Business Taxation, April 2010).

[28] Melissa Costa and Jennifer Gravelle, "U.S. Multinational Corporations: Effective Tax Rates and Business Locations," in National Tax Association, *Proceedings of the 103rd Annual Conference* (Chicago, 2010), www.ntanet.org/publications/nta-proceedings/ 222.html.

[29] Jane Gravelle, *Tax Havens: International Tax Avoidance and Evasion,* CRS Report for Congress R40623 (Congressional Research Service, September 3, 2010).

[30] Harry Grubert, "Foreign Taxes and the Growing Share of U.S. Multinational Company Income Abroad: Profits, Not Sales, are Being Globalized," *National Tax Journal*, vol. 64, no. 2 (2012), pp. 247–281.

[31] See, for example, Kimberly A. Clausing, "The Revenue Effects of Multinational Firm Income Shifting," *Tax Notes* (March 28, 2011), pp. 1580–1586, and "Multinational Firm Tax Avoidance and Tax Policy," *National Tax Journal*, vol. 62, no. 4 (December 2009), pp. 703–725; Martin Sullivan, "U.S. Multinationals Shifting Profits Out of the United States," *Tax Notes* (March 10, 2008), pp. 1078–1082, and "Shifting Profits Offshore Costs U.S. Treasury $10 Billion or More," *Tax Notes* (September 27, 2004), pp. 1477–1481; and Charles W. Christian and Thomas D. Schultz, "ROA-Based Estimates of Income Shifting by U.S. Multinational Corporations," in James Dalton and Beth Kilss, eds., *IRS Research Bulletin: Recent Research on Tax Administration and Compliance—Proceedings of the 2005 IRS Research Conference,* Publication 1500 (Washington, D.C., 2005), pp. 57–72, http://go.usa.gov/gP2R.

[32] For estimates of the revenues that would accrue from adopting some of those options, see Joint Committee on Taxation, *Estimated Budget Effects of the Revenue Provisions Contained in the President's Fiscal Year 2013 Budget Proposal*, JCX-27-12 (March 14, 2012), http://go.usa.gov/gPrA; and Congressional Budget Office, *Reducing the Deficit: Spending and Revenue Options* (March 2011).

[33] See National Committee on Fiscal Responsibility and Reform, *The Moment of Truth: Report of the National Commission on Fiscal Responsibility and Reform* (December 2010), http://go.usa.gov/ fO7.

[34] See White House and Department of the Treasury, *The President's Framework for Business Tax Reform* (February 2012), http://go.usa.gov/fOv.

[35] Eliminating deferral would remove the territorial features of the current tax system but would still not result in a purely worldwide tax system unless the limit on the foreign tax credit was eliminated as well.

[36] See Eric J. Allen and Susan C. Morse, "Firm Incorporation Outside the U.S.: No Exodus Yet" (unpublished paper, University of California, Hastings College of Law, October 2011), www.works.bepress.com /susanmorse/10.

[37] That estimate differs from the tax expenditure for deferral because of adjustments made to account for firms' behavioral responses (for example, choosing to restructure in favor of foreign branches rather than subsidiaries) in the estimates for policy options. See Congressional Budget Office, *Reducing the Deficit: Spending and Revenue Options* (March 2011), p. 186.

[38] For a comparison of options to eliminate deferral and exempt dividends, see Rosanne Altshuler and Harry Grubert, "Corporate Taxes in the World Economy: Reforming the Taxation of Cross-Border Income," in John W. Diamond and George R. Zodrow, eds., *Fundamental Tax Reform: Issues, Choices, and Implications* (MIT Press, 2008).

[39] Unlike dividends, other types of active income (such as interest payments, fees, or royalties) are taxed when they are earned because they flow directly to the parent company. All passive income is taxed as it is earned under subpart F of the Internal Revenue Code.

[40] There could be efficiency gains for the U.S. economy to the extent that the overall tax on capital was reduced. Determining the net effect is difficult and depends on the details of the option.

[41] Territorial approaches are sometimes referred to as exemption systems because they exempt, subject to anti-abuse rules, foreign income from taxation.

[42] Kimberly A. Clausing, "Corporate Tax Revenues in OECD Countries," *International Tax and Public Finance,* vol. 14, no. 2 (April 2007), pp. 115–133.

[43] For discussion of the effects of exempting dividends, see Rosanne Altshuler and Harry Grubert, "Where Will They Go If We Go Territorial: Dividend Exemption and the Location Decisions of U.S. Multinational Corporations," *National Tax Journal,* vol. 54, no. 3 (December 2001), pp. 787–809; and Harry Grubert, "Enacting Dividend Exemption and Tax Revenue," *National Tax Journal,* vol. 54, no. 3 (December 2011), pp. 811–827.

[44] Congressional Budget Office, *Reducing the Deficit: Spending and Revenue Options* (March 2010), pp. 187–188.

[45] Net income, rather than gross income, would be allocated, causing the deductions for expenses also to be allocated proportionately to foreign income. As a result, deductions against foreign income would be higher than they are under the current system.

[46] For discussion of this approach, see Reuven S. Avi-Yonah, Kimberly A. Clausing, and Michael C. Durst, "Allocating Business Profits for Tax Purposes: A Proposal to Adopt a Formulary Profit Split," *Florida Tax Review,* vol. 9, no. 5 (2009), pp. 497– 553.

[47] See Federation of Tax Administrators, "State Apportionment of Corporate Income" (May 2012), www.taxadmin.org/fta/rate/ tax_stru.html.

[48] For a discussion of the consequences of such a change, see Michael Devereux and Simon Loretz, *The Effects of EU Formula Apportionment on Corporate Tax Revenues,* Working Paper WP 07/06 (Oxford University Centre for Business Taxation, April 2007), www.sbs.ox.ac.uk/centres/tax/papers/Pages/paperWP0706.aspx.

[49] For a discussion of the complexity of implementing formula apportionment, see Joanne Martens Weiner, *Formulary Apportionment and Group Taxation in the European Union: Insights from the United States and Canada,* Taxation Papers, Working Paper 8 (European Commission, 2005), http://ec.europa.eu/taxation _customs/common/publications/services_ papers/working _papers/index_en.htm.

[50] Harry Grubert and Rosanne Altshuler, "Corporate Taxes in a World Economy: Reforming the Taxation of Cross-Border Income," in John W. Diamond and George Zodrow, eds., *Fundamental Tax Reform: Issues, Choices and Implications* (MIT Press, 2008).

[51] Joint Committee on Taxation, *Estimated Budget Effects of the Revenue Provisions Contained in the President's Fiscal Year 2013 Budget Proposal,* JCX-27-12 (March 14, 2012), http://go.usa.gov/gPrA.

[52] Joint Committee on Taxation, *Estimated Budget Effects of the Revenue Provisions Contained in the President's Fiscal Year 2013 Budget Proposal,* JCX-27-12 (March 14, 2012), http://go.usa.gov/gPrA.

End Notes for Appendix

[1] For each country in which subnational corporate taxes are deductible from national taxes, as in the United States, the combined statutory tax rate is the sum of the national and subnational tax rates minus the product of the national and subnational statutory rates, which amounts to the value of the deduction.

[2] Japan added a 10 percent surtax for three years, raising the rate to 28.01 percent (excluding local taxes).

[3] For a comparison of the average U.S. tax rate with that of selected other countries, including major trading partners, see Kevin Markle and Douglas Shackelford, *Cross Country Comparisons of Corporate Income Taxes*, Working Paper 16839 (National Bureau of Economic Research, February 2011) www.nber.org/papers/w16839.

[4] See Congressional Budget Office, *Corporate Income Tax Rates: International Comparisons* (November 2005).

In: Taxing U.S. Multinational Corporations
Editor: Angelique Gilder
ISBN: 978-1-62618-145-8

Chapter 2

MOVING TO A TERRITORIAL INCOME TAX: OPTIONS AND CHALLENGES*

Jane G. Gravelle

SUMMARY

Among potential tax reforms under discussion by Congress is revising the tax treatment of foreign source income of U.S. multinational corporations. Some business leaders have been urging a movement toward a territorial tax, which would eliminate some U.S. income taxes on active foreign source income.

Under a territorial tax, only the country where the income is earned imposes a tax. Territorial proposals include the Grubert-Mutti proposal (included in President Bush's Advisory Panel on Tax Reform proposal in 2005) and, more recently, a draft Ways and Means Committee proposal and a Senate bill, S. 2091. The Fiscal Commission also proposed a territorial tax. Proposals have, however, also been made to increase the taxation of foreign source income, including S. 727, and proposals by President Obama.

Although the United States has a worldwide system that includes foreign earnings in U.S. taxable income, two provisions cause the current system to resemble a territorial tax in that very little tax is collected. Deferral delays paying taxes until income is repatriated (paid as a dividend by the foreign subsidiary to its U.S. parent). When income is repatriated, credits for foreign taxes paid offset the U.S. tax due. Under cross-crediting, unused foreign tax credits from high tax countries or on highly taxed income can be used to offset U.S. tax on income in low tax countries.

Some proponents of a territorial tax urge such a system on the grounds that the current system discourages repatriations. Economic evidence suggests that effect is small, in part because in normal circumstances a large share of income is retained for permanent reinvestment. Amounts held abroad may have increased, however, as firms lobbied for another repatriation holiday (similar to that adopted in 2004) that allowed firms to exempt most dividends from income on a one-time basis.

Opponents are concerned about encouraging investment abroad. A territorial tax is generally not viewed as efficient because it favors foreign investment, but that increased

* This is an edited, reformatted and augmented version of a Congressional Research Service publication, CRS Report for Congress R42624, from www.crs.gov, prepared for Members and Committees of Congress, dated July 25, 2012.

outflow of investment is likely to have a small effect relative to the U.S. economy. Artificial shifting of profits into tax havens or low tax countries is a current problem that could be worsened under some territorial tax designs, and proposals have included measures to address this problem.

Proposals also address the transitional issue of the treatment of the existing stock of unrepatriated earnings. The Ways and Means proposal would tax this stock of earnings, but at a lower rate, and use the revenues to offset losses from other parts of the plan, which would lead to a long-run revenue loss. S. 2091 has a similar approach. The Grubert-Mutti proposal does not have a specific transitional tax, but would raise revenue largely due to its disallowance of parent overhead expenses aimed at reducing profit shifting. The other two proposals also contain provisions to address profit shifting.

In addition there are complicated issues in the design of a territorial tax, such as how to treat branches and dividends of firms in which the corporation is only partially owned. A number of issues arise from the ending of foreign tax credits, with perhaps the most significant one being the increased tax on royalties, which are currently subject to tax, have low or no foreign taxes, and would lose the shield of excess credits.

The final section of the report briefly discusses some alternative options, including those in S. 727 and in the Administration proposals. It also discusses hybrid approaches that combine territorial and worldwide systems in a more efficient way, including eliminating the disincentive to repatriate.

One such approach is a minimum tax on foreign source income, which is proposed by the President in the context of current rules, but could be combined with a territorial system.

INTRODUCTION

Tax reform is a perennial issue before Congress. One area of increasing attention is the taxation of U.S. companies on the income they earn abroad. Recently, proposals have been made to, in some cases, decrease taxes and in others to increase these taxes.

Businesses leaders have been urging a movement toward a territorial tax, which would generally eliminate U.S. income taxes on active foreign source income. Such a proposal (presumably based on one developed by Grubert and Mutti) was included in the President's Advisory Panel on Tax Reform in 2005,[1] more recently in a draft proposal by Ways and Means Committee Chairman Dave Camp,[2] and in a bill, S. 2091, introduced by Senator Enzi. The National Commission on Fiscal Responsibility and Reform (referred to as the Fiscal Commission) also proposed a territorial tax in general terms.[3]

Proposals have also been made to move in the opposite direction and increase the taxation of foreign source income, including S. 727, introduced by Senators Wyden and Coats, which would use the significant revenues gained to help finance a corporate income tax rate cut. President Obama has included increased taxes on foreign source income in his budget outlines and, more recently, in his framework for business tax reform, as a revenue source for rate reduction.[4] Because of various features in the current tax system, the U.S. tax system already bears a close resemblance, in terms of revenue collected, to a territorial tax. Tax on the income of foreign subsidiaries is deferred until repatriated (paid as dividends to the U.S. parent) and tax can be avoided by not repatriating income. The system limits credits claimed for foreign taxes paid to U.S. tax on foreign income. The limit, however, is on an overall basis, permitting unused credits from high-tax countries to shield income from low-tax countries, or income that bears little foreign tax, from being taxed in the United States. Because firms have flexibility in timing repatriations, the residual effective tax rate on foreign income is estimated at only 3.3%.[5] Some types of income, such as royalties, are treated more favorably under the current system than they would be under a territorial tax.

Economists have traditionally analyzed the foreign tax system in terms of economic efficiency. Economic theory tends to support, on efficiency grounds, a worldwide system in which income from U.S. investment earned abroad is subject to the same tax, or as close to the same tax as possible, as that on domestic investment. It does not support a territorial tax, and most proposals in the past were to move closer to an effective worldwide tax (see *Appendix*). At the same time, if such a change is not feasible, another question becomes whether moving to an explicit territorial tax would be better or worse than the present system. The fundamental issues are

- the effects on disincentives to repatriate income,
- to what extent the revision will divert investment from the United States,
- the effects on artificial profit shifting,
- transition issues,
- administrative and compliance considerations, and
- the revenue consequences.

There is no single blueprint for a territorial tax and the answers to these questions depend, to some extent, on specific design choices.

This report first explains how the international tax system works and describes the magnitude and distribution of foreign source income and taxes. The report then focuses on alternative features of a territorial tax and their consequences. It also contains, in a final section, a brief discussion of options that move in the opposite direction and other alternatives that do not fit into either the territorial or worldwide approach (such as current taxation of foreign source income but at a lower rate).[6]

How the International Tax System Works

The current U.S. tax system is a hybrid. It has some elements of a residence-based or worldwide tax, where income of a country's firms is taxed regardless of its location. It also has some elements of a source based or territorial tax, where all income earned within a country is taxed only by that country regardless of the nationality of the firms. The provisions that introduce territorial features are deferral and cross-crediting. There are a number of complex interactions that will affect both the design of a territorial or other tax revision and the consequences of those changes.

Deferral

Deferral allows a firm to delay taxation of its earnings in foreign subsidiaries until the income is paid as a dividend to the U.S. parent company. Although a territorial tax is often focused on exempting foreign source income that under current law is taxed when repatriated, there are four basic categories of foreign source income, three of which are not eligible for deferral. They are profits of foreign incorporated subsidiaries; current payment income, such as royalties and interest payments; branch income; and Subpart F income.

Profits of Foreign Incorporated Subsidiaries

U.S. multinationals are not currently taxed on the profits of their subsidiaries incorporated abroad (except for "Subpart F Income" discussed below). Rather they defer payment of taxes until the income is received by the parent as a dividend (repatriated). U.S. tax is then due on the dividend and, because the dividend is after foreign tax, an additional amount (called a gross-up) is added to taxable income to reflect the foreign taxes paid and place the income on a pre-tax basis.[7] A foreign tax credit is then allowed against this U.S. tax.

Current Payment Income

Current payment income is income that is received as a direct payment, such as royalties and interest. It is taxed currently. This income is usually deductible as an expense in the foreign country and, indeed, may not constitute true foreign source income, at least in the case of royalties that could be viewed as more like export income.

Branch Income

Branch income is income from operations that are carried out without a separately incorporated foreign subsidiary. Income of operations organized as foreign branches rather than as separately incorporated subsidiaries is also taxed currently. For tax purposes, branch gross income and deductions are combined with parent income just as if the operation were taking place in the United States. Although branch income is not eligible for deferral, it can be a beneficial form of organization in some cases. If a firm is experiencing a loss, which may be the case with start-ups or mineral or exploration companies, the losses can only reduce U.S. income if the operation is in branch form. In some cases, dividends may attract an additional withholding tax, although for most trading partners these taxes are eliminated or minimized through tax treaties. Non-tax reasons may also cause a firm to choose the branch form; this form, for example, may be particularly beneficial for financial firms in which the branch operation is backed by the assets of the worldwide firm.

Subpart F Income

Subpart F income, named after the section of the Internal Revenue Code that imposes the rules, is income that can easily be shifted to low tax jurisdictions. Subpart F income includes passive income, such as interest and dividends, and certain sales and service income flowing between A variety of tax rules can affect the degree and nature of cross-crediting: separating income and credits into baskets with cross-crediting only allowed within the basket; characterizing certain royalty and export income as foreign source; restricting the use of excess credits generated from oil and gas extraction; and interest and other expense allocation rules. In addition, a provision that effectively allowed claiming of foreign tax credits when the associated income was not subjected to U.S. tax, termed foreign tax credit splitting, may have affected past practices and data. This provision was restricted in 2010.

Firms whose foreign tax payments are larger than those permitted to be credited under the foreign tax credit limit rules are said to be in an excess credit position. Firms whose tax payments are smaller are in an excess limit position.[10]

Foreign Tax Credit Limit Baskets

While the United States has had a variety of limit rules in the past,[11] it currently has an overall limit that allows cross-crediting, separated into two significant baskets based on the type of income: an active or general basket and a passive basket. About 95% of income is in the general basket so there is much scope for cross-crediting.[12] Therefore, companies that have paid taxes higher than the U.S. rate can still (within each basket) offset U.S. taxes on income earned in low-tax countries. Higher tax rates can also offset taxes on income generally taxed at low or no rates; one example is royalties associated with active operations, which fall in the active basket and may be shielded from U.S. tax by excess foreign tax credits. Another is foreign source income from export sales, discussed below under the "Title Passage Rule."

Separate Limit on Oil and Gas

The law also contains separate restrictions on certain other types of income, one of importance, as measured by foreign income affected, being oil and gas extraction income. A separate provision disallows credits paid on oil and gas extraction income in excess of the U.S. tax due, although they can be carried over to future years. This treatment has the effect of placing oil and gas extraction income in a separate basket, because generally this income is subject to high foreign taxes. For example, if the U.S. tax on foreign oil and gas extraction income is 35% and the foreign tax is 50%, the extra 15% credit cannot be used to offset tax on other income. This treatment has the same effect as placing this oil and gas extraction income in a separate basket. If the tax on oil and gas extraction income were lower than the U.S. tax, this income would be eligible to have the additional U.S. tax offset by excess credits on other income because income from oil and gas extraction income is not actually in a different basket.

Allocation of Deductions

Another feature that may contribute to the generation of excess foreign tax credits is the allocation of overhead and other deductions that are not taken for foreign tax purposes. While many deductions can be traced to a particular source of income, the parent firm's costs for interest, research, and other overhead (e.g. administration) is allocated between domestic and foreign uses for purposes of the foreign tax credit limit. This allocation lowers the amount of foreign source income. Because these reductions in income are not recognized by the foreign jurisdiction, the result could be to generate excess credits, even in countries whose general effective tax rate is actually lower than that of the United States.

These allocations are necessary for determining net income by source. Borrowing is generally done at the parent level. In addition, the interest allocation limits the ability of firms who are in the excess credit position to avoid U.S. tax by borrowing in the United States rather than in low-tax countries where the deduction is less valuable.

The rule, however, has some imperfections. Foreign subsidiaries may also have overhead costs, particularly interest, which are not recognized in income because dividends are received net of deductions. In 2004, a revision that would have allowed elective allocation of worldwide interest, was adopted but did not go into effect immediately. This elective worldwide interest allocation rule has been delayed on several occasions; currently it is scheduled to take place in 2021.

Title Passage Rule

There is a special rule called the title passage rule (or the inventory sales source exception rule) that allows half of manufacturing export income (and all of sales of inventory) to be sourced as income in the country in which the title passes. Because this title passage can be arranged in foreign countries, this income is foreign source income and thus eligible for cross-crediting. This provision is effectively an export subsidy for firms with excess foreign tax credits. The title passage rule is important in considering a territorial tax because cross-crediting, at least for active income, would, in theory, disappear. Export income, as well as royalties, would be subject to higher tax rates in some cases with elimination of foreign tax credits.

Foreign Tax Credit Splitting (Now Restricted)

Prior to 2010, there was also a possibility of claiming foreign tax credits for income that had not actually been subject to tax due to differing rules across countries as to entity status.[13] P.L. 111- 226 disallowed any consideration of a foreign tax credit unless the underlying income was reported. Although this provision was estimated to gain relatively little revenue (about $0.4 billion annually),14 it is hard to be certain how prevalent these activities were. These arrangements may affect the data currently available by increasing the ability of firms to offset, for example, royalties with excess credits.

The Magnitude and Distribution of Foreign Source Income and Taxes, Actual and Potential

Before discussing the issues and consequences of reforms, it is useful to get a "lay of the land." How important are the various sources of foreign income, how much tax do they generate currently, and how much might they generate with various reforms? Because individual tax return data are not available, this issue can only be explored by combining aggregate data available and various analyses that have been done by researchers with access to tax returns. This section discusses the current sources of foreign income, the potential magnitude of foreign income not reported, the sources of tax liability, and the potential size of foregone taxes due to deferral and cross-crediting.

Current Sources of Realized Foreign Income

Table 1 shows the distribution of foreign source income by type for firms claiming and receiving foreign tax credits for 2007 and 2008, to the extent that sources can be identified. This data set should capture most of foreign source income reported by U.S. multinationals on their tax return (i.e., not deferred). (Although some data are available for 2009, these data may be skewed because of the economic slowdown that spread abroad).

Total foreign source net income was $392.5 billion in 2007 and $413.4 billion in 2008. In the data, oil and gas extraction income is reported separately, so that dividends do not include that income.

Table 1. Distribution of Foreign Source Income Realized in the United States by Type, 2007 and 2008

Type of Income	Share of Taxable Income, 2007 (%)	Share of Taxable Income, 2008 (%)
Dividend Payments	19.2	22.2
Includable Income (Subpart F)	16.6	16.5
Deemed Taxes (Gross Up)	12.9	16.9
Export Income	3.7	3.5
Royalties, and License Payments (Gross)	26.0	25.7
IC-DISC	2.3	0.0
Other	19.4	15.2

Source: Statistics of Income, International Statistics, Returns With Foreign Tax Credits, http://www.irs.gov/ taxstats/bustaxstats/article/0,,id=210069,00.html; Royalties and License Payments adjusted to eliminate rents based on data from Bureau of Economic Analysis, Trade in Services, 1999-2010, http://www.bea. gov/scb/pdf/2011/07%20July/0711_itaq-tables.pdf. Foreign taxes withheld as reported in the IRS data are added to royalties. Total taxable income for royalties from the Commerce Department data was increased by withholding taxes of approximately $4 billion.

Notes: Newly provided data for 2008 and 2009 separate the deemed tax gross up; for 2008, 73% of these taxes were associated with dividend payments and the remainder with Subpart F. See Internal Revenue Service http://www.irs.gov/pub /irs-soi/08colinecount.pdf.

Note that the third item in the table is related to the first two. Because dividends and Subpart F income are on an after-tax basis, the dividends must be increased by the taxes paid for corporate taxpayers electing a foreign tax credit. Most of the deemed paid taxes are probably associated with dividend payments (73% for 2008 when data first because available)[15] because Subpart F income is usually subject to lower foreign taxes. Accordingly, the data suggest an estimate of 30% to 35% of foreign source income that arises from these dividends.

The table also shows that royalties are significant parts of foreign source income, accounting for about a quarter of foreign source income, suggesting that the consequences of changes in the law for this income might be significant.

In *Table 1*, the measure of net income was income net of all deductions (but before adjustments). Some of these deductions were overhead costs that are allocated based on formulas.

In *Table 2,* shares are calculated based on income before these allocated deductions. With this approach, it is also possible to calculate the share of interest income and oil and gas extraction income.

In *Table 2*, foreign source income before non-allocable deductions is $615.4 billion in 2007 and $614.6 billion in 2008. Non-allocable deductions accounted for 36% of this income in 2007 and 33% in 2008.

Table 2. Distribution of Realized Foreign Source Income Before Non-Allocable Deductions, 2007 and 2008

Type of Income	Share of Taxable Income, 2007 (%)	Share of Taxable Income, 2008 (%)
Dividend Payments	12.2	14.9
Includable Income (Subpart F)	8.3	11.1
Deemed Taxes (Gross Up)	10.6	11.4
Export Income	2.3	2.3
Royalties, and License Payments (Gross)	16.6	17.3
IC-DISC	1.4	0.0
Oil and Gas Extraction Income	10.2	15.9
Service Income	2.8	3.2
Interest	21.3	18.4
Other (rents, other branch income)	14.3	5.3

Source: Statistics of Income, International Statistics, Returns With Foreign Tax Credits, http://www.irs.gov/ taxstats/bustaxstats/article/0,,id=210069,00.html; Royalties and License Payments adjusted to eliminate rents based on data from Bureau of Economic Analysis, Trade in Services, 1999-2010, http://www. bea.gov/scb/pdf/ 2011/07%20July/0711_itaq-tables.pdf. Foreign taxes withheld as reported in the IRS data are added to royalties. Total taxable income for royalties from the Commerce Department data was increased by withholding taxes of approximately $4 billion.

Notes: Newly provided data for 2008 and 2009 separate the deemed tax gross up; for 2008, 73% of these taxes were associated with dividend payments and the remainder with Subpart F. See Internal Revenue Service http://www.irs.gov /pub/irs-soi/08colinecount.pdf.

Dividend payments and their related tax gross ups are smaller as a share (25% to 30%) when pretax income is considered. Their true importance probably lies somewhere between the shares in *Table 1* and *Table 2* given the imperfections in allocation rules. Note however, that oil and gas extraction income can arise from a subsidiary and is simply reported separately. Including oil and gas income in dividends would bring the totals back up toward 35% to 40% of income. Oil and gas extraction income, however, has little or no reason not to be repatriated because the taxes due on these earnings are generally larger than the U.S. tax (which is why they are treated separately in a way that effectively results in a separate basket). *Table 2* also shows the importance of interest income in the totals for foreign source income (although a full measure of the importance of interest would require information on income of financial institutions through branches).

Deferred Income

Table 1 and Table 2 report realized income (direct, repatriated, branch, and Subpart F). Total foreign source income also includes deferred income. How large is this deferred income on an annual basis? Estimates in this section indicate that close to half of foreign source income is subject to U.S. tax, but less than a quarter of active income of foreign subsidiaries of U.S. firms that can be deferred is currently repatriated.

There are no precise data sources to estimate this effect. Based on IRS statistics for controlled foreign corporations, available for 2008, which accounted for $177 billion of distributions out of pre-tax income to U.S. parents (about 78% of the total distributions), total deemed and distributed income was 27% of total pre-tax income. Subpart F income was 12.1% of pre tax income and dividends were 14.7%.[16] As a share of after tax income, dividends were 18.1% of income and Subpart F 14.3% income, for a total of 32.4%. These ratios might be somewhat understated because of the possibility of non-U.S. shareholders, but that is likely to be unimportant.

Commerce Department data (Table 6.16D: Corporate Profits by Industry) reports $511 billion and $582 billion of rest of world corporate profits in 2007 and 2008, on an after-tax basis.[17] Considering distributions after foreign tax in 2007, the ratios are 14.7% for dividends and 12.7% for Subpart F income, for a total of 27.4%. These ratios are 15.7% for dividends, 12.0% for Subpart F, and 27.8% for the total for 2008.

These numbers do not capture deemed taxes. Using IRS data on controlled foreign corporations and based on the ratios of deemed taxes to distributions in Table 1 (with 73% of deemed taxes associated with active dividends), the share of pre-tax profits including taxes for 2008 was 19.7% for dividends and 14.7% for Subpart F. Because Subpart F is not voluntary, the share of dividends out of pre-tax profits net of Subpart F income is 23%.

A study of the new M-3 form that reconciles tax and book income finds that for firms with positive taxable and book income, 9% of the foreign source income is actively paid as a dividend and 47% is subject to U.S. tax (including royalties and other direct). Dividends as a share of total income are 19%, the same share as in Table 1. The ratios would be similar to those above if deemed taxes were included.

Overall, it appears that close to half of foreign source income is reported as taxable income in the United States, but less than a quarter of the income over which firms have discretion, active income of foreign subsidiaries, is subject to U.S. tax. Rates of deferral vary significantly by location. For 2008, in the aggregate 33% of after tax income of controlled foreign corporations was distributed, 18% as discretionary dividends and the remaining 15% as Subpart F income. Canadian subsidiaries, however, distributed 44%, with 36% as discretionary payments and the remaining 8% as Subpart F. However, for Switzerland, a significant tax haven country, 19% was paid out, 10% as dividends and the remaining 9% as Subpart F. These shares are not available for 2007, and 2006 is probably not very representative, at least for tax haven countries, because it was immediately after the repatriation holiday enacted in 2004 that permitted a one-time dividend payment with an 85% exclusion.[18]

In determining the consequences of present and proposed systems, it is also important to note the repatriated income is not random. Firms presumably choose to repatriate income that can be most easily shielded by foreign tax credits. Some evidence of this effect can be found in the M-3 study, in which the residual U.S. tax on foreign source income was only 3.3% even though half of income was reported and a significant share was in royalties that had little foreign tax (to be used for credits) attached.

Sources of Tax Liability

To examine this issue, consider the data in *Table 3* on foreign tax credits, which indicate the foreign taxes paid, and credits claimed.

Table 3. Foreign Tax Payments and Credits, 2007 and 2008

Item	2007 ($ billions)	2008 ($ billions)
Current Foreign Taxes Paid	99.1	156.2
Minus Reduction (Largely for Oil and Gas Taxes)	10.3	14.7
Plus Carryover	29.2	49.7
Equals Total Foreign Tax Credits Available	117.9	191.2
Foreign Tax Credit Limit	114.0	122.5
Foreign Tax Credits Claimed	86.5	100.4
Residual U.S. Tax (Limit Minus Claim)	29.5	22.1

Source: Statistics of Income, International Statistics, Returns With Foreign Tax Credits, http://www.irs.gov/ taxstats/bustaxstats/article/0,,id=210069,00.html.

Even though a significant share of the income was royalties and other direct income that should have been taxed, the effective U.S. residual tax rate on foreign source income as measured for tax purposes was only 7% in 2007 and 5% in 2008.[19] Moreover, the size of the tax suggests that royalties were being shielded from tax by excess credits. The royalties were $101.9 billion and $106.4 billion. Had they been fully subject to a 35% tax rate the tax on this source of income (offset by approximately $4 billion in withholding taxes) would have been around $32 billion and $33 billion respectively, larger than total taxes paid. The indication that royalties are shielded from tax is reinforced by evidence from 2000 tax returns, which traced the $12.7 billion of U.S. residual taxes to foreign sources.[20] *Table 4* shows the distribution of the shares paid. In 2000, there were nine foreign tax credit limit baskets. Only three accounted for a significant share: passive (4.6% of the total), financial services (21.3% of total), and the residual general limit basket (71.3% of the total).[21] Active dividends in the general basket accounted for only 10.2% of total taxes and dividends in financial services accounted for 2.4%. The largest share was due to royalties, interest, and branch income in the active basket. Financial branch income and financial interest each accounted for 18% so that the financial income basket bore a share of taxes out of proportion to its share of income, presumably in part because interest income was subject to tax. The remainder, 16.5% was due to the passive basket, which was largely composed of Subpart F income.

Table 4. Estimated Sources of Tax Revenue on Foreign Source Income, 2000

Type of Income	Share of Taxes Paid (%)
Dividends Non-Financial Services	10.2
Dividends Financial Services	2.4
Active Royalties, Interest and Export (Non-Financial)	33.9
Financial, Branch Income	18.1
Financial, Interest	18.1
Passive (Largely Subpart F)	16.5

Source: Harry Grubert and Rosanne Altshuler, "Corporate Taxes in the World Economy: Reforming the Taxation of Cross-border Income," in Fundamental Tax Reform: Issues, Choices, and Implications, Ed. John W. Diamond and George R. Zodrow, Cambridge, MIT Press, 2008, pp. 326-327.

If current taxes were distributed in the same manner now as they were in 2000, then taxes on active dividends for 2007 would have been responsible for a residual U.S. tax of around one-half of 1% on total foreign source active income potentially paid out as dividends.[22] The combination of selective deferral and cross-crediting appears to have essentially eliminated any U.S. tax on active income of foreign subsidiaries.

The same study that estimated data for *Table 4* estimated that two-thirds of royalties were shielded by tax credits. It is possible, however, that more tax is collected on royalties currently because of the declines in foreign tax rates and the elimination of foreign tax credit splitting.

Current and Potential Tax Collections

To consider a year that should be more normal (i.e., past the effects of a slow recovery from the recession) *Table 5* estimates three components of potential foreign taxes for FY2014: foreign taxes projected to be collected, additional taxes collected as a result of the repeal of deferral, and additional taxes collected if, in addition to repealing deferral, a per country foreign tax credit were imposed.

Those provisions taken together should result in a close approximation of a true worldwide system that eliminated deferral and largely eliminates cross-crediting.

Table 5. Current and Potential Tax Collections on Foreign Source Income, FY2014

Provision	Effect on Revenues ($billions)	Share of Current Total U.S. Corporate Tax (%)
Current Tax	32.1	7.5
Gain from Ending Deferral	18.4	4.3
Additional Gain from Per Country Foreign Tax Credit	45.9	10.9
Limit		
Total Share of All	96.4	22.5
Addendum: Eliminate Title Passage Rule	6.3	1.6
Addendum: Repeal Worldwide Interest Allocation	3.6	0.8

Source: Current Tax extrapolated from 2007 data based on changes in corporate tax revenues. Gain from Ending Deferral and Title Passage Rule from Joint Committee on Taxation, Estimates Of Federal Tax Expenditures For Fiscal Years 2011-2015, January 17, 2012, JCS-1-12. Gain from Per Country Foreign Tax Credit Limit from Joint Committee on Taxation estimates at http://wyden. senate.gov/imo/media/doc/Score.pdf; Worldwide interest allocation based on FY2019 cost adjusted to FY2014 based on projected corporate tax revenues; FY2019 cost at Joint Committee on Taxation, General Explanation Of Tax Legislation Enacted In The 111th Congress, JCS-2-11, March 24, 2011.

This table shows the importance of cross-crediting, by showing the effects of moving to a per country foreign tax credit limit given deferral is eliminated. Because of this importance, a territorial tax, which would eliminate foreign tax credits, can have consequences beyond the active income it is designed to remove from the U.S. tax base, since excess credits currently shield royalty and export income from U.S. tax.

Table 5 also shows the separate revenue consequences of two other provisions: the title passage rule and the effect of worldwide allocation of foreign source income.

ISSUES IN CONSIDERING TERRITORIAL TAXATION

Several issues arise when considering moving from the present hybrid tax system to a territorial tax: the effect on repatriations, the effect on the location of real investment, the consequences for artificial profit shifting, transition, administrative and compliance issues, and the revenue consequences.

Effect on Repatriations

One criticism of the current system is that while collecting very little revenue from foreign subsidiaries, it nevertheless discourages repatriations. The negative effect of the current system on repatriations is the major economic rationale cited by the Ways and Means Committee's press release proposing a territorial tax.[23] This argument also ties the lower repatriation rates to less investment and fewer jobs in the United States.

Before discussing the potential effects, however, note that the repatriation argument alone is not a sufficient justification for a territorial tax. The tax effect on repatriation could be eliminated by moving in the opposite direction, ending deferral. Or it could be achieved by a variety of hybrid approaches such as taxing a fixed share of profits currently and exempting the remainder, or allowing an exemption combined with a minimum tax that is smaller than the U.S. tax rate. All of these approaches create a system where taxation is not triggered by repatriation.

Would the elimination of the tax triggered by repatriations (which could be achieved by either a territorial tax or elimination of deferral) increase repatriations significantly? And if so, would those increased repatriations result in more investment and jobs in the United States?

Although the projections vary with data source and with shares of pre-tax and after-tax income, estimates in the previous section suggest that about a third of foreign subsidiaries' earnings was repatriated, with discretionary distributions net of Subpart F income around 23%. Does that imply that the remaining two thirds of income (or 77% of income net of Subpart F distributions) would be repatriated? It is unlikely that much of an increase would occur, as discussed below, and even more unlikely that it those repatriations would be translated into investment.

Several considerations suggest that the increase in repatriations would be limited. First, regardless of tax considerations, much of foreign source earnings would be retained abroad to be reinvested in the enterprises there. Historical evidence on corporate rates of return and growth rates in the United States suggest that about 60% of nominal income is typically retained to maintain the real capital stock and allow it to grow normally at a steady state.[24] The remainder, 40%, would be distributed. Thus we might expect, using the estimates above, at best to see an increase of 7% of earnings, or 17% of earnings net of Subpart F income.

Second, these repatriation rates are probably at an unusually low level because they followed the large one time repatriation (generally in 2005) from the temporary repatriation holiday enacted in 2004. Not only had large sums been repatriated to take advantage of a one time tax exemption which reduced the need for repatriations immediately after the holiday, but more might have been retained abroad than usual in anticipation of another holiday.[25] Historical data indicate that repatriation rates fell towards the end of the 1990s and continued to be low from 2000 to 2008.[26] Data were provided every other year and did not include 2005, the year most repatriations occurred under the repatriation holiday. Over the period 1968-2008, the average repatriation rate was 40%; for 2000-2008 it was 20%. In addition to the anticipation and aftermath of repatriation holidays, the growth of high-tech and dot.com firms that were expanding rapidly and not initially paying dividends may also have affected these payout ratios.[27] The evidence from tax data is also consistent with studies examining repatriation rates over an earlier period of time using financial data that found rates of around 40%.[28] Since a 40% rate is about the rate that might be expected in a no-tax world, these results suggest that the repatriation tax has had relatively little effect on a permanent basis. If firms came to believe another repatriation holiday or territorial tax were not in store, and the high-tech industries achieved a steady state growth, repatriation rates might rise to more normal levels.

Third, there is direct evidence that shifting to a territorial tax would not have large effects. Some initial evidence indicates that the Japanese shift to a territorial tax increased repatriations in the first year by about 20%.[29] Applied to current realizations rates, it would increase realizations by about 4% of total earnings; compared to the 40% rate it would increase realizations by about 8% of earnings. Since a larger first year effect might be expected, as pent up earnings are returned, such an increase is quite modest. Preliminary results from a study of the UK territorial tax shift, while subject to revision, suggest an increase of 6% of earnings.[30] A statistical study of U.S. affiliates in different countries facing different taxes suggested that repatriations would increase by about 13%, which would be 2.5% to 5% of earnings.[31]

Moreover, some theory and research suggests the effects would be negligible on a permanent basis. Theoretical considerations indicate that the repatriation tax should not matter because firms will eventually have to repatriate earnings. This theory, referred to as the "new view" is related to a similar theory about why domestic firms pay dividends to their individual shareholders even though it triggers a dividend tax. In both cases, the idea is that eventually shareholders will want to receive their dividends in excess of amounts needed for steady state reinvestment and dividends will be paid either currently, or in the future with interest. In either case, the same present value of tax will occur. While this "new view" for dividends paid in the U.S. to its individual shareholders could be rejected on the grounds that firms can return cash to the economy by repurchasing shares, such an option is not available for dividend payments between a multinational affiliate and its parent.

If the theory correctly describes behavior, then one would expect that, regardless of the repatriation tax a similar share of earnings would be paid in dividends with or without a repatriation tax. A large empirical literature has developed to study repatriation behavior, finding a variety of results. For example, some early evidence suggested that repatriation rates are sensitive to tax, but subsequent research showed that it might be due to transitory effects.[32] Evidence that repatriations were more likely from highly taxed subsidiaries (where taxes generated would be offset by foreign tax credits) relative to low taxed ones suggested that taxes have effects on repatriations.[33] However, another study found that the repatriations tax became less important given alternative strategies for returning cash for the United States.[34]

These strategies included making passive investments abroad with the parent company borrowing against them, or having low tax subsidiaries make equity investments in high tax subsidiaries which in turn repatriated income with attached foreign tax credits.[35] These strategies would indicate differential repatriation rates exist between high and low tax subsidiaries but they are not necessarily meaningful. Most recently, a study suggested taxes had some effect, but a limited one, on repatriations; this study also showed over a long period of time payout shares of about 40%.[36]

The recent pressure for a repatriation holiday and reports of large amounts of accumulated unrepatriated earnings probably comes largely from firms that have intangible assets, have been growing rapidly abroad and thus retaining earnings for that purpose, and perhaps shifting profits arbitrarily.[37] They may have also been delaying repatriations in anticipation of another holiday.

As affairs settle into more of a steady state, there may be a greater need to distribute to pay shareholders, so this phenomenon may be largely transitory.

Even if repatriations increase under a permanent territorial tax, those repatriations may not result in additional investment, but are likely to be paid out as dividends, or substitute for borrowing by the parent company.[38] Job creation is not the primary focus here in any case, as in the long run, reduce jobs.

The economy will tend to create jobs naturally. As an illustration, consider that in 1961 and in 1991 the unemployment rate was the same, 6.7%. Employment, however, rose from 66 million to 117 million, as the economy accommodated the baby boom and the entry of women into the labor force. Permanent provisions that encourage capital to move abroad can change the types of jobs and reduce wages, but not overall employment.[39]

Location of Investment

Historically, the central issue in evaluating a foreign tax regime has been the effect on the allocation of investment. Economic theory seeking efficiency objectives supports taxing investments at the same rate wherever they are invested; this approach would maximize worldwide output by investing capital where it earns the highest pre-tax return. For example, if the after tax return is 7% and the U.S. tax is an effective 30% while the foreign tax rate is zero, and investments are perfect substitutes, the total pre-tax return at the margin on an investment in the United States is 10% (0.07/(1-0.30) while the return in the foreign location is only 7%. Allowing foreign source income to be exempt causes capital to move to a less productive use, where it earns a pre-tax return of 7%, when it could earn a 10% return in the United States.[40]

The equating of taxes on a firm's investment is most closely associated with a residence based tax system. Given the need for limits on foreign tax credits, this system would be most closely approximated by a system that eliminates deferral and imposes a foreign tax credit limit on a country by country basis. If the objective were not worldwide optimization or efficiency, but maximizing U.S. welfare, the rules would be more stringent by allowing foreign taxes as a deduction rather than a credit.[41]

Assessing Arguments for a Territorial Tax

What, then, is the justification for moving in the opposite direction, to a territorial tax? One may be that if, for political or other reasons, it is not possible to move closer to a residence-based system, it is possible to design a territorial tax system that is an improvement over the current rules. This argument is made by Grubert and Mutti,[42] and their proposal was incorporated in President Bush's Advisory Commission's tax reform proposals.[43] Grubert and Mutti proposed, along with exempting active dividends from tax, to provide for an allocation of overhead costs of the firm (such as interest) between taxable and tax exempt income. For example, if 10% of income is exempt because of the dividend exemption then 10% of interest and other overhead costs would be disallowed. They also note that that the elimination of foreign tax credits would mean that royalty, export and other income would not be shielded from U.S. tax with excess foreign tax credits. As a result, this proposal is projected to raise revenue, a result also found by the Joint Committee on Taxation, and the overall tax rate on foreign source income would rise.[44] Grubert and Mutti also note that repatriations would not trigger a tax and that such a change would reduce the cost of tax planning to avoid the repatriation tax.

The argument that a territorial tax that could improve economic efficiency, or at least make it no worse, should be distinguished from arguments that do not stand up to economic reasoning. For example, moving to a territorial system because other countries have generally done so does not mean such a system is desirable either for them or for the United States. Many policies exist in other countries, such as a value added tax or national health insurance, policies that many oppose and that have not been adopted in the United States. The issues may differ as well. European countries, for example, are geographically and politically closer than the United States is to other countries. The European Union also has provisions on freedom of capital movement and establishment that prevent the type of anti-inversion laws that the United States has, to prevent U.S. firms from relocating their headquarters.[45] These rules may influence decisions to adopt territorial systems as well as decisions to lower corporate tax rates, which has occurred in the United Kingdom recently.

Similarly, the argument that because most other countries do not tax their foreign subsidiaries, the United States also should not do so in order to allow its firms to compete abroad does not stand up to economic analysis. A country does not compete in the manner that a firm does, because its resources (labor and savings provided by its citizens) do not disappear if another firm undercuts prices; they are simply used in a different way. That is, a country does not compete with the rest of the world, it trades with them, both its products and its capital. It can generally be shown that the United States would still be better off, or at least no worse off, if it taxes foreign and domestic investments by its firms at the same rate, even if other countries do not.[46]

Finally, arguments made based on empirical studies that indicate that increased foreign investment of multinationals is correlated with more, not less, domestic investment do not show that overall U.S investment is not reduced by more favorable foreign treatment, and may simply identify firms that are growing.

In any event, the aggregate amount of capital owned by U.S. citizens and the allocation of that capital are separate issues. Even if savings responds to the overall U.S. tax burden, of two revenue neutral regimes, the one that taxes capital equally in both locations would be more efficient.

There are some arguments that have been made that bear consideration. Perhaps the most important of these is that U.S. firms can change their nationality by moving their headquarters abroad, merging with foreign companies, or incorporating abroad. However, anti-inversion rules adopted in 2004 are likely to prevent large-scale shifting of headquarters of existing firms, while mergers and incorporating abroad are probably largely determined by non-tax factors and could be addressed with legislative revisions.[47] Evidence suggests that very little incorporation of true U.S. firms occurs abroad[48] and this effect could be addressed with legislation (such as basing taxation on where effective management occurs) if necessary.

Arguments have also been made that the higher taxes on returns to capital investments would prevent U.S. firms from exploiting intangible assets abroad.[49] However, there are many ways of exploiting intangibles without engaging directly in manufacturing or other activities, such as licenses, franchises, and contract manufacturing.[50] Products embodying U.S. innovations could also be produced in the United States and exported.

Likely Effects of International Tax Revision on Investment

What are the likely effects of altering the international tax system on investment? There are several reasons that these effects would probably be modest, although they would depend on the particular design features of the reform.

First, most countries where physical investment might take place, such as manufacturing, tend to have taxes that are not much different from those that apply in the United States: average effective rates of 27% and marginal effective rates of about 20%.[51] The average effective tax rate on foreign subsidiaries of U.S. parents is estimated to be lower than that of U.S. firms in general (about 16% versus 26% with a 3% residual U.S. tax on foreign earnings), but that partially reflects profit shifting to low tax countries, since the effective rate in tax haven countries was 5.7%.[52] Overall effective tax rates abroad for foreign subsidiaries of U.S. companies also vary by industry. Industries with a lot of intangible assets have lower tax rates. For example, computer and electronic product manufacturing had an effective tax rate of 8.7% and finance 11.3%.[53]

Second, to the extent that firms expect largely to avoid U.S. taxes under the current system, either through permanent reinvestment of profits or tax planning, moving to a territorial tax would not make much difference in inducing outflows of capital, especially if anti-base erosion provisions (such as treating income earned in tax haven countries as Subpart F Income) are adopted. Nevertheless, since firms' investments are only observed under the current deferral and foreign tax credit system, it is possible that significantly more capital would be invested abroad, especially in lower tax jurisdictions.

Moving in the opposite direction, by ending deferral and possibly cross-crediting (with a per country foreign tax credit limit) would reduce capital investment abroad by retaining more outbound capital in the United States.

Nevertheless, effects from either revision are unlikely to be important to the overall U.S. economy or to U.S. welfare; estimates of the effect of cutting the U.S. corporate tax rate by ten percentage points, which would presumably have larger effects by attracting inbound capital as well is estimated to increase U.S. output by only about 2/10^{ths} of 1% and U.S. income by 2/100^{ths} of 1%.[54] The effects of moving to a territorial tax would be negative (decrease U.S. output) because they increase the return on outbound capital, but would be smaller in magnitude because the effects are smaller. Based on relative sizes of revenue effects, a ten percentage point rate reduction would lose about 29% of corporate revenue, while, based on the estimates in *Table 5,* eliminating all taxes on foreign source income would lose about 7.5% of corporate revenue, or a quarter of the amount. Eliminating deferral alone would gain revenue equal to about 15% of the absolute change from a ten percentage point rate reduction, while eliminating deferral and cross-crediting would be about 53% of the change. This last change could be more significant than the domestic rate reduction but nevertheless not large relative to the U.S. economy.

All of these effects are small, relative to output, for several reasons. First, although capital flows respond to differential tax rates, capital is not perfectly mobile.[55] Even if it were, the large size of the U.S. domestic economy and capital stock and the constraints of production (capital must combine with labor to be productive) limit the effect to 1/2 of 1% of output and a negligible effect on income.[56] The corporate tax itself is also small as a cost factor: about 2% of GDP. Thus even a 10 percentage point rate reduction would be slightly over 1/2 of 1% of GDP, while most international revisions would be even smaller. Finally, most of these gains would not accrue to U.S. income: for inbound capital most of the gain would be profit to foreign investors, and for outbound capital drawn back, profits were already in existence and merely change location.

The analysis in this section suggests that while there may be concerns about the effects of international reforms on investments, either reducing U.S. investment in the case of a territorial tax or increasing it by moving towards a residence based tax (e.g., eliminating deferral and cross-crediting) these effects are likely quite modest.

Treatment of Royalties and Export Income

One effect of the current system that might be changed by moving to a territorial system is the reduction in the beneficial treatment of royalties and export income through the use of excess foreign tax credits. The current benefits for royalties encourage firms to exploit intangibles in foreign operations rather than in the United States, while the export subsidy causes prices and magnitudes of exports to be too large.

Royalties, in particular, are a difficult issue to address because increased taxes on royalties paid from foreign subsidiaries would encourage manufacturing of goods in the United States but, as will be discussed in the next section, also creates an incentive to understate royalties and artificially shift intangible income into untaxed active earnings of foreign subsidiaries that are exempt. Ideally, such profit shifting should be addressed by anti-abuse provisions.

Artificial Profit Shifting

The third issue, which primarily involves revenue, is artificial profit shifting—that is, shifting profits into low-tax jurisdictions that are then exempt from U.S. tax. Profit shifting also exists under the current system because of deferral. Evidence of profit shifting is clear from the distribution of shares of U.S. subsidiary profits as a percentage of GDP, where profits as a percentage of output were typically less than 1%-2% in the G-7, were significantly larger in the larger tax-haven countries (7.6% in Ireland and 18.2% in Luxemburg), and were more than 600% and 500% respectively in Bermuda and the Cayman Islands.[57] The estimates of magnitude vary substantially reaching up to $90 billion and ranging from about 14% to 29% of corporate revenues.[58] They have been growing as well.[59]

In general, most of this profit shifting apparently arises from either leveraging (borrowing in high-tax jurisdictions) or shifting of the location of profits from intangibles. It is not surprising, therefore, that low-tax rates tend to be associated with manufacture of drugs and electronics, and the information and communications industries.

Profit shifting is a policy problem even without a move to a territorial tax. One of the concerns about moving to a territorial tax is the possibility that it will increase the already significant and growing estimated level of profit shifting. Under current law, firms that have shifted profits to low-tax jurisdictions may still have to face eventual taxation. The considerable lobbying for a repatriation holiday such as that in 2004 may be a sign of this concern.[60] With a simple territorial tax with no anti-abuse provisions, profit shifting could increase substantially.

There is little to clarify the likely magnitude of this effect. Evidence for European countries has also indicated significant profit shifting, benefiting most European countries largely at the expense of Germany.[61] Germany has since lowered their corporate tax rate (and profit shifting may have played a role in that decision). However, it is difficult to draw conclusions from the experiences of these very different countries, who already have territorial systems but also have in most cases had measures to address base erosion.

If the new view of dividends is correct, and companies expect to pay taxes on excess profits with interest when deferred, then the move to a simple territorial tax (without any anti-base erosion measures) could increase profit shifting, perhaps considerably. However, if this view is not correct and firms expect to escape tax indefinitely, then going to a territorial tax might not make much difference.

Unfortunately, while there is a relatively powerful theoretical justification for the new view, the empirical evidence has been mixed. At the same time, however, as noted above, the lobbying for a repatriation holiday supports the new view and the expectation that profit shifting might increase insignificantly.

One particular potential effect on profit shifting involves royalties. Because royalties are protected to some extent by excess foreign tax credits, moving to a territorial tax would eliminate that protection and increase the tax on royalties. This change in taxation would create a further incentive to shift intangible income into the earnings of foreign subsidiaries and out of royalties.

Aside from the issue of the effect of a territorial tax (and of its particular design features) on profit shifting, other reforms might be considered that might address profit shifting either in the current system or in a system revised in ways other than moving to a territorial tax. These reforms might include provisions reforming the current system proposed by President Obama (and earlier by former Ways and Means Committee Chairman Rangel), which would tax excess earnings from intangibles as subpart F income and rules that would disallow some portion of overhead expenses to the extent income is not taxed.

Fundamentally, as long as a system allows for differential taxes, whether between the U.S. and foreign source income or between types of foreign source income, there is likely to be profit shifting.

Companies appear willing to exploit relatively small differentials in tax as illustrated by the double-Irish, Dutch sandwich technique that allowed firms to not only avoid the U.S. tax, but to avoid the 12.5% Irish tax as well, and establish taxation in Bermuda, with a zero tax rate.[62] The only tax system that eliminates differential taxes is the elimination of deferral, possibly combined with a separate tax credit limit basket for royalty income.

Transition

An important issue in moving to a territorial tax is how to treat accumulated unrepatriated earnings, which were generated under a worldwide system. One approach would be to deem all accumulated earnings as repatriated and pay taxes, with a number of years allowed to pay these taxes. The provision might create a hardship for firms to the extent that income is tied up in non-liquid form, unless the period of time for paying the tax were extensive. In addition, it would be a retroactively harsh tax compared with the present system, because a significant portion of earnings need never be repatriated. During normal times, estimates suggest that more than half of retained earnings abroad is probably reinvested in the firms activities. Note also that while perhaps 60% or so of the flow of income would be retained abroad, a much larger share of the stock of unrepatriated earnings would be likely to be permanently reinvested abroad. Another option is to treat these earnings the same as newly generated earnings and exempt them in the same way. This approach would create a windfall benefit, especially to the degree that firms have been holding off repatriating and engaging in aggressive profit shifting because of a potential tax holiday.

A third option would be to treat dividends as paid out of accumulated earnings until these earnings are exhausted, while applying the full tax rate and foreign tax credit rules. This approach, however, would continue the disincentive to repatriate for some time.

None of these approaches may be entirely satisfactory. Intermediate proposals that are under consideration would tax this income but at a lower rate. One, in the Ways and Means proposal, is to deem all this earnings repatriated prior to the law changes, apply the provisions of the 2004 tax holiday (85% exclusion of income with proportional foreign tax credits), which would impose a small tax, and allow it to be paid over a period of time. On average this may be a reasonable compromise, because, although a significant fraction of income is exempt, a significant fraction of this income would probably never have been repatriated.

A second intermediate option is to allow firms to elect the holiday (with an extended pay out period) and to tax any remaining dividends at the full tax rate until all of the remaining earnings is paid out as dividends. This voluntary approach allows firms to avoid undesirable forced payouts, but prolongs the effective movement to a territorial tax.

Striking a balance between limiting the windfall benefits and the associated revenue loss compared with a baseline, providing firms with terms that allow the funds to pay (since a lot of accumulated earnings are not liquid) and avoiding prolonged coverage of dividends under the old system is one of the most difficult problems in crafting a shift to a territorial tax. As will be discussed subsequently, the proposals have included a variety of approaches.

While accumulated untaxed earnings are an important issue, there are other transition issues relating to the shift from the current system to a territorial tax. These include unused foreign tax credits associated with previously taxed income and foreign loss carryovers. How credits and losses might be treated may depend largely on the treatment of existing earnings accumulated abroad and how other features of the foreign tax credit are modified.

Administration and Compliance

Arguments have often been made that moving to a territorial tax would simplify administration and compliance. Grubert and Mutti, in their proposal for a territorial tax, stressed the cost of tax planning associated with repatriating income while paying minimal tax. Thus a territorial tax would add value by simplifying repatriation policy. U.S. parents could receive dividends from their subsidiaries without concerns about the tax consequences. However, the same simplification would occur if deferral were ended, because firms would have no choice about paying taxes or arranging for optimal cross-crediting. Hybrid approaches such as taxing a share of income currently would also eliminate the scope for tax planning around repatriation.

Although repatriation tax planning would be eliminated, if a territorial tax increased profit shifting incentives, tax planning in that area could increase. And, as will be shown in the discussion of design issues, provisions considered to combat income shifting can add considerable complexity to the tax code.

Revenue Issues

A shift to a territorial system could potentially gain revenue, in part because relatively little tax is collected on foreign operations. In any case, it is unlikely that large revenue losses would occur unless the move to a territorial tax includes other provisions (such as lower tax rates on royalties) or induces pronounced income shifting responses. If *Table 4* shares of income are applied to estimates of current taxes paid on foreign source income listed in *Table 5*, the taxation of dividends of foreign subsidiaries is quite small, a little over $4 billion in FY2014, or about 1% of corporate revenues. Branch income is slightly under $6 billion, so if this income is also exempted in a move to a territorial tax, the total effect would be about $10 billion. The two together are about 2% of corporate revenues. Taxes on royalties and export income (which along with nonfinancial interest would be somewhat over $10 billion, or about 2% of revenues) could increase with the loss of foreign tax credits, leading to a relatively small net loss or possibly a small gain.

There is considerably more revenue to be gained by moving in the opposite direction, as some proposals do. Eliminating deferral and providing a per country foreign tax credit limit could triple the revenue collected on foreign source income, raising $64 billion or about 15% of corporate taxes, according to the estimates in *Table 5*. Other intermediate changes could raise revenues; eliminating deferral alone would raise about $18 billion in revenue, and the combination of President Obama's budget proposals for international taxation would raise $16 billion.[63]

Some proposals for moving to a territorial tax aim for revenue neutrality, but also propose to use transitional revenues (from taxes on accumulated untaxed earnings) to achieve this revenue neutrality in the budget horizon. Because transitional gains are temporary, this approach results in a long-run revenue loss.

Design Issues in a Territorial Tax

Moving to a territorial tax goes far beyond a simple matter of exempting foreign source income from U.S. tax. There are issues of transition, the treatment of current flow through income, and the retention and perhaps revision of anti-abuse rules. In this section, three proposals are outlined: the Grubert Mutti proposal, the discussion draft provided by Ways and Means Committee Chairman, and Senator Enzi's bill, S. 2091. The latter two proposals are similar in general approach. Note that the Grubert Mutti proposal is a general outline, while the Ways and Means Discussion Draft and S. 2091 are in legislative language and are more detailed.

The Grubert Mutti Proposal

This proposal has been circulating for some time as a general proto-type of a move to a territorial tax, and has been estimated to raise revenue, primarily due to increased taxes on royalties and allocation of parent company expenses between taxable and exempt income.[64] A proposal of this nature was included in President Bush's Advisory Panel Proposal in 2005.[65]

- Exemption of dividends for active foreign income by U.S. shareholders with a 10% or more interest and eliminate foreign tax credits.
- Foreign branches treated the same as subsidiaries.
- Royalties and interest paid to the U.S. parent are taxable.
- Current anti-abuse rules for passive income(Subpart F) would be retained, although some aspects would become obsolete (primarily the inclusion of dividend payments between subsidiaries).
- Parent's overhead expenses, such as interest, would be allocated in proportion to untaxed income and disallowed.
- Active foreign losses could not offset domestic income.
- Capital gains and losses from the sale of productive assets would be exempt.
- Income from U.S. exports would not be classified as foreign source income.

The proposal does not address the treatment of existing accumulated earnings abroad or profit shifting via intangible assets, although one of the proposal's authors has indicated that their plan should probably include a tax on accumulated earnings, but at a lower rate.[66]

This proposal has been estimated to raise revenue of approximately $6.9 billion in 2014.[67] If the shares of revenue in *Table 4* remain the same for 2014, about 30% of current tax on foreign source income or slightly under $10 billion (based on aggregates from *Table 5*) is collected on active dividends and branch income. The additional taxes on royalties and export income plus limits on the deduction of overhead expenses presumably raise about $17 billion (replacing the lost revenue and generating additional amounts).

Ways and Means Chairman Camp's Discussion Draft

In October 2011, Ways and Means Chairman Dave Camp released a discussion draft outlining an approach to a territorial tax (hereafter Discussion Draft). This proposal includes some options and unsettled issues, and there is not as yet a revenue estimate. Note also that the intention expressed in press releases at that time was to couple the move to a territorial tax with a general tax reform that would reduce the top corporate rate from 35% to 25%. This rate matters since some provisions allow a proportional tax benefit. Since the other changes that might be needed to achieve this reduction have not been yet spelled out, no observations on the effects if any remaining revision will be included, outside of noting the consequences of the rate change for specific territorial provisions.

The following summary of these provisions does not include all of the detailed nuances of the proposal, which are contained in a technical draft discussion.[68]

- Allows a 95% deduction for the foreign source portion of dividends for 10% U.S. corporate shareholders of foreign subsidiaries that are controlled foreign corporations (CFCs). A holding period of one year for stock in foreign corporations is required. If the rate is reduced to 25%, dividends would be taxed at 1.25%; at the current rate, they would be taxed at 1.75%. (CFCs are those where 50% of the stock is owned by five or fewer 10% U.S. shareholders.)
- 10% corporate shareholders of non controlled corporations (where 50% of the stock is not owned by five or fewer 10% U.S. shareholders, called 10/50 corporations) can elect the same treatment as CFCs.
- Foreign branches are treated the same as subsidiaries; the draft also considers the possible inclusion of partnerships in this treatment.
- Anti-abuse (Subpart F) provisions are retained, although these rules would be revised in light of the other changes; these details are to be considered subsequently. Dividends paid between CFCs are exempt.
- Capital gains on sales of stock in active eligible subsidiaries are also eligible for a 95% exclusion.
- Accumulated untaxed earnings will be taxed with an 85% exclusion and apportionment of associated foreign tax credits in the same fashion as the 2004 repatriation holiday, except that all earnings will be taxed rather than earnings that are voluntarily repatriated. No actual repatriation is necessary. Firms can pay the tax in installments with interest over eight years. Assuming this provision applies before changes in the statutory tax rate, the effective rate is 5.25% less any apportioned foreign tax credits.
- The foreign tax credits associated with active dividends and with foreign branch income are disallowed (those for Subpart F are retained). All foreign tax credits would be in one basket, presumably because the active basket would no longer be relevant. The proposal also eliminates the allocation of parent interest that presently applies to determine the foreign tax credit limit: only directly associated expenses will be applied to determine foreign income. It would also repeal the provision preventing the splitting of foreign tax credits.
- A provision that requires the inclusion in income of investments of deferred income (income that is not taxed because it is not distributed) in U.S. property is repealed. This provision exists to prevent firms from effectively repatriating earnings without declaring dividends that are subject to the tax.
- Three anti-base-erosion options, two directed at intangible income, are considered. Option A is similar to a proposal made by President Obama in his budget proposals, that would tax excess earnings on intangibles (in excess of 150% of costs) in low tax jurisdictions as Subpart F. The inclusion would be phased out between a 10% and a

15% rate. Option B would tax income that is subject to an effective foreign tax rate below 10% unless it qualifies for a home country exception. The home country exception applies when a firm conducts an active trade or business in the home country, has a fixed place of business, and serves the local market. Option C would tax all foreign income from intangibles (whether earnings by the foreign subsidiary or royalty payments) but allow a deduction for 40%, resulting in a tax rate of 15% at a 25% statutory tax rate.

- Additional base-erosion provisions (sometimes call thin-capitalization rules) relating to interest would restrict the deduction for interest if the company failed to meet either of two tests: if debt to equity ratios in the U.S. differed from the total debt to equity ratio worldwide and if interest expenses exceed a certain share of adjusted income (generally taxable income before the deduction of interest and depreciation). The smaller of the excess interest under either test would be disallowed, but the percentage has not been specified.
- The draft indicates that the two extenders, exception from Subpart F of active financing and active insurance income and the look-through rules, would be considered separately.

Senator Enzi's Bill (S. 2091)

Senator Enzi has introduced S. 2091 which is similar in many respects to the Ways and Means Discussion Draft. His bill is a separate bill that does not include a general tax reform or lowering of the corporate rate.[69]

- The Enzi proposal provides the same 95% dividend exemption and election option for 10/50 companies as the Discussion Draft.
- Foreign branches would not be treated as subsidiaries.
- Anti-abuse rules (Subpart F) would be retained, but the inclusion of foreign base company sales and service income would be eliminated.
- Capital gains on the sale of stock would be eligible for the exclusion to the extent they would be treated as a dividend under Section 1248 (which treats gains as dividends to the extent of earnings and profits).
- Firms could elect to tax accumulated earnings with a 70% exclusion (a 10.5% tax) and no foreign tax credits; otherwise accumulated earnings would be taxed at full rates with foreign tax credits allowed when paid out as dividends and these pre-existing earnings would be deemed to be paid out first.
- Foreign tax credits (and deductions for these taxes) associated with exempt income would be disallowed.
- The Enzi bill does not repeal the provision taxing investments of deferred income in U.S. property.
- For anti-base-erosion provisions a version of Option B in the Discussion Draft along with a version of the first part of Option C would be included. Income in countries with tax rates of half or less than the U.S. rate (17.5%) would be subject to tax. However, operations that conduct an active business, with employees and officers

that contribute substantially, would be excepted except to the extent the income is intangible income of the CFC. The CFC's intangible income would be Subpart F income. These rules provide more scope for exemption as compared to the rules in the Discussion Draft which would require exempt income to carry out activities serving the home country market. The bill also includes the first part of Option C, allowing a 17.5% tax rate on intangible income (such as royalties) earned by a domestic corporation. Intangible income would be placed in a separate foreign tax credit basket.

- The bill does not contain the thin capitalization rules (such as allocating interest between U.S. firms and their foreign subsidiaries).
- The bill makes the two extenders, the exception from Subpart F for active financing and active insurance income and the look-through rules, permanent. It also applies the worldwide interest allocation for purposes of the foreign tax credit in 2013, rather than 2021.

Analysis and Commentary on the Proposals

Some insights into issues and trade offs may be noted by observing the difference between these proposals. In addition, the Discussion Draft proposals invited commentary, which has appeared in a number of venues including testimony before a Ways and Means Subcommittee on Select Revenue Measures hearing on November 27, 2011. This section examines the alternative approaches in light of the issues discussed earlier and general design considerations.

Repatriation Incentives

While the Grubert-Mutti proposal has no tax that is triggered by repatriation, the other two territorial proposals do, due to the 5% "haircut" resulting from the proposed 95% exemption. In addition, the Discussion Draft also allows firms to choose an alternate completely tax free method of repatriation since investment in U.S. assets is not taxed, even at a 5% share. Presumably, the expectation is that the tax due to the 5% inclusion in income (1.25% at a 25% rate and 1.75% tax at a 35% rate) is too small to matter. At least one commentator, however, has singled this issue out as a potentially serious one indicating that as long as tax planning to avoid even a small tax is costless, firms will undertake it.[70] One option for the Discussion Draft, which would not eliminate the small repatriation tax but would eliminate the costless avoidance, would be to continue to tax these transactions, or to tax 5% of them. An approach that could eliminate the repatriation tax trigger arising from the 5% exclusion altogether is to include 5% of income whether repatriated or not, and make dividends entirely exempt.

S. 2091 also has an additional temporary repatriation trigger arising from its transition rule, which allows firms to elect to repatriate under a 70% exclusion without credits, but would tax dividends until any remaining accumulated funds are exhausted. Presumably, firms would repatriate funds voluntarily from low tax jurisdictions, and then repatriate funds from countries with high foreign taxes until the backlog is exhausted.

The Grubert Mutti proposal does not have any special provision for accumulated untaxed earnings and dividends paid out of those earnings. Basically this provision was not addressed although, as noted above, the authors would expect some transition rule similar to the other proposals; this treatment was not incorporated into their revenue estimates.

Effects on Tax Burden and Investment

Although the Discussion Draft leaves a number of options open, its objective to be revenue neutral indicates that it is more beneficial to U.S. multinational firms than the Grubert-Mutti proposal that raises revenue. Moreover the Discussion Draft proposes to finance part of the revenue loss through the one time revenue gain from the tax on existing accumulated earnings. Senator Enzi has indicated an intention for his bill to be revenue neutral as well, although it has not been scored.[71]

Some elements that increase the tax burden on foreign source income (offsetting the loss from exempting dividends and in some cases branch income) are the allocation of deductions and taxation of royalties in the Grubert-Mutti proposal and the 5% inclusion of dividends in the other two proposals. The base erosion provisions may or may not increase taxes depending on which option is chosen and the extent to which firms can use the active trade or business exception to avoid the tax. Some of the reason for these differences in revenue effect is that the 5% inclusion appears to be significantly smaller than overhead costs (even excluding interest). One comment also noted that the 5% inclusion does not take account of a firm's individual circumstances.[72]

Altshuler and Grubert estimate that overhead expenses outside of interest and research expenditures are 10% of pretax earnings.[73] Moreover, their proposal would disallow the deduction regardless of whether dividends are paid out, while the 5% inclusion would apply only to dividends paid. Assuming that about 40% of earnings are paid out in a steady state the 5% provision would be 2% of total earnings. Thus the provision in the Grubert-Mutti proposal would be about five times the size of the provision in the Discussion Draft and S. 2091.

Presumably interest would also be significant. The Grubert-Mutti proposal has a direct allocation rule for the parent's interest presumably based on allocations of assets.[74] The proposal does not spell out specifics, but interest allocation could be net or gross, and it could involve only the parent interest or worldwide interest. Turning to years of 2006 and 2007, net interest as a share of combined interest and pretax earnings of nonfinancial corporations in the National Income and Product Accounts was 15% in 2006 and 21% in 2007.[75] The 2006 measure may be more appropriate as a steady state guide since profits had begun to decline in 2007. According to tax statistics, for manufacturing the share was 13% in 2006 and 18% in 2007.[76] Gross interest, the basis of the current allocation rules for the foreign tax credit limit, would be much larger, ranging from 34% to 39% of profits plus interest payments. In a related article, by Altshuler and Grubert, the analysis assumes that debt accounts for a third of the capital stock.[77] The Discussion Draft has thin capitalization rules that are based on two alternative tests: an allocation provision for net interest based on parent versus subsidiary debt-equity ratios taking into account worldwide debt and an alternative based on an as-yet-unspecified share of adjusted income, so that the effects on interest are uncertain. S. 2091 has no allocation rule.

Grubert and Mutti could have an allocation for research and development expenditures but apparently do not.[78] Thus, they have no provision that addresses profit shifting from intangibles.

If these costs were included, for 2006 for manufacturing they were 18% of the total of earnings and research costs.[79] Neither the discussion draft nor S. 2091 have such an allocation, although they have some options that affect base erosion that could address intangibles.

Without more specific guidelines, it is difficult to determine the share of income that would be taxed under the Grubert Mutti proposal. Using net interest, the ratio for manufacturing in 2006 relative to net income is about 15% and the overhead costs add another 10%, taxing about 25% of income, whether paid as a dividend or not. In contrast, assuming 40% of income is paid as a dividend, the 5% inclusion in the Discussion Draft and S. 2091 would tax about 2%. At a 35% rate, these effects would impose additional taxes of 8.75% (0.25 times 0.35) under the Grubert Mutti plan and 0.7% (0.05 times 0.35 times 0.40).

If the allocation of interest is made based on worldwide costs (and not just U.S. parent costs), the allocation could be smaller and firms could shift interest costs to their foreign subsidiaries and deduct them so that the effect would be only the difference between the U.S. and foreign rate. In addition, with an overall allocation, this interest cost would presumably be shifted to high tax countries. The United States would still gain revenue but some of it would be offset (from the firm's point of view) by lower tax payments to foreign countries. At the extreme, only the overhead allocation of 10% would affect taxes, leading to a 3.5 percentage point tax increase.

Both the Discussion Draft and S. 2091 include specific anti-base erosion measures which are not included in the Grubert Mutti proposal and these may to some extent substitute for cost allocation provisions. These provisions relate less to investment than to profit shifting and are discussed in the next section.

Incentives could also be affected by the treatment of royalties whose tax burden would rise as excess foreign tax credits disappear. This higher tax on royalties could encourage both more exports of products with technology embodied (as the cost of exploiting intangibles abroad increases). It could also encourage more research to be performed abroad in low tax CFCs although this effect is unclear since such research would not have a benefit as an investment (expensing and the R&D credit) as is the case in the United States.

S. 2091 also provides that royalty income will be taxed at a 17.5% rate, which reduces the additional taxes that would arise from the loss of foreign tax credits on other incomes. A lower tax on royalties is an option in the discussion draft. Under S. 2091, intangibles that fall under the anti-base erosion rules would be taxed at the full rate, 35%.

As noted earlier, none of the shifts in investment are likely to be large relative to the U.S. economy. Thus, even if the provisions induce more research to be performed abroad, the consequences would not be likely to be significant.

Artificial Profit Shifting

There are several different anti-profit shifting regimes discussed in the proposals: the full allocation of deductions in Mutti and Grubert, the interest allocation rules plus one of three options in the Ways and Means Draft, and the combination of components of two of the three options for S. 2091. Although a more detailed discussion is presented below, Table 6 summarizes the discussion. Grubert and Mutti address artificial profit shifting by allocating deductions, including overhead administrative costs and interest. For interest deductions, this allocation method should address the shifting facilitated through leveraging, although their proposal may only allocate parent company expenses.

Table 6. Summary of Discussion in Text of Base Erosion Provisions of the Proposals

Grubert and Mutti	
Allocation of Deductions	Allocation of overhead costs and interest is simple. It might be desirable to employ worldwide allocation. Allocation would automatically impose an additional tax on shifted profits. Grubert and Mutti have no provisions to address profit shifting through intangibles.
Ways and Means Discussion Draft	
Interest restrictions	Worldwide allocation of interest may be effective in dealing with leverage. The ability to meet an alternative less restrictive test may undermine the effects; it is not clear what the purpose of this alternative is.
Plus Option A	Provisions to tax as U.S. connected income intangible earnings in excess of 150% of costs for countries with rates below 15% (phased out between 10% and 15%) would discourage profit shifting of this nature. It creates an incentive to shift costs to low tax countries and could encourage firms to relocate. Measuring effective tax rates and identifying affected income would be complicated.
Or Plus Option B	Provisions to tax income in countries with rates below 10% as U.S. income would exclude Ireland, and would encourage firms to shift to slightly higher tax rate countries, or perhaps encourage tax havens to increase taxes, both of which would increase taxes paid to foreigners. Measuring effective tax rates could be complicated. Firms may be able to avoid the U.S. tax through the home country exception.
Or Plus Option C	This provision, which taxes all intangible income as U.S. income at a lower rate is not triggered by the country's tax rate and effectively imposes a minimum tax of 15% on intangible income. It thus imposes a lower tax rate on income in low tax jurisdictions but does not induce shifting to other countries. It also imposes the same tax rate on royalties, reducing the incentive to shift these profits into a subsidiary, but compared to a plan without this feature, encouraging production abroad. Distinguishing intangible income would be difficult. This royalty provision might violate WTO rules against export subsidies.
S. 2091 (Enzi)	
No Deduction Allocation	This bill has no provision for restricting leveraging directly.
Option B Version	Income in countries with taxes less than half the U.S. rate (17.5%) are subject to U.S. tax, unless there is an active trade or business. A higher rate encompasses more countries, including Ireland. However, it also has an incentive for affected firms to move income to slightly higher tax rate countries and involves complications in measuring effective tax rates. The provision excepts firms that are making a substantial contribution to a business, a more easily avoided rule than the one in the Discussion Draft which allows an exception only for production for the home market.
Plus Part of Option C	Would also tax royalties at 17.5%, which could in some cases encourage income to be received as royalties. It would encourage exploitation of intangibles abroad and might violate the WTO.

Source: CRS analysis of proposals.

A more comprehensive approach is to allocate world wide expenses.[80] They discuss this world wide approach as well, which would lose revenue compared to allocating only parent company costs and could potentially cause an overall revenue loss. For intangible profits, they do not address the tax on income shifted abroad. Rather they disallow a portion of the associated investment costs (research and development costs and other overhead costs such as marketing). Their anti-abuse program has the virtue of simplicity and because an increase in profits abroad triggers a tax (in the form of foregone deductions) it reduces the incentive to shift profits through that effect as well.

The Ways and Means Discussion Draft addresses the shifting due to leveraging by restricting interest deductions. They impose the lesser of two restrictions. The first is an allocation of interest based on worldwide interest and assets, much like the Grubert and Mutti approach. The second is a limit on interest relative to modified income, and since the limit is not spelled out, the extent of that restriction is yet to be determined. If a high enough ratio of interest to modified income is allowed then the interest allocation would not be very effective and since modified income is prior to not only interest but depreciation and some other production expenses, the ratio would have to be relatively low to be broadly effective. The effectiveness would need to be explored once a percentage is determined. The value of this alternative is not readily apparent given that the first restriction, the allocation rule, provides a reasonable method. The Enzi bill has no interest allocation provisions.

A specific base erosion provision outside of interest has not been chosen in the discussion draft, and it is difficult to determine how effective the base erosion proposals are likely to be. Both Options A and Option B hinge on being in a low tax country and the tax rate is relatively low, only 10%. Option A, which phases out the U.S. taxation of excess intangibles between 10% and 15% may only partially affect Ireland, for example, which has a statutory tax rate of 12.5% and Option B would miss it altogether. These tax rates are effective rates, which is appropriate, but which could be difficult to measure.[81] Options A and C require the identification of intangible income, which is not necessary for B; this problem has been identified as an important complicating factor in several comments.[82]

By triggering current taxation of intangibles when the return exceeds 150% of costs, Option A provides an incentive to push deductible development and marketing costs into the CFC, a point made in Ways and Means hearing.[83] Once a firm falls into the excess profit class a dollar of cost moved to the CFC will decrease income subject to U.S. taxation by $1.50, while increasing taxable income in the United States by $1.00 (although if the tax code retained the production activities deduction and income were eligible for it, this additional dollar would increase taxable income by $0.91).

tion B, which triggers full U.S. taxation of some income in countries with tax rates below 10% would create incentives to move profits to countries with tax rates higher than the 10% level but lower than the U.S. 25% level. Ireland is a possibility, but there are many potential locations which might not currently be used as tax havens which would become so, including a number of former eastern block countries. It is also possible that jurisdictions that cater largely to U.S. multinationals would raise their own taxes to prevent U.S. firms from leaving. In either case, total U.S. income (the sum of taxes and company profits) would be reduced because a third party (the other countries) would collect a higher share of U.S. firms profits. Option B also is formulated as a cliff: once the country reaches a trigger level all income is subject to full U.S. taxes. Option B exempts from inclusion income derived in the home country (an active trade or business with income derived from the sale of property for use in the country or services provided in the country). These rules may be exploited by firms to avoid the tax.

The drawbacks of option B could also potentially affect option A as well. Since the lower taxes would apply to profits equal to 150% of costs, the lower taxes paid in countries with rates below 10% on this portion of profits would have to be traded off against higher taxes on the excess profits. However, in countries where the costs are small relative to profits firms might also have incentives in this case to shift locations.

Option C, which applies this system only to intangibles and is not triggered by a specific tax rate would also have the merit of not inducing undesirable behavioral changes. Option C would also apply this lower tax to royalties, although at least one analysis has suggested that a lower tax rate on royalties might violate WTO rules on export subsidies.[84] Several critics have pointed out the complication of measuring intangible income which would be a drawback. However, it would still require the measurement of affected income, adding complexity.

The purpose of option B could be accomplished is a way that does not encourage these undesirable behavioral responses by imposing a minimum (combined U.S. and foreign) tax on all foreign source income. Consider, for example, the 60% share of income taxed that comprises the second half of Option C. If a 15% minimum tax were imposed, it would only affect income in those countries with effective tax rates of below 15% but it would not produce incentives to move to a higher tax country.

Option B does appear to have relatively effective provisions defining an active operation that can avoid the tax in the Ways and Means Discussion Draft, although whether companies could work around them remains to be seen. The Enzi bill has a weaker rule, which would might more easily allow firms to justify an exception to the tax authorities and to the courts. The Enzi bill provision is triggered by a higher tax rate, which should capture Ireland.

One witness at the Ways and Means Hearing also noted that there is no distinction in the Discussion Draft between intangibles created in the United States and in other foreign countries: any intangible income could trigger a U.S. tax even if developed outside the United States.[85]

Option C of the Ways and Means Discussion Draft and S. 2091 also contains a reduced tax rate for royalties. Under Option C, royalties would be taxed at the same rate as intangible income generated inside the CFC which would eliminate the incentive to shift newly taxed royalties into tax exempt CFC income. If two thirds of royalties were exempt before due to sheltering by foreign tax credits, this change would be a slight relative tax increase (since 40% is taxed), but if the share is lower due to small excess credits and elimination of the splitter rules it could be a tax cut. Similar points could be made about S. 2091.

Transition

The Grubert-Mutti proposal appears to exempt dividends regardless of their source, a view that is probably consistent with their emphasis on reducing tax complexity, such as planning around repatriation. This approach provides a windfall benefit. However, as the Grubert and Mutti study is a general outline, the authors may simply not have addressed transition issues. One of the authors has indicated that it would be appropriate to impose a lower tax on the accumulated unrepatriated earnings in an approach similar to the Ways and Means Discussion Draft.[86]

The Ways and Means Discussion Draft would tax all accumulated earnings before implementation of the reform, but with an 85% exclusion, which may or may not provide a windfall since it might largely apply to earnings that would probably never be repatriated. These earnings would not have to be actually repatriated, but could be deemed repatriated, a benefit that is important if these funds are tied up in illiquid investments. Taxes would be offset by a proportional share of foreign tax credits. In a steady state, most accumulated earnings, based on past evidence and new view theory would be earnings that are permanently reinvested. However, since earnings may have accumulated at higher rates through anticipation of another repatriation holiday, more of these earnings may be planned for distribution.

One critic suggests that the deemed repatriation provision which is extended to individuals as well may not be appropriate for taxpayers not eligible for the dividend exemption.[87] Another suggests that firms may have trouble measuring the total amount of unrepatriated earnings.[88]

S. 2091 has a repatriation tax that differs from the Ways and Means provision in that it is elective on a CFC by CFC basis, the exclusion is smaller at a 70% exclusion and no foreign tax credits would be allowed.

However, for income that is not elected to be taxed, the dividend relief would not occur until these accumulated earnings are exhausted. Since firms might eventually wish to repatriate earnings, this rule should create an incentive to repatriate, however, the elective aspect allows firms not to repatriate if their conditions are such that a move of this nature would be difficult (i.e., lack of funds to pay the tax).

Current tax treatment is governed in some respects by tax treaties and these treaties may now come into conflict with the new proposed rules. Interactions with treaties would need to be addressed.

An issue to be determined is the treatment of foreign tax credits and losses that have been carried over. For the Grubert-Mutti proposal and the Ways and Means Discussion Draft, which are aimed at a full break from the old system, it seems appropriate to allow foreign tax credit carryovers to lapse (if any foreign tax credit carryovers remain after the taxation of accumulated earnings).

That is apparently the intent of the deemed repatriation tax.[89] S. 2091 would presumably continue carryovers for entities not covered (such as branches) and tax credits associated with accumulated income not yet taxed. Treatment of losses under the Discussion Draft has not been addressed, but presumably would continue under S. 2091 which continues aspects of the pre-existing system.

Administrative and Technical Issues

Many of the major rules discussed above would complicate tax administration. The Grubert-Mutti proposal appears to involve the least amount of complication as it has a simple exclusion, somewhat reduces the scope of Subpart F, and has a straightforward anti-abuse provision in the form of the allocation of deductions. There is no scope for a repatriation tax. Although the Ways and Means Discussion Draft is not fully fleshed out, it retains a small repatriation tax that could lead to tax planning (the 5% inclusion of dividend income), and its anti-abuse provisions could be quite complicated. S. 2091 could also potentially lead to a continued repatriation incentive.

This section addresses some other specific issues that have technical and administrative implications.

Including Branches

Including branch company income under the territorial rules is contained in two of the proposals, Grubert and Mutti and the Ways and Means Discussion Draft, but not in S. 2091. There is a good reason for including branches in the scope of the territorial tax, since, if branch income is not allowed or if firms can opt out, then firms could continue to use branches versus subsidiaries for tax planning, to allow the recognition of losses but not positive earnings. Moreover, while there are non-tax reasons for operating as a branch, including branches would equalize the treatment of branch and subsidiary operations.

Nevertheless, one comment suggests that the approach in the Discussion Draft, which treats branches as if they are CFC's subject to all of the other provisions of the proposal comes with additional complications. It is difficult to: measure income of an entity that does not legally exist as if it were separate, determine when a foreign branch exists as designed in the proposal, determine the formation or liquidation of an operation that is not a separate entity, and address the rules that apply to intra-company payments. In addition, firms might shift to operating as a partnership. This comment suggests that branch income simply be exempt from the tax without defining them as CFCs[90] Another comment raises a number of specific tax issues that need to be addressed when branches are included, including whether taxes will be triggered by reorganization and the treatment of inter-branch payments.[91]

10/50 Election

The Grubert Mutti proposal includes 10/50 corporations in their exemption system, while the Ways and Means Discussion Draft and S. 2091 allow it as an election. (Recall that a 10/50 company is one where the corporation has a 10% or more share but the company is not controlled by five or less 10% U.S. shareholders). Presumably companies would prefer to elect the exempt treatment especially as they will lose the foreign tax credits associated with dividends.

One comment suggested that 10/50 corporations that wish to elect inclusion may have difficulties because they will become subject to Subpart F rules but may not be able to obtain the information on Subpart F income because they do not control the firm. In addition, 10/50 firms may not be able to compel the cash dividend payments needed to pay tax given the tax on accumulated earnings under the Ways and Means Discussion Draft,[92] and may not be able to determine the size of those accumulated earnings.[93] A concern was also expressed that the tax on accumulated deferrals would include income generated before the taxpayer purchased shares in the company.[94] In S. 2091, a similar argument could be made about the elective repatriation, which these firms may not be able to take advantage of.

Foreign Tax Credit Revisions

The Ways and Means Discussion Draft eliminates foreign tax credits for CFC's, branches, and 10/50 corporations except for those associated with Subpart F income. It also eliminates the foreign tax credit baskets, splitter rules, and allocation of indirect expenses to foreign source income (including interest allocation rules).

One comment suggests that these changes are problematic because individuals will still be eligible for foreign tax credits.[95] Another adds that these changes in the foreign tax credit would encourage countries to reinstate foreign withholding tax and abrogate treaties because the changes effectively eliminate the limits of current law that credits are limited to foreign source income.[96]

Thin Capitalization Rules and Interest Allocation

One comment raised the question of whether strengthened thin capitalization rules that limit debt would be extended to U.S. subsidiaries of foreign parents (where presumably weaker rules already apply), or at least that intentions in this area might need to be made clear.[97] Although the legislation is focused on U.S. multinationals and their foreign operations, profit shifting can also occur across foreign parents and their U.S. subsidiaries, the current focus of thin capitalization rules.

Another comment pointed out that with more restrictive interest allocation rules firms might want to shift borrowing abroad so that interest could be deducted in other jurisdictions, but that this change might increase borrowing costs.[98] One option that might be considered is to allow loans from the parent to foreign subsidiaries at the borrowing rate of the parent or allow the parent to guarantee subsidiary loans without triggering effective dividends.

Continuing Subpart F

Some discussion of the treatment of the existing anti-abuse rules under Subpart F has occurred. At least one commentator questions why Subpart F, which was developed as a general anti-deferral provision, should continue as is with respect to certain types of income, when income is now generally exempt. One example is foreign to foreign base company income relating to sales and services, which is active income.[99]

Grubert and Mutti suggest that Subpart F should be retained to address profit shifting but modified by eliminating taxes on dividends and also on deemed dividends from investments in the United States. The Ways and Means Discussion Draft makes these two changes although they do not account for the 5% inclusion in income for either. They indicate a further consideration of Subpart F will be made. Grubert and Mutti suggest that the case for other rules such as the foreign base company rules relating to sales and services and interest would be strengthened under a territorial tax. Presumably they are referring to income shifted out the United States. S. 2091, however, specifically excludes this income from Subpart F.

Grubert and Mutti prepared their analysis before check-the-box rules (and the look-through rules) that allow CFC's to disregard their related foreign subsidiaries, which have undermined Subpart F, became so important. The Ways and Means Discussion Draft indicates that these issues will be considered separately and S. 2091 would make the look-through rules (as well as the exclusion of active financing income), currently part of extenders and having expired after 2011, permanent One comment suggested that tax reform should address the leakage in Subpart F including checkthe-box and the look-through rules[100] At the same time, one of the concerns about check the box and look through rules is that the result would not be greater U.S. tax collections but an increase in taxes paid to other countries. For example, if a subsidiary's interest payments from loans to its own high tax subsidiary could not longer be disregarded for purposes of Subpart F with an end to these rules, the response could be to no longer make the loan causing additional tax to be collected by the higher tax foreign country. This outcome would not be beneficial for the U.S. overall since it would reduce the sum of U.S. private profits and U.S. taxes. One comment, for example, notes that exemption would cause firms to have every incentive to reduce foreign taxes paid, and broadening of Subpart F rules should not undo that incentive.[101]

A final comment about Subpart F income is that, since this income is deemed repatriated and not actually paid out, there will be an additional tax under the Discussion Draft and S. 2091on 5% of income when these earnings are actually paid out as dividends.[102] Thus, 5% of income would be subject to double taxation.

Revenue Consequences

The Grubert-Mutti proposal is projected to raise revenue on a permanent basis, although the gain is small, less than 2% of corporate revenues. Both the Ways and Means Discussion Draft and S. 2091 aim to be revenue neutral over the budget horizon. However, both also rely on a one time revenue gain from taxing existing accumulated earnings. Since this gain is transitory, these proposals will lose revenue on a permanent basis. Since the proposals have not been scored, there is no way to determine how large the permanent revenue loss would be, but it is likely to also be small.

ALTERNATIVES TO A TERRITORIAL TAX

As noted in the prior discussion, there are alternatives to a territorial tax that could address issues associated with repatriation and profit shifting as effectively or perhaps more effectively than the territorial tax provisions. These alternatives fall into three main groups: ending deferral and possibly limiting cross-crediting to move closer to a true worldwide system, reforming the existing system in more limited ways, particularly to address profit shifting, and a hybrid between ending deferral and a territorial tax, such as a minimum tax, which would eliminate the repatriation tax trigger. By traditional theory all of these approaches would probably attract capital back to the United States and improve efficiency in the allocation of capital, although they may create a need to further address shifting of headquarters.

These proposals are summarized briefly. Many of them are addressed in more detail in other CRS reports.[103] Note that many of the same issues that arise with a territorial tax would need to be addressed in some cases, such as dealing with the transition, and dealing with operations outside of CFCs.

Ending Deferral

Ending deferral, as shown in *Table 5,* is estimated to raise $18.4 billion in FY2014. A deferral option is also included in the CBO budget options study and is estimated to raise $11.1 billion in revenue in FY2014.[104] The smaller revenue gain may reflect a provision that eliminates the current interest allocation provision for purposes of the foreign tax credit limit. It would tax income of foreign subsidiaries, while allowing foreign tax credits as in current law. Current taxation would eliminate any disincentive to repatriate, and would also reduce the benefits and scope for profit shifting. Cross-crediting would still be available. It would be more consistent with efficient resource allocation, although issues of shifting headquarters might need to be addressed further. As with territorial tax proposals, transition issues would arise which could be addressed in a fashion similar to that in the Ways and Means Discussion Draft. The revision would require the measurement of earnings under U.S. law, which could add complexity, although such measurement would also be needed for most base erosion measures as well. As with the territorial tax, issues would arise in extending the treatment to 10/50 corporations that have a large U.S. shareholder but are not controlled by a group of large U.S. shareholders, since information on earnings may not be available. This change would, however, permit the elimination of Subpart F.

Ending Deferral and Ending Cross-Crediting Via a Per Country Limit

A greater level of taxation and a more effective provision to discourage artificial profit shifting, which would also eliminate disincentives to repatriate, is to combine ending deferral with a per country limit on foreign tax credits, preventing tax haven income from being shielded by foreign tax credits. This proposal is part of S. 727, the Wyden and Coats general tax reform plan, and is combined with a repatriation holiday similar to that enacted in 2004. This provision was estimated to raise $64.3 billion in FY2014 (see *Table 5*). This larger revenue gain aided in the reduction of the corporate tax rate in that bill to 24%. This provision would require country-bycountry measures of foreign taxes paid as well as income (focusing on income earned within that country and not adjusting for intercompany dividends). Provisions would need to be enacted to prevent firms from using holding companies to avoid the per country limit and check the box and look through rules would probably need to be revised.

Measures to Modify the Current System: the President's Proposals

The President has made several proposals that address international tax issues.

The FY2013 budget outline contains several revisions which overall would raise $16.8 billion in FY2014. Note that some of these are complex to explain, and are described in more detail in a Treasury Department document.[105]

- Disallowing interest deductions of parent companies to the extent that income is deferred. This provision is similar to the allocation proposal in Grubert and Mutti but confined to interest and affecting deferred income. An earlier tax reform proposal by Chairman Rangel (H.R. 3970 in the 110th Congress, 2007) would have allocated a broader range of deductions, not just interest. This provision would reduce, although not eliminate, the disincentive to repatriate. ($5.9 billion).
- Limiting foreign tax credits available to the same share of total credits as the overall share of income that is repatriated. This approach would limit tax minimization by repatriating income to absorb foreign tax credits. ($5.5 billion).
- Treating excess intangibles profits as U.S. income, the same provision as Option A is the Ways and Means Discussion Draft, although the budget proposal does not specify the magnitude of the cost mark-up. ($2.5 billion). The proposal would also clarify some rules relating to the valuation of intangibles. ($0.1 billion).
- U.S. insurance companies can reduce taxes by purchasing reinsurance from foreign affiliates, with a deduction of the premiums by the U.S. firm but no tax on the income of the foreign affiliate. This provision would disallow these deductions under certain circumstances. ($0.2 billion).

- Stricter limits on interest deductions would apply to U.S. subsidiaries of firms that inverted (moved their headquarters abroad) prior to the anti-inversion rules adopted in 2004. ($0.4 billion).
- Foreign taxes paid in part to receive a benefit (i.e., the firm is paying a tax in a dual capacity) would not be credited unless the income tax is generally imposed on the country's own residents as well as foreign persons. The current rule does not require the tax to be imposed on the country's residents. This provision typically relates to taxes being substituted for royalties in oil producing countries. ($1.0 billion).
- A codification of regulations that impose on a foreign corporation or nonresident alien tax on gain from a partnership interest to the extent the gain reflects property effectively connected with U.S. business. ($0.2 billion).
- A provision to prevent a foreign affiliate from avoiding characterization as a dividend by making the distribution through a related affiliate with limited earnings and profits, causing the distribution to adjust the cost basis of stock rather than create dividend income. ($0.3 billion).
- Preventing foreign tax credits from offsetting tax on the gain from certain types of asset acquisitions. (0.1 billion).
- A provision that prevents the reduction of earnings and profits without the reduction in foreign tax credits that can currently occur in some transactions. ($20 million).

The Administration also presented a framework for tax reform that mentioned five elements: the allocation of interest for deferred income (first bullet point above), a tax on excess intangibles (third bullet point), a minimum tax on foreign source income in low tax countries, disallowing a deduction for the cost of moving abroad and providing a 20% credit for costs of moving an operation from abroad to the United States.[106]

The minimum tax on foreign source income, which would be a potentially important provision, is not discussed in detail. A minimum tax that could be imposed in the framework of an effective territorial system is discussed below.

Partial or Targeted End to Deferral

A variety of more limited ways of reducing or partially eliminating deferral include eliminating deferral for specified tax havens, eliminating deferral in countries with tax rates that are below the U.S. rate by a specified proportion, eliminating deferral for income from the production of goods that are in turn imported into the United States, eliminating deferral for income from the production of goods that are exported to any other country from the foreign location, and requiring a minimum payout share. These provisions would partially achieve the goals of a general elimination of deferral.[107]

Formula Apportionment

Another approach to addressing income shifting, whether in the current system or a revised territorial system, is through formula apportionment. With formula apportionment, income would be allocated to different jurisdictions based on their shares of some combination of sales, assets, and employment. This approach is used by many states in the United States and by the Canadian provinces to allocate corporate income. In the past, a three factor apportionment was used, but some states have moved to a sales based system. Studies have estimated a significant increase in taxes from adopting formula apportionment.[108] The ability of a formula apportionment system to address some of the problems of shifting income becomes problematic with intangible assets which, unlike production income, cannot be allocated based on tangible assets.[109] There is also a problem of coordinating with other countries so that income would not be double-taxed or never taxed.[110]

Hybrid Approaches: Minimum Tax, Partial Territorial Tax

Using the basic territorial approach embodied in the Ways and Means Draft Discussion, it would be possible to generate a relatively straightforward hybrid approach, by a modification of Base Erosion Option B to impose a simpler general minimum tax with no exceptions for active trade or business. Such a revision would technically begin with an elimination of deferral and per country foreign tax credit limit. Income, however, would be taxed at a lower tax rate. This approach would avoid the incentives to shift to a slightly higher tax jurisdiction. Moreover, it would be simpler, because it would not require any measure of a specific type of income, would not require a measure of effective tax rate, and would not require a determination of the type of activity to allow an exception. It would use U.S. rules for measurement of income, but would apply a lower statutory rate to taxable income. Foreign tax credits would need to be allowed on a country by country basis. For example, suppose the statutory rate to be applied were half the U.S. rate, or given current rates, 17.5%. In that case any income from a country with an effective tax rate on taxable income at that level (and probably a lower effective rate overall) would not be subject to U.S. tax. Such a tax regime would only affect tax havens and low tax jurisdictions.[111]

An alternative would be to require income to be repatriated (or deemed repatriated) but subject some share of it to U.S. tax and exempt the rest. An appropriate share of foreign tax credits would be disallowed. For example, if half of income is taxed, the system would be 50% a territorial tax and 50% a world wide tax without deferral. Foreign tax credit limits could be allowed on an overall basis or country by country. This approach bears some resemblance to the foreign tax credit pooling proposal in the President's budget except there is no discretion about repatriation. Comments made on the combining of a minimum tax with a territorial system suggested that the tax rate would be important, with two observers suggesting a rate of 20%, similar to the rate used by Japan, and indicating that a 10% tax rate is too low.[112]

Both of these proposals would have the effect of eliminating the repatriation disincentive as well as reducing the incentive to shift profits (or at least the cost). Unlike proposals to tax this income at full U.S. rates, such a minimum tax is less likely to shift income to other jurisdictions that have higher rates than the United States.

In any proposal aimed at tax havens, there is a possibility that the haven or low tax country would raise its taxes and capture some of the profits. This problem is more significant with a minimum tax that it would be with full elimination of deferral, which would remove the incentive to profit shift altogether. Tax havens attracting other country's firms might be reluctant to raise taxes and it might be possible to deny credits for taxes that are increased for that purpose.

APPENDIX. HISTORY OF INTERNATIONAL TAX RULES

As this history indicates, most of the proposals made over the years, whether adopted or not, moved not toward a territorial tax and a reduction in taxation of foreign source income, but toward a worldwide tax and increased taxation.

Deferral of tax on income from foreign incorporated subsidiaries dates from the earliest years of the income tax based reflecting legal principles of the time. The earliest income tax allowed a deduction for foreign taxes, which was replaced by an unlimited credit in 1918. In 1921 an overall limit on the foreign tax credit. similar to current law, was adopted. Beginning in 1932, a per country limit was allowed or required, although regulations that sourced income to holding companies allowed firms to achieve overall limits on their own. The per country limit was eliminated in 1976, although income was sorted into passive and active baskets to prevent this type of cross-crediting.

A number of proposals for changing the system were made but were not (or have not yet been) adopted. Eliminating deferral was proposed by President Kennedy and President Carter. The Kennedy proposals led to the anti-abuse rules (Subpart F) that tax passive and easily shifted income currently.

The Burke Hartke proposal in the 1970s would have repealed deferral and allowed a deduction rather than a credit for foreign taxes. A per country limit was proposed by the Reagan Administration as part of the Tax Reform Act of 1986, but the legislation expanded the number of baskets from two to several instead. The baskets were reduced to two again in legislation in 2004. The main consequence according to tax data, was to include income from financial services in the general basket.

Legislative proposals which would have increased taxation of international income by allocating parent company expenses, such as interest, to deferred income and not allowing it as well as allowing overall foreign taxes to be considered Proposals similar to those of President Obama were included in tax reform legislation proposed by then Ways and Means Committee Chairman Rangel in 2007. A predecessor to the Wyden Coats bill was the Wyden Gregg bill in the 111th Congress. International tax provisions are discussed in detail, through 1989, in William P. McClure and Herman B. Bouma, "The Taxation of Foreign Income from 1909 to 1989: How a Tilted Playing Field Developed," *Tax Notes*, June 19, 1989, pp. 1379.

End Notes

1 The President's Advisory Panel on Federal Tax Reform, Final Report, November 1, 2005, at http://govinfo.library.unt.edu/taxreformpanel/final-report/index.html. The Grubert-Mutti proposal was the territorial proposal under discussion for a number of years. It is outlined in Harry Grubert and John Mutti, Taxing International Business Income: Dividend Exemption Versus the Current System (Washington, DC, AEI Press, 2001). It is discussed in further detail in Rosanne Altshuler and Harry Grubert, "Where Will They Go if We Go Territorial? Dividend Exemption and the Location Decisions of U.S. Multinational Corporations," National Tax Journal (December 2001), pp. 787-809. Because the current U.S. tax system

collects little revenue, and because of features of the Grubert-Mutti proposal to allocate parent company deductions, this proposal would raise revenue.

[2] See various discussions and drafts at the Ways and Means Committee website, at http://waysandmeans.house.gov/taxreform/.

[3] The National Commission on Fiscal Responsibility and Reform, The Moment of Truth, at http://www.fiscalcommission.gov/sites/fiscalcommission.gov/files/documents/TheMomentofTruth12_1_2010.pdf.

[4] The President's Framework for Business Tax Reform: A Joint Report by the White House and the Department of the Treasury, February 2012, at http://www.treasury.gov/resource-center/tax-policy/Documents/The-PresidentsFramework-for-Business-Tax-Reform-02-22-2012.pdf.

[5] Melissa Costa and Jennifer Gravelle, "Taxing Multinational Corporations: Average Tax Rates," presented at a Conference of the American Tax Policy Center, October 2011, and forthcoming in Tax Law Review at http://www.americantaxpolicyinstitute.org/pdf/Costa-Gravelle%20paper.pdf.

[6] Fundamental economic issues are discussed in CRS Report RL34115, Reform of U.S. International Taxation: Alternatives, by Jane G. Gravelle.

[7] This discussion generally refers to foreign subsidiaries that are sometimes wholly owned and sometimes partially owned by a U.S. parent. The tax law defines a controlled foreign subsidiary or a controlled foreign corporation (CFC) as one in which the U.S. firm has a 10% share and 50% of the shares are owned by five or fewer 10% U.S. shareholders. A corporation in which a U.S. firm owns a 10% share but 50% is not owned by five or fewer 10% shareholders is called a non controlled Section 902 corporation or a 10/50 corporation. Smaller share ownership is portfolio investment. New data from the Internal Revenue Service reports dividends from firms that are less that 20% owned, more than 20% owned and wholly owned at 7%, 65%, and 27%, although any of these firms could potentially be CFC's and the payout ratios may differ. Filled in 1120 form at http://www.irs.gov/pub/irs-soi/08colinecount.pdf.

[8] Check-the-box allows a firm, including a subsidiary of a U.S. firm, to choose to disregard (not recognize) its own subsidiary as a separate entity and consolidate that income with the parent (higher tier subsidiary) firm. For example, if a U.S. parent's subsidiary in a low-tax country lends money to its own subsidiary in a high-tax county (with deductions for interest paid), the interest income received by the low-tax subsidiary would normally be taxed as Subpart F income even if this income is not repatriated to the U.S. parent. Check-the-box allows the high-tax subsidiary to be disregarded for tax purposes so that no interest income appears.

[9] See David R. Sicular, "The New Look-Through Rule: W(h)ither Subpart F?" Tax Notes, April 23, 2007, pp. 349-378 for a discussion of this provision.

[10] Fewer excess credit firms in recent years also led to transactions designed to generate foreign tax credits, but these have now been limited by regulation. See Steven Schneider, Regulations Address Foreign Tax Credit Generator Structures, at http://www. taxlawroundup.com/2011/07/regulations-address-foreign-tax-credit-generator-transactions/.

[11] A per country limit was used in the past at various times, but because it did not have look-through rules, holding companies could be used to accomplish the effects of an overall limit. While an overall credit limit has been used for some time, between 1986 and 2004, the credit was applied within nine different baskets.

[12] Scott Luttrel, "Corporate Foreign Tax Credit, 2007," Internal Revenue Service, Statistics of Income Bulletin, 2011, at http://www.irs.gov/pub/irs-soi/11cosumbulcorpforeign.pdf. There are two very small baskets for income from countries sanctioned by the United States and income resourced by treaty, which accounted for less than two-tenths of a percent. Prior to 2007 when there were nine baskets, but the only important difference was a separation of the financial services basket, with 19.7% of income, from the general basket.

[13] These treatments were referred to as reverse hybrids, and they occurred when, from the U.S. perspective, the subsidiary has its own subsidiary where profits can be deferred, but from the foreign perspective the subsidiary and its own subsidiary are the same firm. The top tier subsidiary thus confronts a foreign tax it is liable for and which could be claimed as a credit even though the income is not reported because it is eligible for deferral. It is the reverse of the check the box arrangement.

[14] This provision was adopted in the P.L. 111-226. See Joint Committee on Taxation, General Explanation Of Tax Legislation Enacted In The 111th Congress, JCS-2-11, March 24, 2011, for the revenue estimate for this provision and for several other revisions of the foreign tax credit to address abuses. See also CRS Report R40623, Tax Havens: International Tax Avoidance and Evasion, by Jane G. Gravelle.

[15] See Internal Revenue Service http://www.irs.gov/pub/irs-soi/08colinecount.pdf.

[16] Internal Revenue Service, Statistics of Income, Controlled Foreign Corporations, at http://www.irs.gov/taxstats/bustaxstats/article/0,,id=96282,00.html. Firms represented in these statistics have a 50% ownership or more.

[17] Department of Commerce, Bureau of Economic Analysis, Table 6.16D, at http://www. bea.gov/international/ di1usdop.ht.m.

[18] For 2006 total payments were 25% with 12% as discretionary dividends. The data for Canada were similar, but in Switzerland 16% was paid out in total but only 3% as dividends.

[19] Residual U.S. tax in Table 3 divided by net income from statistics reported in Table 1.

[20] Harry Grubert and Rosanne Altshuler, "Corporate Taxes in the World Economy: Reforming the Taxation of Cross-border Income," in John W. Diamond and George R. Zodrow, eds., Fundamental Tax Reform: Issues, Choices, and Implications (Cambridge: MIT Press, 2008).

[21] Data on distribution by basket from Scott Luttrell, Corporate Foreign Tax Credit, 2000, Internal Revenue Service, Statistics of Income, at http://www.irs.gov/pub/irs-soi/00cftcar.pdf.

[22] Pre-tax income would range from $112 billion for 2007 to $142 billion for 2008 (with deemed tax apportioned 73% on active dividends. 12.6% of the total tax in Table 3 would result in $3.7 billion in 2007 and $2.8 billion in 2008, for an effective tax rate of 3.3% and 1.6% on dividends received. However, estimates above indicate that only about 23% of dividends are paid out, so that these tax rates need to be multiplied by 0.23, yielding rates of 0.36% to 0.76%.

[23]Camp Releases International Tax Reform Discussion Draft , October 26, 2011, at http://waysandmeans.house.gov/ News/DocumentSingle.aspx?DocumentID=266168.

[24] If the rate of return were 10%, the steady state nominal growth rate were 6% (a typical value reflecting a real growth rate of 3% and an inflation rate of 3%), then the remainder would be paid out as a 4% dividend yield. These are typical historical values in the United States. Thus, in a steady state growth model with these values, 60% of nominal earnings would be retained in any case (and would be retained if taxes did matter), and 40% paid out.

[25] See CRS Report R40178, Tax Cuts on Repatriation Earnings as Economic Stimulus: An Economic Analysis, by Donald J. Marples and Jane G. Gravelle. Another repatriation holiday was voted on in the Senate in 2009, but not adopted.

[26] Data from 1992 to 2008 were from Internal Revenue Service Statistics of Income, Data on Controlled Foreign Corporations, http://www.irs.gov/taxstats/bustaxstats/article/ 0,,id= 97151,00.html. Data from 1968-1992 reported in James R. Hines, Jr., The Case Against Deferral: A Deferential Consideration, National Tax Journal ,Vol. 52, September 1999, pp. 385-404.

[27] The evidence does not support the idea that the fall in repatriations was due to check-the-box, which was first announced at the beginning of 1997. Subpart F income did not begin to decline as a share of income until 2004.

[28] Mehir A. Desai, C. Fritz Foley, and James R. Hines, Jr., Dividend Policy Inside the Multinational Firm, Financial Management, March 22, 2007, at http://www.thefreelibrary. com/Dividend+policy+inside+the+multinational+ firm.- a0167305683.

[29] Testimony of Mr. Gary M. Thomas Before the Committee on Ways & Means, U.S. House of Representatives, Hearing on How Other Countries Have Used Tax Reform To Help Their Companies Compete in the Global Market and Create Jobs, May 24, 2011, at http://www.whitecase.com/files/Uploads/Documents/GThomas-HWM-Testimony24May2 011.pdf.

[30] Peter Egger, Valeria Merlo, Martin Ruf, and Georg Wamser, The Consequences of the new UK Tax Exemption System: Evidence from Micro-level Data, Working Paper, January 26, 2012.

[31] Mehir A. Desai, C. Fritz Foley, and James R. Hines, Jr., "Repatriation Taxes and Dividend Distortions," National Tax Journal, Vol. 54, December 2001, pp. 829-851.

[32] See Rosanne Altshuler, T. Scott Newlon, and William C. Randolph, "Do Repatriations Matter? Evidence from Tax Returns of Multinationals," in The Effects of Taxation on Multinational Corporations, Ed. by Martin Feldstein, James r. HInes, Jr. and R. Glenn Hubbard, Chicago: University of Chicago Press, 1995, pp. 253-277.

[33] Mehir A. Desai, C. Fritz Foley, and James R. Hines, Jr., "Repatriation Taxes and Dividend Distortions," National Tax Journal, Vol. 54, December 2001, pp. 829-851.

[34] Rosanne Altshuler and Harry Grubert, "Repatriation Taxes, Repatriation Strategies and Multinational Financial Policy, Journal of Public Economics, Vol 87, 2002, pp. 73-107.

[35] Some methods of returning cash to the United States involve corporate reorganizations. See Jesse Drucker, "Dodging Repatriation Tax Lets Companies Bring Home Cash," Bloomberg, December 29, 2010, http://www.bloomberg.com/ news/2010-12-29/dodging-repatriation-tax-lets-u-s-companies-bring-home-cash. html. For an in depth discussion of methods, see Hal Hicks and David J. Sotos, "The Empire Strikes Back (Again) – The Killer Bs, Deadly Ds and Sec. 367 As The Death Star Against Repatriation Rebels,".

International Tax Journal, May-June 2008, pp. 37-58. The Internal Revenue Service has periodically attempted to address various methods of repatriating cash without paying tax, most recently in July 2012. See Richard Rubin, "IRS Ends Deals That Let Companies Avoid Repatriation Tax," Bloomberg, July 13, 2011, at http://www.bloomberg.com/news/2012-07-13/irs-ends-deals-that-let-companies-avoidrepatriation-tax.html.

[36] Mehir A. Desai, C. Fritz Foley, and James R. Hines, Jr., Dividend Policy Inside the Multinational Firm, Financial Management, March 22, 2007, at http://www. thefreelibrary.com/Dividend+policy+inside+the+ multinational +firm.- a0167305683.

[37] CRS Report R40178, Tax Cuts on Repatriation Earnings as Economic Stimulus: An Economic Analysis, by Donald J. Marples and Jane G. Gravelle.

[38] The repatriations under the repatriation holiday, enacted on the basis of increasing investment, were largely used to repurchase shares, the equivalent of paying dividends. See CRS Report R40178, Tax Cuts on Repatriation Earnings as Economic Stimulus: An Economic Analysis, by Donald J. Marples and Jane G. Gravelle, for a review of the evidence.

[39] Using repatriations to increase employment in an underemployed economy in the short run are unlikely to be effective because transferring foreign earnings into U.S. dollars is contractionary and likely overwhelms any direct spending effects. See CRS Report R40178, Tax Cuts on Repatriation Earnings as Economic Stimulus: An Economic Analysis, by Donald J. Marples and Jane G. Gravelle.

[40] Note that economic analysis has focused on efficient allocation of investment, rather than the effects on jobs because in the long run (the focus of a permanent tax law), an economy will tend to naturally create jobs.

[41] The issues discussed in this section are discussed in more detail in CRS Report RL34115, Reform of U.S. International Taxation: Alternatives, by Jane G. Gravelle.

[42] Harry Grubert and John Mutti, Taxing International Business Income: Dividend Exemption Versus the Current System," Washington, DC, The AEI Press, 2001.

[43] The President's Advisory Panel on Federal Tax Reform, Simple, Fair and Pro-Growth: Proposals to Fix America's Tax System, November, 2005, at http://govinfo.library. unt.edu/taxreformpanel/.

[44] The proposal is estimated to raise revenues by $6.9 billion in FY2014. See Congressional Budget Office, Reducing the Deficit: Spending and Revenue Options, March, 2011, p. 187, http://www.cbo.gov/sites/default /files/cbofiles/ ftpdocs/120xx/doc12085/03-10-reducing thedeficit.pdf.

[45] Countries can adopt anti-abuse provisions that are more limited. See Marco Rossi, "European Commission Blesses Italy's Anti-Inversion Rules," at http://www.euitalianinternationaltax. com/2011/05/articles/european-commissionblesses-italys-antiinversion-rules/.

[46] See Jane G. Gravelle, Does the Concept of Competitiveness Have Meaning in Formulating Corporate Tax Policy? November 2011, forthcoming, Tax Law Review, at http://www.americantaxpolicyinstitute.org/pdf/ Jane%20 Gravelle%20paper.pdf. Critiques of competitiveness arguments were also made, primarily with respect to trade policy, by Paul Krugman, See "Competitiveness: A Dangerous Obsession," Foreign Affairs, Vol. 73, No. 2 (March-April, 1994), pp. 28-44. Links to the journal can be found at http://www. foreignaffairs.com/issues/1994/73/4.

[47] Mergers that involve shifting the location of incorporation do occur occasionally. The announced merger of Eaton Corporation and Cooper Industries is an example of how mergers can be used to shift headquarters although even in this case the stated primary reason was non-tax issues. Cooper was already incorporated in Ireland, but is effectively a U.S. company with management in Houston. See Robert Schoenberger, "Eaton Corporation Plans to Buy Cooper Industries, Move Incorporation to Ireland," The Plain Dealer, May 12, 2012. http://www.cleveland.com/business/ index.ssf/2012/05/eaton_corp_plans_ to_merge_ with.html. Aon's shift of incorporation to the U.K. will trigger a shareholder level capital gains tax. See "Aon Shareholders May Pay Hefty Taxes With Headquarters Shifting to London," Ameet Sachdev's Chicago Law, at http://articles. chicagotribune.com/2012-01-20/business/ct-biz-0120- chicago-law-20120120_1_aon-global-aon-corp-tax. Among solutions to limit tax motivated international mergers is imposing a tax on shareholder gain at ordinary rates.

[48] Susan Morse and Eric Allen, "Firm Incorporation Outside the U.S.: No Exodus Yet," December 2011, at http://papers.ssrn.com/sol3/papers.cfm?abstract_id=1950760.

[49] This idea is most recently addressed in Mihir Desai and James Hines, "Evaluating International Tax Reform," National Tax Journal, Vol. 56, September 2003, pp. 487-502.

[50] See CRS Report RL34115, Reform of U.S. International Taxation: Alternatives, by Jane G. Gravelle, for a more detailed discussion of this issue.

[51] See CRS Report R41743, International Corporate Tax Rate Comparisons and Policy Implications, by Jane G. Gravelle.

[52] Melissa Costa and Jennifer Gravelle, Taxing Multinational Corporations: Average Tax Rates, Presented at a Conference of the American Tax Policy Center, October 2011, and forthcoming in Tax Law Review, at http://www.americantaxpolicyinstitute.org/pdf/Costa-Gravelle%20paper.pdf.

[53] Charles Duhigg and David Kocieniewski, "How Apples Sidesteps Billions in Taxes," New York Times, April 29, 2012, p.1, 20-21. at http://www.nytimes.com/ 2012/04/29/business /apples-tax-strategy-aims-at-low-tax-states-andnations.html?pagewanted=all.

[54] See CRS Report R41743, International Corporate Tax Rate Comparisons and Policy Implications, by Jane G. Gravelle.

[55] The overall evidence suggests an elasticity of around three which is used in the calculations above; see Jennifer C. Gravelle, Corporate Tax Incidence: Review of General Equilibrium Estimates and Analysis, Working Paper 2010-03, May 2010, at http://www.cbo.gov/sites/ default/files/cbofiles/ftpdocs/115xx/doc11519/05-2010-working_papercorp_tax_incidence-review_of_gen_eq_estimates.pdf. See Harry Grubert and Rosanne Altshuler, "Corporate Taxes in the World Economy: Reforming the Taxation of Cross-border Income," in Fundamental Tax Reform: Issues, Choices, and Implications, Ed. John W. Diamond and George R. Zodrow, Cambridge, MIT Press, 2008 who reference a number of studies showing that investment by multinationals is sensitive to tax rates. A review is also contained in Michael Smart , Repatriation Taxes and Foreign Direct Investment: Evidence From Tax Treaties, Working Paper, June 20, 2010, at http://www.sbs.ox.ac.uk/ centres/tax/symposia/Documents/2010/05%20Smart.pdf; and in Lars Feld and Jost Heckemeyer, "FDI and Taxation: A Meta Study," Journal of Economic Surveys, Vol 25, April, 2011, pp.233-272. The working paper version is at http://www.cesifo-group.de/ portal/pls/portal/docs/1/1186528.PDF.

[56] Estimates from CRS Report R41743, International Corporate Tax Rate Comparisons and Policy Implications, by Jane G. Gravelle, based on perfect mobility of capital and perfect product substitution.

[57] CRS Report R40623, Tax Havens: International Tax Avoidance and Evasion and CRS Report R41743, International Corporate Tax Rate Comparisons and Policy Implications, both by Jane G. Gravelle. Data on earnings and profits of controlled foreign corporations were taken from Lee Mahoney and Randy Miller, Controlled Foreign Corporations 2004, Internal Revenue Service Statistics of Income Bulletin, Summer 2008,http://www.irs.ustreas. gov/pub/irs-soi/ 04coconfor.pdf. Data on GDP from Central Intelligence Agency, The World Factbook, https://www.cia.gov/library/ publications/the-world-factbook. Most GDP data are for 2008 and based on the exchange rate but for some countries earlier years and data based on purchasing power parity were the only data available.

[58] See CRS Report R40623, Tax Havens: International Tax Avoidance and Evasion and CRS Report R41743, International Corporate Tax Rate Comparisons and Policy Implications, both by Jane G. Gravelle. For the most recent estimates see Kimberly A. Clausing "The Revenue Effects of Multinational Firm Income Shifting Tax Notes, March 28, 2011, pp. 1580-1586, who finds estimates for 2008 from $57 billion to $90 billion and Martin Sullivan, "Transfer Pricing Costs U.S. at Least $28 Billion," Tax Notes, March 22, 2010, pp. 1439-1443.

[59] Martin Sullivan, "Transfer Pricing Abuse Is Job-Killing Corporate Welfare," Tax Notes August 2, 2010, pp. 461-468.

[60] The lobbying group has apparently ended at least part of their campaign. See "WIN America, Tax Repatriation Holiday Lobby Group, Ends Advocacy Work" Reuters, http://www. huffingtonpost.com/2012/04/23/win-america-taxrepatriation-holiday_n_1447581.html?ref=business. For a report on the repatriation holiday and its issues see CRS Report R40178, Tax Cuts on Repatriation Earnings as Economic Stimulus: An Economic Analysis, by Donald J. Marples and Jane G. Gravelle.

[61] Harry Huizinga and Luc Laeven, "International Profit Shifting Within Multinationals: A Multi-Country Perspective," Journal of Public Economics, vol. 92. 2008, pp.1164-1182.

[62] Jesse Drucker, "Google 2.4% Rate Shows How $60 Billion Lost to Tax Loopholes," Bloomberg, October 21, 2010, at http://www.bloomberg.com/news/2010-10-21/google-2-4-rate-shows-how-60-billion-u-s-revenue-lost-to-taxloopholes.html.

[63] Department of the Treasury, General Explanations of the Administration's Fiscal Year 2013 Revenue Proposals, February 2012, http://www.treasury.gov/resource-center/tax-policy/ Documents/General-Explanations-FY2013.pdf.

[64] Harry Grubert and John Mutti, Taxing International Business Income: Dividend Exemption Versus the Current System (Washington, DC, AEI Press, 2001).

[65] The President's Advisory Panel on Federal Tax Reform, Simple, Fair and Pro-Growth: Proposals to Fix America's Tax System, November, 2005, at http://govinfo. library.unt. edu/taxreformpanel/.

[66] Author's conversation with Harry Grubert, July 2, 2012.

[67] Congressional Budget Office, Reducing the Deficit: Spending and Revenue Options, March 20, 2011, p. 187. http://www.cbo.gov/sites/default/files/ cbofiles/ftpdocs/120xx/doc12085/ 03-10-reducingthedeficit.pdf

[68] Documents, including bill language, technical discussions and shorter summaries can be found at the Ways and Means Committee website at http://waysandmeans.house.gov /taxreform/.

[69] Ernst & Young has provided a summary of this bill, "Senator Enzi Introduces and International Tax Reform Bill," http://www.ey.com/Publication/vwLUAssets/ Senator_ Enzi_introduces_ an_international_tax_reform_bill/ $FILE/Senator%20Enzi%20introduces%20reform%20bill.pdf, March 1, 2012.

[70] Jeffery M. Kadet, "Territorial W&M Discussion Draft: Change Required," Tax Notes, January 23, 2012, pp. 463-464.

[71] See Senator Enzi's press release, at http://www.enzi.senate.gov/uploads/3.pdf.

[72] Comments of Stephen Shay, KPMG, Will the U.S. Shift to a Territorial System: A Discussion of Chairman Camp's Territorial Tax Draft, http://www.us.kpmg.com/microsite /taxnewsflash/Corporate/2011/tgi-exec-sum-territorialtax.pdf.

[73] Rosanne Altshuler and Harry Grubert, "Where Will They Go if We Go Territorial? Dividend Exemption and the Location Decisions of U.S. Multinational Corporations," National Tax Journal, December 2001, pp. 787-809.

[74] The proposal refers to allocating the parents interest to firms and not worldwide interest, although a worldwide allocation would be an option.

[75] See data from Economic Report of the President at http://www.gpo.gov/fdsys/pkg/ERP-2012/pdf/ERP-2012-table15.pdf.

[76] Internal Revenue Service, http://www.irs.gov/taxstats/article/0,,id=170692,00.html. In 2006, the manufacturing sector has 247 billion of interest payments, $183 billion of interest income and $481 billion in net income. In 2007, these numbers were $304 billion, $203 billion and $468 billion respectively.

[77] Rosanne Altshuler and Harry Grubert, "Where Will They Go if We Go Territorial? Dividend Exemption and the Location Decisions of U.S. Multinational Corporations," National Tax Journal, December 2001, pp. 787-809.

[78] Ibid.

[79] International Revenue Service statistics, at http://www.irs.gov/taxstats/article/ 0,,id= 164402, 00.html.

[80] When the Grubert Mutti proposal was developed, worldwide allocation was not in the law. Harry Grubert, in a conversation on July 5, 2012, indicated that worldwide allocation would be appropriate.

[81] This measurement problem is pointed out by Harrington, Subcommittee on Select Revenue Measures, Ways and Means Committee, November 27, 2011, testimony of John L. Harrington, at http://waysandmeans.house.gov/ UploadedFiles/Harringtonsrm1117.pdf.

[82] This complication of Options A and C is pointed out by Stephen Shay and Paul Oosterhuis, KPMG, Will the U.S. Shift to a Territorial System: A Discussion of Chairman Camp's Territorial Tax Draft, at http://www.us. kpmg.com/ microsite/taxnewsflash/Corporate/ 2011/tgi-exec-sum-territorial-tax.pdf and by Michael Reilly, discussion reported in Shamik Trivedi, "Agreement on Territorial Plans Unlikely Despite Commonalities," Tax Notes, February 20, 2012, pp. 949-950.

[83] Subcommittee on Select Revenue Measures, Ways and Means Committee, November 27, 2011, Testimony of T. Timothy Tuerff, at http://waysandmeans.house.gov/Uploaded Files/Tuerffsrm1117.pdf.

[84] Kristen A. Parillo, "Camp Plan Would Likely Violate WTO Rules, Buckley Says," Tax Notes, December 12, 2011, pp. 1327-1328.

[85] Subcommittee on Select Revenue Measures, Ways and Means Committee, November 27, 2011, testimony of David G. Noren, at http://waysandmeans.house.gov/ UploadedFiles/ Norensrm1117.pdf.

[86] Conversation with Harry Grubert, July 2, 2012.

[87] Subcommittee on Select Revenue Measures, Ways and Means Committee, November 27, 2011, testimony of John L. Harrington, at http://waysandmeans.house.gov/ UploadedFiles/ Harringtonsrm1117.pdf. He notes that the purpose may be able to deal with individuals transferring their earnings to corporate form, but suggests that should be dealt with in a more targeted fashion.

[88] Subcommittee on Select Revenue Measures, Ways and Means Committee, November 27, 2011, testimony of Paul W. Oosterhuis, at http://waysandmeans.house.gov/UploadedFiles/ Oosterhuissrm1117.pdf.

[89] See comment of Ray Beeman , KPMG, Will the U.S. Shift to a Territorial System: A Discussion of Chairman Camp's Territorial Tax Draft, at http://www.us.kpmg.com /microsite/taxnewsflash/Corporate/2011/tgi-exec-sumterritorial-tax.pdf.

[90] Subcommittee on Select Revenue Measures, Ways and Means Committee, November 27, 2011, testimony of John L. Harrington, at http://waysandmeans.house.gov/ UploadedFiles/ Harringtonsrm1117.pdf.

[91] Subcommittee on Select Revenue Measures, Ways and Means Committee, November 27, 2011, testimony of T. Timothy Tuerff, at http://waysandmeans.house.gov/Uploaded Files/Tuerffsrm1117.pdf.

[92] Subcommittee on Select Revenue Measures, Ways and Means Committee, November 27, 2011, testimony of John L. Harrington, at http://waysandmeans.house.gov/UploadedFiles/ Harringtonsrm1117.pdf.

[93] Subcommittee on Select Revenue Measures, Ways and Means Committee, November 27, 2011, , testimony of Paul W. Oosterhuis, at http://waysandmeans.house.gov/UploadedFiles/ Oosterhuissrm1117.pdf.

[94] Report on comment of Jose Murillo at an Ernst and Young Conference, Kristen A. Parillo and Marie Sapirie, "Territorial Plan Drafters Aware of Transition Concerns," Tax Notes, November 14, 2011, pp. 810-812.

[95] Subcommittee on Select Revenue Measures, Ways and Means Committee, November 27, 2011, testimony of John L. Harrington, at http://waysandmeans.house.gov/Uploaded Files/Harringtonsrm1117.pdf.

[96] Kristen A. Parillo, "Camp Plan Would Dramatically Affect Withholding, Buckley Says" Tax Notes, November 21, 2011, pp. 948-949, reporting comments by John Buckley.

[97] Subcommittee on Select Revenue Measures, Ways and Means Committee, November 27, 2011, testimony of John L. Harrington, at http://waysandmeans.house.gov/Uploaded Files/Harringtonsrm1117.pdf.

[98] Subcommittee on Select Revenue Measures, Ways and Means Committee, November 27, 2011, Testimony of T. Timothy Tuerff, at http://waysandmeans.house.gov/UploadedFiles/ Tuerffsrm1117.pdf. See also Paul Oosterhuis, , KPGM, Will the U.S. Shift to a Territorial System: A Discussion of Chairman Camp's Territorial Tax Draft, at http://www.us.kpmg.com/microsite/taxnewsflash/Corporate/2011/tgi-exec-sum-territorial-tax.pdf.

[99] Subcommittee on Select Revenue Measures, Ways and Means Committee, November 27, 2011, testimony of John L. Harrington, at http://waysandmeans.house.gov/ UploadedFiles/ Harringtonsrm1117.pdf.

[100] Kristen A. Parillo, "Camp Plan Would Dramatically Affect Withholding, Buckley Says" Tax Notes, November 21, 2011, pp. 948-949, reporting comments by Jeff Vandervolk.

[101] Subcommittee on Select Revenue Measures, Ways and Means Committee, November 27, 2011, testimony of Paul W. Oosterhuis, at http://waysandmeans.house.gov/UploadedFiles/ Oosterhuissrm1117.pdf.

[102] Subcommittee on Select Revenue Measures, Ways and Means Committee, November 27, 2011, Testimony of T. Timothy Tuerff, at http://waysandmeans.house.gov/UploadedFiles/ Tuerffsrm1117.pdf.

[103] CRS Report RL34115, Reform of U.S. International Taxation: Alternatives, by Jane G. Gravelle; CRS Report R40623, Tax Havens: International Tax Avoidance and Evasion, by Jane G. Gravelle.

[104] Congressional Budget Office, Reducing the Deficit: Spending and Revenue Options, March, 2011, p. 186, at http://www.cbo.gov/sites/default/files/cbofiles/ftpdocs/120xx/doc12085/03-10-reducingthedeficit.pdf.

[105] See U.S. Department of Treasury, General Explanations of the Administration's FY2013 Revenue Proposals, February 2012, http://www.treasury.gov/resource-center/tax-policy /Documents/General-Explanations-FY2013.pdf.

[106] The President's Framework for Business Tax Reform: A Joint Report by the White House and the Department of the Treasury, February 2012, http://www.treasury.gov/resource-center/tax-policy/Documents/The-Presidents-Frameworkfor-Business-Tax-Reform-02-22-2012.pdf.

[107] CRS Report R40623, Tax Havens: International Tax Avoidance and Evasion, by Jane G. Gravelle This reports also discusses a variety of minor changes in rules including foreign tax credit provisions.

[108] Slemrod and Shackleford estimate a 38% revenue increase from an equally weighted three-factor system Douglas Shackelford and Joel Slemrod, "The Revenue Consequences of Using Formula apportionment to Calculate U.S. and Foreign Source Income: A Firm Level Analysis," International Tax and Public Finance, vol. 5, no. 1, 1998, pp. 41-57. Clausing and Avi-Yonah estimate a 35% increase in taxes using sales. Kimberly A. Clausing and Reuven A. AviYonah, Reforming Corporate Taxation in a Global Economy : A Proposal to Adopt Formulary Apportionment, Brookings Institution: The Hamilton Project, Discussion paper 2007-08, June 2007.

[109] These and other issues are discussed by Rosanne Altshuler and Harry Grubert, "Formula Apportionment: Is it Better than the Current System and Are There Better Alternatives?" Oxford University Centre for Business Taxation, Working paper 09/01.

[110] CRS Report R40623, Tax Havens: International Tax Avoidance and Evasion, by Jane G. Gravelle, for further discussion.

[111] A 2000 Treasury Study proposed a similar treatment and also discussed a tax at a low rate without foreign tax credits. See U.S. Department of Treasury, The Deferral of Income Earned Through U.S. Controlled Foreign Corporations, p. 91, at http://www.treasury. gov/resource-center/tax-policy/Documents/subpartf.pdf.

[112] These observations were made by Reuven Avi-Yonah and Edward Kleinbard, reported in Julie Martin, "Minimum Tax on Multinationals," Tax Notes, March 19, 2012, pp. 1498-2000.

In: Taxing U.S. Multinational Corporations
Editor: Angelique Gilder
ISBN: 978-1-62618-145-8

Chapter 3

BACKGROUND AND SELECTED ISSUES RELATED TO THE U.S. INTERNATIONAL TAX SYSTEM AND SYSTEMS THAT EXEMPT FOREIGN BUSINESS INCOME*

Joint Committee on Taxation

INTRODUCTION

The House Ways and Means Committee has scheduled a public hearing for May 24, 2011 on the rules in certain foreign jurisdictions for taxing foreign income.

This document,[1] prepared by the staff of the Joint Committee on Taxation, describes the U.S. international tax rules applicable to foreign income of resident taxpayers, provides a general overview of a territorial system of taxation, including a brief discussion of basic design considerations, and summarizes the rules of nine selected countries for the taxation of foreign income.

I. PRESENT LAW: WORLDWIDE TAXATION AND DEFERRAL OF ACTIVE BUSINESS INCOME

A. In General

The United States has a worldwide tax system under which U.S. resident individuals and domestic corporations generally are taxed on all income, whether derived in the United States or abroad.

Income earned directly, including as a result of a domestic corporation's conduct of a foreign business itself (by means of branch operations in the foreign jurisdiction) rather than

* This is an edited, reformatted and augmented version of Staff of the Joint Committee on Taxation, Publication No. JCX-33-11, dated May 20, 2011.

through a separate foreign legal entity, or through a pass-through entity such as a partnership, is taxed on a current basis.

Foreign business income earned by a domestic parent corporation indirectly through a foreign corporate subsidiary generally is not subject to U.S. tax until the income is distributed as a dividend to the domestic corporation.

This rule is circumscribed by the anti-deferral rules of subpart F of the Internal Revenue Code, which provide that a domestic parent corporation is subject to U.S. tax on a current basis with respect to certain categories of passive or highly mobile income earned by its foreign subsidiaries.

To mitigate double taxation of foreign-source income, the United States allows a domestic corporation to claim a credit for foreign income taxes paid by it and its foreign subsidiaries.

Present law provides detailed rules for the allocation of deductible expenses between U.S.-source income and foreign-source income. These rules do not affect the timing of the expense deduction.

A domestic corporation generally is allowed a current deduction for its expenses (such as interest and administrative expenses) that support income that is derived through foreign subsidiaries and on which U.S. tax is deferred. Instead, as is described in more detail in section I.B.2 below, the expense allocation rules apply to a domestic corporation principally for determining the corporation's foreign tax credit limitation.

This limitation is computed by reference to the corporation's U.S. tax liability on its taxable foreign-source income in each of two principal limitation categories.

B. Principal Features

1. Anti-deferral regimes

Subpart F

Under the subpart F rules,[2] 10-percent or greater U.S. shareholders of a controlled foreign corporation ("CFC") are subject to U.S. tax currently on their pro rata shares of certain income earned by the CFC, whether or not the income is distributed to the shareholders. A CFC is defined generally as a foreign corporation with respect to which U.S.10-percent shareholders own more than 50 percent of the combined voting power or total value of the stock of the corporation.

Income subject to current inclusion under subpart F (before consideration of the temporary rules described below) includes, among other categories, insurance income and foreign base company income. Foreign base company income consists of foreign personal holding company income, income from certain transactions involving a related person (for example, income derived from services performed for or on behalf of a related person outside the country in which the CFC is organized), and income attributable to certain oil and gas activities.[3]

Foreign personal holding company income generally comprises the following: (1) dividends, interest, royalties, rents, and annuities; (2) net gains from the sale or exchange of (a) property that gives rise to the preceding types of income, (b) property that does not give rise to income, and (c) interests in trusts, partnerships, and real estate mortgage investment conduits ("REMICs"); (3) net gains from commodities transactions; (4) net gains from certain foreign currency transactions; (5) income that is equivalent to interest; (6) income from notional principal contracts; (7) payments in lieu of dividends; and (8) amounts received under personal service contracts.

Temporary exceptions from foreign personal holding company income, foreign base company services income, and insurance income apply for subpart F purposes for certain income that is derived in the active conduct of a banking, financing, or similar business, as a securities dealer, or in the conduct of an insurance business (so-called "active financing income").[4] So-called "look-through rules" temporarily provide that dividends, interest, rents, and royalties received by one CFC from a related CFC are not treated as foreign personal holding company income to the extent attributable or properly allocable to non-subpart F income of the payor. For these purposes, a related CFC is a CFC that controls or is controlled by the other CFC, or a CFC that is controlled by the same person or persons that control the other CFC. Ownership of more than 50 percent of the CFC's stock (by vote or value) constitutes control for these purposes.[5]

In addition to current U.S. taxation of insurance income and foreign base company income, U.S. 10-percent shareholders are subject to taxation currently on income that is deemed to be distributed when a CFC increases its investment in U.S. property. For this purpose and subject to certain exceptions, U.S. property includes tangible property located in the United States, stock or debt of a related U.S. person, and rights to use certain intangible property in the United States.

Passive Foreign Investment Companies

U.S. shareholders (both individuals and corporations) are effectively taxed currently on earnings of a passive foreign investment company ("PFIC"), regardless of the amount of the PFIC's stock that they own. A PFIC is any foreign corporation: (1) 75 percent or more of the gross income of which is passive, and (2) at least 50 percent of the assets of which produce passive income or are held for the production of passive income.[6] Passive income generally is the same as foreign personal holding company income, as defined for subpart F purposes.[7]

The PFIC rules provide three different methods of taxation. The first is the "excess distribution" regime under which gains from the disposition of PFIC stock and distributions that exceed prior year averages are deemed to have been earned ratably over the U.S. taxpayer's holding period and are subject to an interest charge to reflect the time value of the deferred tax payment.

The excess distribution regime can be avoided if a U.S. shareholder elects to treat the PFIC as a qualified electing fund (a "QEF"). If a QEF election is made, the U.S. shareholder is taxed currently on its share of the QEF's earnings. QEF elections may be made only if the PFIC provides sufficient data to its shareholders that the PFIC's ordinary earnings and net capital gain can be determined each year. For investors in publicly traded PFICs (such as foreign mutual funds), who may not be able to make QEF elections, there is also a mark-to-market election. In that case, the U.S. shareholder includes the annual unrealized gain or loss in its PFIC stock for the year in its taxable income.

2. Foreign Tax Credit

Subject to certain limitations, a domestic corporation is allowed to claim a credit for foreign income taxes it pays. A domestic corporation that owns at least 10 percent of the voting stock of a foreign corporation is allowed a "deemed-paid" credit for foreign income taxes paid by the foreign corporation that the domestic corporation is deemed to have paid when the related income is distributed or included in the domestic corporation's income under the anti-deferral rules.[8]

The foreign tax credit generally is limited to a taxpayer's U.S. tax liability on its foreign-source taxable income (as determined under U.S. tax accounting principles).[9] The limit is computed by multiplying a taxpayer's total U.S. tax liability for the year by the ratio of the taxpayer's foreign-source taxable income for the year to the taxpayer's total taxable income for the year. If the total amount of foreign income taxes paid and deemed paid for the year exceeds the taxpayer's foreign tax credit limitation for the year, the taxpayer may carry back the excess foreign taxes to the previous year or carry forward the excess taxes to one of the succeeding 10 years.[10]

The computation of the foreign tax credit limitation requires a taxpayer to determine the amount of its taxable income from foreign sources in each category by allocating and apportioning deductions between U.S.-source gross income, on the one hand, and foreign-source gross income in each limitation category (described below), on the other. In general, deductions are allocated and apportioned to the gross income to which the deductions factually relate.[11] However, subject to certain exceptions, deductions for interest expense and research and experimental expenses are apportioned based on taxpayer ratios.[12] In the case of interest expense, this ratio is the ratio of the corporation's foreign or domestic (as applicable) assets to its worldwide assets. In the case of research and experimental expenses, the apportionment ratio is based on either sales or gross income. All members of an affiliated group of corporations generally are treated as a single corporation for purposes of determining the apportionment ratios.[13]

The term "affiliated group" is determined generally by reference to the rules for determining whether corporations are eligible to file consolidated returns.[14] These rules exclude foreign corporations from an affiliated group.[15] The American Jobs Creation Act of 2004 ("AJCA") modified the interest expense allocation rules for taxable years beginning after December 31, 2008.[16] The effective date of the modified rules has been delayed to January 1, 2021.[17] The new rules permit a U.S. affiliated group to apportion the interest expense of the members of the U.S. affiliated group on a worldwide-group basis (i.e., as if all domestic and foreign affiliates are a single corporation). A result of this rule is that interest expense of foreign members of a U.S. affiliated group is taken into account in determining whether a portion of the interest expense of the domestic members of the group must be allocated to foreign-source income. An allocation to foreign-source income generally is required only if, in broad terms, the domestic members of the group are more highly leveraged than is the entire worldwide group.

The foreign tax credit limitation is applied separately to "passive category income" and to "general category income."[18] Passive category income includes passive income, such as portfolio interest and dividend income, and certain specified types of income. General category income includes all other income. Passive income is treated as general category income if it is earned by a qualifying financial services entity. Passive income is also treated as general category income if it is highly taxed (that is, if the foreign tax rate is determined to exceed the highest rate of tax specified in section 1 or 11, as applicable). Dividends (and subpart F inclusions), interest, rents, and royalties received by a U.S.10-percent shareholder from a CFC are assigned to a separate limitation category by reference to the category of income out of which the dividends or other payments were made.[19] Dividends received by a 10-percent corporate shareholder of a foreign corporation that is not a CFC are also categorized on a look-through basis.[20]

3. Transfer Pricing

A basic U.S. tax principle applicable in dividing profits from transactions between related taxpayers is that the amount of profit allocated to each related taxpayer must be measured by reference to the amount of profit that a similarly situated taxpayer would realize in similar transactions with unrelated parties. The transfer pricing rules of section 482 and the accompanying Treasury regulations are intended to preserve the U.S. tax base by ensuring that taxpayers do not shift income properly attributable to the United States to a related foreign company through pricing that does not reflect an arm's-length result.[21] Similarly, the domestic laws of most U.S. trading partners include rules to limit income shifting through non-arm'slength pricing.

Section 482 authorizes the Secretary of the Treasury to allocate income, deductions, credits, or allowances among related business entities when necessary to clearly reflect income or otherwise prevent tax avoidance,[22] and comprehensive Treasury regulations under that section adopt the arm's-length standard as the method for determining whether allocations are appropriate. The regulations generally attempt to identify the respective amounts of taxable income of the related parties that would have resulted if the parties had been unrelated parties dealing at arm's length. For income from intangible property, section 482 provides, "In the case of any transfer (or license) of intangible property (within the meaning of section 936(h)(3)(B)), the income with respect to such transfer or license shall be commensurate with the income attributable to the intangible."

II. Territorial System

The remainder of this pamphlet addresses territorial systems of taxation. This section provides an overview of principal features of a territorial taxing system and includes a brief discussion of basic design considerations.[23]

A. Principal Features

1. In General

A strict territorial system, one that bases taxation entirely on whether income is foreign or domestic, would exempt all foreign income. The territorial systems of major U.S. trading partners do not provide this complete exemption. Instead, existing territorial systems exempt foreign income only if the income satisfies certain requirements. For example, exemption may be available only for income attributable to the conduct of a foreign business. Foreign business income may be eligible for exemption only if it is subject to meaningful tax in the foreign jurisdiction or is derived in a jurisdiction that has in force an income tax treaty with the taxpayer's country of residence. Income that does not satisfy the requirements for exemption under existing territorial systems generally is taxed as it is earned or when it is repatriated, and a deduction or credit for foreign income tax imposed on the income may be allowed. The descriptions in section III of the territorial regimes of selected countries provide examples of rules that distinguish between exempt and non-exempt income.

A related question is the mechanism by which exemption of foreign business income is provided under a territorial system. In theory, exemption could be allowed as income is earned, whether directly or through foreign companies. By contrast, territorial systems of the major U.S. trading partners generally provide exemptions for dividends received by resident companies from foreign companies. Dividend exemption may be available only if certain requirements are satisfied, including that the resident company receiving the dividend owns a certain percentage (10 percent, for example) of the stock of the foreign company paying the dividend. Territorial systems that operate by means of a dividend exemption typically tax non-dividend foreign income such as royalties or interest derived directly by resident taxpayers.

The following sections describe additional issues related to the scope of the tax exemption provided under territorial systems of taxation.

2. Expenses

A corporation with foreign operations may incur expenses in generating foreign income that is exempt under a territorial system. A question is whether a territorial system should allow a deduction for these expenses.

Most jurisdictions with territorial systems permit deductions for resident companies' expenses for generating exempt foreign income. Some countries allow these deductions but impose tax on a small percentage of foreign dividends (five percent, for example). A question in designing a territorial system might be whether this tax should be imposed when dividends are paid or when income out of which dividends are paid is earned.

A territorial system that permits a deduction for an expense incurred to produce exempt foreign income may not achieve a matching of taxable income items with deductible expense items. Disallowing a deduction for the expense may, however, cause the expense not to be deductible in any country (because the country in which the income is derived also may not permit a deduction).

A number of countries with territorial systems of taxation deny deductions for a portion of a resident company's interest expense if the resident company, or a multinational group that includes a resident company, has indebtedness (in some cases related-party indebtedness and in other cases related- and unrelated-party indebtedness) that exceeds a threshold level. Countries have different measures of permitted levels of indebtedness. Measures include debt-to-equity ratios and comparisons of domestic and foreign leverage within a group.

A question in this context is whether, if the United States adopted a territorial system, the U.S. present law earnings stripping rules, which deny a deduction for a portion of interest expense on related-party indebtedness when a corporation's debt-to-equity ratio and interest expense in relation to income exceed certain levels,[24] should be retained, modified, repealed, or replaced with other interest limitation rules. Although the earnings stripping rules apply to both foreign-controlled and U.S.-controlled groups, they are important in practice mostly for foreign-controlled groups, in part because income under subpart F generally would result from loans to a U.S. parent corporation from its foreign subsidiary. If a concern in a territorial system is that resident corporations will reduce their U.S. tax liabilities by borrowing (from unrelated or related parties) to produce exempt income, consideration might be given to interest limitation rules that would have more uniformity of application to domestically-controlled and foreign-controlled groups and to unrelated and related party borrowing.

3. Controlled Foreign Company Rules

Many territorial systems impose current taxation on certain items of foreign income derived not only by resident companies directly, but also by foreign companies owned in whole or part by resident companies. As described previously in section II.A.1, these controlled foreign company rules may, among other possibilities, tax foreign income that has been subject to tax in the foreign jurisdiction at less than a threshold rate or that has been derived in a jurisdiction that does not have an income tax treaty with the jurisdiction in which the parent company is organized.

As described above in section I.B.1, the subpart F rules of U.S. law impose current U.S. taxation on U.S. 10-percent shareholders of a CFC for their shares of certain items of investment income or highly mobile income derived by the CFC. If U.S. policymakers were to consider a territorial system of taxation, a question would be whether the subpart F rules should be maintained, modified, repealed, or replaced with other rules that impose tax on certain foreign income.

4. Gain or Loss on the Sale of Foreign Subsidiary Stock

Territorial taxing systems that operate by means of a dividend exemption have different rules for the taxation of a resident company's gain or loss from the sale of stock of a foreign subsidiary. One possible rule is that gain from the sale of this stock is exempt to the extent the gain represents earnings of the foreign subsidiary that would be exempt if distributed to the parent company as a dividend. Gain from the sale of foreign subsidiary stock may, however, also be attributable to unrealized appreciation in assets of the foreign subsidiary that produce income that is either exempt or currently taxable (or in part exempt and in part currently taxable) under the territorial rules. In theory, gain might be exempt to the extent it represents unrealized appreciation in exempt-income-producing property. Other possible rules include a complete tax exemption for gain from the sale of foreign subsidiary stock or taxation of the entire amount of the gain. Rules for losses from the sale of foreign subsidiary stock would also be necessary.

5. Foreign Branches

There are two broad alternatives for the taxation of foreign branches of resident companies under a territorial taxing system. Under one alternative, a foreign branch might be taxed in the same manner as a foreign subsidiary. Transactions between the foreign branch and the domestic headquarters would be treated as if they were transactions between a foreign subsidiary and a resident company. In a dividend exemption system, certain payments made by the foreign branch would be treated as dividends and would be exempt under rules equivalent to those applicable to actual dividend payments made by foreign subsidiaries. More broadly, taxpayers and the Internal Revenue Service would be required to account separately for transactions that under present law are intra-company activities and for earnings and profits and other items of foreign branches.

Alternatively, a foreign branch's foreign income might be wholly exempt, wholly taxable, or partly exempt and partly taxable as it is earned. This treatment of foreign branch income might avoid possible administrative complications of accounting for intra-company transactions and branch items, but by providing differing tax rules for branch and subsidiary income, it might treat similarly situated taxpayers differently and could introduce new tax considerations into the decision whether to operate abroad through branches or subsidiaries.

The treatment of foreign branch losses in a territorial system might warrant particular consideration. A basic question is whether the treatment of foreign branch losses should follow the treatment of foreign branch income, or whether the rules for losses and income might vary from one another.

Foreign partnerships present issues similar to (but in some situations more complicated than) those raised by foreign branches.

6. Intangible Property Income

As described previously, in dividend exemption systems non-dividend payments from foreign subsidiaries to resident companies typically are fully taxable. These non-dividend payments may include, among other items, royalties for the use of intangible property such as patents or other know-how.

Over time, full taxation of foreign royalties could affect taxpayer decisions about where to develop and own intellectual property, although many non-tax factors also affect these decisions, and the development and ownership decisions are separable from one another. In the short run, however, in the absence of perfect administration of arm's-length-based transfer pricing rules, a resident company could reduce the amount of its taxable royalties in respect of existing intangible property by interacting with foreign related parties at non-arm's-length terms (by, for instance, characterizing as exempt dividends all or a portion of payments that as an economic matter are royalties because they are for the use of the intangible property). As described in section I.B.3, transfer pricing rules generally are intended to ensure an arm's-length division of income when related parties transact with one another. Transfer pricing is important under U.S. present law because it determines how much income is subject to current U.S. taxation. Transfer pricing rules could be expected to remain significant under a territorial system because those rules would determine, in part, how much income could be repatriated in the form of exempt dividends. Transfer pricing disputes between the government and taxpayers under present law often involve pricing of related party transactions in intangible property.

To address concerns about the effects of a territorial system on where intellectual property is developed and owned, consideration might be given to rules providing favorable tax treatment of income related to intangible property. Some countries with territorial systems provide reduced tax rates on income attributable to taxpayer-developed patents or other intellectual property (sometimes referred to colloquially as "patent box" regimes). As one alternative, a limited exemption could be provided for a resident company's royalty income received from a foreign subsidiary for the subsidiary's use of intangible property in the conduct of a foreign business.

Alternatively, or in conjunction with rules providing favorable treatment of intangible property income, concerns about the effects of a territorial system on the location of development and ownership of intellectual property could be addressed by making U.S. present law transfer pricing or subpart F rules more stringent. Recent proposals to provide more stringent rules have prompted debate that might be relevant to discussions about adoption of a territorial system.[25]

B. Transition

If the United States adopted a territorial system of taxation, various transition issues would need to be considered. One issue is the treatment of earnings attributable to periods before the enactment of the territorial legislation. One approach is to have the exemption system apply only in respect of CFC earnings generated after the effective date. Under this approach, the pre-enactment rules would apply to previously untaxed earnings.

A variation of this transition rule is to provide a limited period in which taxpayers may make an election to repatriate some or all of their pre-effective date earnings at a reduced tax rate (perhaps under rules similar to the temporary, elective dividends received deduction enacted in 2004 for repatriated earnings[26]).

An alternative approach would exempt from tax all CFC earnings and profits paid as dividends after the effective date of the new system. A variation of this approach would deem all pre-effective date earnings repatriated under present law rules (at the regular tax rate or at a reduced rate), perhaps over a multi-year period.

III. Territorial Systems of Selected Countries

A. Australia[27]

1. In General

Australian resident corporations are subject to income tax on a worldwide basis, at a marginal rate reaching 30 percent. Various exclusions, credits, and other special rules operate to provide a participation exemption for certain categories of foreign-source income. Income that may be entirely or partially exempt include dividends paid out of active earnings of a foreign affiliate, capital gains from a foreign permanent establishment, and foreign branch profits.

The scope of the exemption for foreign-source dividends encompasses dividends from non-portfolio investments in which the Australian company owns at least a 10-percent voting interest, without any required holding period, as well as dividends paid by controlled foreign companies out of income that was previously taxed. These exemptions parallel the result applicable to most dividends under the imputation system since 1987, which is intended to avoid the imposition of tax on corporate earnings both at the corporate level when earned and at the shareholder level when distributed. Under the imputation system, an Australian resident receives credit for the tax previously paid on the income underlying the dividend from an Australian corporation. Dividends are "franked" to identify the amount of tax paid with respect to the underlying income funding the dividend. The recipient reports the dividend, grossed-up by the amount of the tax paid, and claims a credit in the "franked" amount.

2. Expenses

Deductions for expenses incurred in generating the profits that result in exempt non-portfolio foreign dividends and foreign branch profits are not generally allowed, nor are credits permitted for foreign income tax paid with respect to the foreign exempt income. Expenses incurred in financing debt are excepted from the general rule of disallowance, provided that the expenses satisfy the thin capitalization rules. Those rules limit the portion of debt expenses that may be deducted when the entity's debt-to-equity ratio exceeds certain limits. The limits vary depending on whether the investing entity is inbound, outbound, or both, and whether the investing entity is an approved deposit-taking institution, with a safe harbor debt-to-equity ratio of three-to-one available in most cases. The rules apply economic substance principles to determine whether instruments are to be treated as debt or equity. The expenses that may be limited under these rules include interest payments or loan fees that an entity would otherwise be entitled to deduct, but not rental expenses on certain leases and some foreign currency losses.

The thin capitalization rules affect both Australian and foreign entities that have multinational investments, regardless of whether they hold the investments directly or through Australian entities. Under the thin capitalization rules, the amount of debt used to fund the Australian operations of both foreign entities investing into Australia (inbound) and Australian entities investing overseas (outbound) is limited. The thin capitalization rules for any given income year do not apply to Australian resident entities that have no cross-border investments, to foreign entities that have no investments (such as assets) or permanent establishments in Australia, or to entities that meet any of the threshold tests described below.

There are three threshold tests. The first two ensure entities with relatively small debt deductions (less than AUD$250,000 (US$254,588) in the tax year) or small overseas investments (an outbound investor that is not foreign controlled and whose Australian assets are at least 90 percent of worldwide assets) are not subject to the thin capitalization rules.[28] A third threshold test provides that debt deductions incurred by special purpose entities, established to manage certain risks, are not limited by these thin capitalization rules.

3. Controlled Foreign Company Rules

Australia currently has an accruals taxation system, similar to the antideferral regime under the subpart F rules in the United States.[29] Under the accruals taxation system, most foreign-source income of a controlled foreign company is taxed, if at all, on the basis of a notional dividend to an Australian owner or shareholder. The portion taxable to the owner or shareholder is determined by reference to the ownership share attributed to the shareholder, known as an attributable taxpayer. An attributable taxpayer is an Australian entity that has a controlling interest, inclusive of interests held by associates, of a specified level.

Controlled foreign company status is determined by one of three control tests: strict control, assumed controller test or the de facto control test. Strict control exists if at least 50 percent of the company is owned or may be acquired by a group of five or fewer Australian one-percent entities (resident Australian entities that own at least one-percent of the foreign company), including their associates or members.

The assumed controller test is met if an Australian entity and its members or associates own or are entitled to acquire at least a 40 percent interest in the company, and the remaining interest is not controlled by an unrelated party or parties. The de facto control test is met if a group of five or fewer Australian entities effectively controls the company.

The holder of a 10-percent interest is an attributable taxpayer, regardless of which of the three control tests is met for controlled foreign company status. In addition, an Australian one-percent entity may be an attributable taxpayer if it is one of a group of five or fewer owners holding de facto control of the foreign company.

The attributable taxpayer is deemed to have received a dividend equal to its pro rata share of assessable earnings in the tax year accrued. When those earnings are actually distributed, the dividend is exempt from taxation as previously taxed income.

The amount of assessable income of a controlled foreign company under the accruals taxation system depends upon the conduct of an active business, the character of the income as "adjusted tainted income," and whether the company is resident in a listed country.

Adjusted tainted income includes all passive income as well as income from sales or services transactions with related parties. Listed countries are defined by statute as foreign jurisdictions that impose income tax on a basis comparable to that of Australia. The listed countries are Canada, France, Germany, Japan, New Zealand, the United Kingdom, and the United States.

Income derived from a company in a listed country that operates an active business in that country is eligible for exemption from Australian tax unless the income was both tainted and eligible for a tax concession in the listed country.

Income derived by a company resident in an unlisted country qualifies for exemption from accruals taxation only if the company conducts an active business in that jurisdiction and the income is not "adjusted tainted income."

4. Gain or Loss on the Sale of Foreign Subsidiary Stock

Gain from the disposition of stock in certain foreign companies is subject to exemption if the following conditions are met. The company whose stock is being sold must have operated an active business abroad. The taxpayer must hold at least a 10-percent voting interest in the company.

Finally, the taxpayer must meet a holding period of 12 months within the two-year period preceding the sale of stock.

In addition, a capital loss with respect to the disposal of a branch asset may be nondeductible if the gain from disposal of such an asset would have been exempt.

5. Foreign Branches

Active business income earned by a foreign branch or permanent establishment of an Australian resident company is generally exempt from accruals taxation, depending upon the character of the income as "adjusted tainted income" and whether the company's residence is in a listed country. Adjusted tainted income includes all passive income as well as income from sales or services transactions with related parties.

Income of branches in a listed country that operate an active business in the listed country is exempt from Australian tax unless the income was both tainted and eligible for a tax concession in the listed country.

Branches that reside in unlisted countries qualify for exemption of income from accruals taxation only if they conduct an active business in that jurisdiction and the income is not "adjusted tainted income."

6. Intangible Property Income

Australia does not have a special regime governing the taxation of foreign-source income from intangible property. Resident companies are taxable on royalties from all sources.

Both the controlled foreign company rules and the exemption for foreign branch profits provide that tainted royalty income is treated as passive income, and is thus currently taxable.

Tainted royalty income is royalty income derived from assigning any intangible property or right to such property other than an assignment by a foreign branch or subsidiary of property it substantially developed to an unrelated party in the course of carrying on the business of the branch or subsidiary.

B. Canada[30]

1. In General

Like the United States, Canada generally subjects Canadian resident corporations to current taxation on worldwide income while providing deferral for income earned by a foreign corporation in which the Canadian resident corporation is a shareholder and relief from double taxation by way of a foreign tax credit mechanism. Nonetheless, Canadian law applies the principles of territorial taxation by exempting certain qualifying distributions out of active earnings of certain foreign subsidiaries located in treaty jurisdictions. For 2011, the combined federal and provincial corporate income tax rate generally ranges from 26.5 percent to 32.5 percent (25 percent to 31 percent for 2012) depending on the province in which the Canadian resident corporation is located.[31]

Dividends received by a Canadian resident corporation out of certain active earnings of a foreign affiliate may be wholly or partially exempt from Canadian taxation. This exemption is accomplished by providing the Canadian resident corporation with a deduction equal to all or a portion of the eligible dividend received from the foreign affiliate. For this purpose, a foreign affiliate is defined as a nonresident corporation in which the Canadian taxpayer's equity percentage is at least one percent, and the equity percentage of the taxpayer and related persons is collectively at least 10 percent.

The amount of the deduction is determined based on whether the dividend is paid out of exempt surplus, taxable surplus, or preacquisition surplus. A 100-percent dividends received deduction is allowed to the extent the dividend is paid out of exempt surplus. Exempt surplus includes income of a foreign affiliate attributable to an active business carried on in a designated treaty country. A designated treaty country is one with which Canada has a treaty that is in force for the year in question. Additionally, exempt surplus treatment has also been extended to countries with which Canada does not have a tax treaty in force but with which Canada has entered into a comprehensive tax information exchange agreement ("TIEA").

Taxable surplus includes income from an active business carried on in a country that is not a designated treaty country on which foreign income and withholding taxes have been paid. While not exempt from Canadian taxation, dividends out of taxable surplus may carry with them a deduction attributable to the underlying foreign taxes imposed on the foreign affiliate. The deduction is computed by multiplying the relevant tax of the foreign affiliate by a fraction equal to one over the Canadian corporate tax rate and is intended to have an economic effect similar to that of a foreign tax credit.

Payments made by foreign affiliates that are not out of exempt surplus or taxable surplus are generally treated as distributed out of preacquisition surplus. Payments out of preacquisition surplus are treated as a return of capital and deductible in computing taxable income. However, such amounts reduce the adjusted cost base of the shares and may trigger gain to the extent in excess of the adjusted cost base.

A December 2008 report issued by the Canadian Ministry of Finance appointed Advisory Panel on Canada's System of International Taxation had, as one of its recommendations, that the existing exemption system be expanded to cover all foreign active business income earned by foreign affiliates.[32]

2. Expenses

Canada does not have rules that disallow a deduction for expenses of a Canadian resident corporation to the extent those expenses are attributable to exempt foreign dividends.[33]

However, Canada does have thin capitalization rules designed to limit the ability of nonresidents of Canada to withdraw profits through deductible interest payments.

In general, the thin capitalization rules limit the deductibility of interest paid or payable by a Canadian corporation to specified nonresidents if the debt of the Canadian corporation exceeds two times the equity of the Canadian corporation. When this occurs, a prorated portion of any interest paid is not allowed in computing income of the Canadian corporation. The disallowed amount is treated as a dividend that must be paid out of earnings accumulated after Canadian tax.

For purposes of applying these rules, a specified nonresident is a nonresident shareholder who, either alone or together with persons with whom the shareholder does not deal at arm's-length, owns shares that meet a 25-percent vote or value test.

3. Controlled Foreign Company Rules

Canada's foreign accrual property income ("FAPI") rules, which were originally modeled after the U.S. subpart F rules, are designed to prevent Canadian resident shareholders from being able to avoid or defer Canadian taxation by earning certain types of passive or mobile income through a controlled foreign affiliate. The FAPI of a controlled foreign affiliate is imputed to a Canadian resident in proportion to the Canadian resident's participating percentage (i.e., the percentage of shares held directly or indirectly) in the controlled foreign affiliate at the end of the tax year. For this purpose, a foreign corporation is treated as a controlled foreign affiliate in cases in which the Canadian corporation has *de jure* control giving it the ability to elect a majority of the board of directors of the foreign corporation. This control generally occurs if the Canadian corporation has more than 50 percent of the voting power of all outstanding shares of stock. A foreign corporation may also be treated as a controlled foreign affiliate under an alternative test that looks to whether there is a collection of persons that control the corporation consisting of the taxpayer, persons that do not deal at arm's-length with the taxpayer, up to four other Canadian residents, and all persons who do not deal at arm's-length with Canadian residents.

In general, FAPI consists of foreign direct investment income of a passive nature (such as dividends, interest, rent and royalties) and certain capital gains. Additionally, FAPI also includes the following:

1. income from the rendering of services if the cost of those services is deductible in calculating the income of the controlling shareholders or of a related person from a business carried on in Canada;
2. income from the sale of property if either:
   - the cost of the property will be included in the income of the taxpayer or a non-arm's-length person in calculating income from a business carried on in Canada; or
   - the property sold by the foreign affiliate was not produced or processed in the country in which the foreign affiliate was established;
3. income from the insurance of persons resident in Canada or of property situated in Canada;
4. interest and rental income on debt and lease obligations of persons resident in Canada; and
5. income from an investment business, defined as a business that has as its principal purpose the earning of income from property (unless such activities constitute the principal business of the foreign affiliate and the foreign affiliate has more than five full-time employees in the business).

However, items (2), (3), and (4) do not apply in cases in which more than 90 percent of the foreign affiliate's income of that type is derived from transactions with arm's-length entities.

In the 2007 Budget, the Ministry of Finance announced that FAPI will be extended to include business income earned in a country with which Canada has neither a tax treaty nor a TIEA. The extension of the FAPI concept is scheduled to occur on a country-by-country basis, subject to negotiations with that country. In the case of a non-treaty, non-TIEA country that was in the process of negotiating a TIEA with Canada on March 19, 2007, FAPI treatment will apply if the negotiations are not successfully completed before 2014. In the case of other non-treaty, non-TIEA countries (i.e., Canada proposes TIEA negotiations, or negotiations start without a Canadian proposal, after March 19, 2007), FAPI treatment will apply only if those negotiations are not successfully completed by the fifth anniversary of the earlier of the start of TIEA negotiations and the date on which Canada proposed the TIEA negotiations.

4. Gain or Loss on the Sale of Foreign Subsidiary Stock

The sale of stock of a foreign subsidiary generally is subject to Canadian taxation under the general rules applicable to capital gains and losses of Canadian resident corporations. As a result, 50 percent of capital gains are taxable and included in the corporation's taxable income at ordinary rates. Likewise, 50 percent of capital losses are deductible, but generally only against capital gains. Any excess of allowable capital losses over taxable capital gains in the current year can be carried back three years and forward indefinitely, to be applied against net taxable capital gains from those years, except in the case of an acquisition of control. For purposes of applying these rules, there is no particular holding period requirement.

The December 2008 Advisory Panel Report included in its recommendations that the exemption system be extended to capital gains and losses realized on the disposition of shares of a foreign affiliate in cases in which the shares derive all or substantially all of their value from active business assets.

5. Foreign Branches

Income of a foreign branch of a Canadian resident corporation is taxable in Canada when earned. In computing the taxable profit or loss of the foreign branch, a Canadian taxpayer can usually take a deduction for the same types of expenses that would have been available for such expenses had they been incurred in Canada. The Canadian resident corporation is allowed a foreign tax credit with respect to any foreign income or profits tax imposed on the foreign branch.

6. Intangible Property Income

Canada does not have a special tax regime or tax rate that applies to intellectual property income. Therefore, royalty income received by a Canadian corporation is currently taxable at the applicable corporate income tax rate discussed above.

C. France[34]

1. In General

French resident companies, defined as those that have their legal seat in France or are effectively managed and controlled from France, generally are taxed on a territorial basis. Accordingly, business income and losses realized through enterprises operating outside France generally are not taken into account for French tax purposes. Nevertheless, tax is imposed on worldwide income from passive foreign sources (for example, royalties, interest, and dividends that do not qualify for the participation exemption), unless it can be shown that such income is connected to foreign business operations. French tax law generally does not provide for foreign tax credits, so income subject to foreign tax that is not exempt from tax in France is taxable in France net of any foreign tax paid.[35]

French resident parent companies may elect a participation exemption in respect of certain dividends received from their resident and nonresident subsidiaries. To qualify for the regime, the parent must have a participation in the subsidiary that represents at least five percent of the voting rights and financial rights in the subsidiary and must have held the participation for at least two years (or commit to hold the shares for at least two years). The participation exemption is not complete, however, and an amount equal to five percent of the dividend must be added to the parent company's income (effectively, there is a 95-percent participation exemption). This amount is deemed to correspond to nondeductible expenses incurred in connection with earning the dividends, although if the company demonstrates that the actual expenses are less, it need include in income only an amount equal to the actual expenses.

If a subsidiary is located in a country identified as a noncooperative state or territory, the participation exemption is not available with respect to dividends paid by that subsidiary. A noncooperative state or territory is defined as a state or territory that (1) is not a member of the European Union, (2) is reviewed and monitored by the Organisation for Economic Cooperation and Development Global Forum on Transparency and Exchange of Information, (3) has concluded 12 or fewer tax information exchange agreements, and (4) has not signed a tax information exchange agreement with France.

The standard corporate tax rate is 331/3 percent.[36] In addition, companies whose turnover exceeds €7,630,000 ($10,177,886) are subject to an additional social security surtax of 3.3

percent levied on the portion of their aggregate corporate tax that exceeds €763,000 ($1,017,789). The result is a combined tax rate of 34.43 percent.

2. Expenses

In general, a French resident company may fully deduct expenses that support exempt dividends. However, the five-percent portion of a dividend that is subject to tax under the participation exemption is deemed to correspond to a management charge related to earning the exempt dividend. If a company demonstrates that the actual charges are less than that five percent, the company is taxed only on the actual charges.

Despite the broad allowance of deductions for expenses related to exempt dividends, deductions for interest paid to related parties (and to third parties on loans that are secured by related parties) may be limited. In general, related-party interest deductions are limited if the interest paid exceeds three thresholds: (1) an amount determined using a formula incorporating a related-party debt-to-equity ratio of 1.5-to-1; (2) 25 percent of adjusted current profits (i.e., operating profits before the deduction of taxes, related-party interest, depreciation and amortization, and certain lease payments) for the year; and (3) interest income received from related parties. If interest exceeds all three thresholds, the interest deduction is limited to an amount equal to the highest of the three thresholds plus €150,000 ($200,090). The excess interest deductions may be carried forward, although they are reduced by five percent annually starting with the second carry-forward year. A safe harbor is available that nevertheless allows a company to fully deduct interest that does not satisfy the three thresholds if the company can demonstrate that its debt-to-equity ratio does not exceed the debt-to-equity ratio of the worldwide group to which it belongs.

In addition, a French resident company is not allowed to deduct direct expenses of, and certain head office expenses attributed to, foreign branch operations, which generate income exempt from French taxation.

3. Controlled Foreign Company Rules

France has controlled foreign company rules that apply to provide for taxation of the profits of certain foreign entities or permanent establishments. A pro rata portion (which is 100 percent in the case of a wholly owned subsidiary or branch) of the profits are taxable to a French resident company if (1) the French resident company directly or indirectly holds a participation of more than 50 percent (whether voting rights or financial rights, or both) in the foreign entity (or permanent establishment), and (2) the foreign entity (or permanent establishment) is subject to an effective rate of tax in its country of residence that is at least 50 percent lower than the rate of tax that would apply in France. An anti-abuse rule reduces the participation threshold to five percent if more than 50 percent of the interests in the foreign entity (or permanent establishment) are controlled by French resident companies or by foreign entities directly or indirectly controlled by French resident companies.

The controlled foreign company rules generally do not apply to an entity (or permanent establishment) resident in another member of the European Union, unless the French tax authorities can demonstrate that the entity (or permanent establishment) is part of an artificial arrangement intended solely to avoid French tax. In addition, the controlled foreign company rules do not apply to an entity (or permanent establishment) resident outside the European Union if the entity (or permanent establishment) is principally engaged in commercial or industrial economic activities in its country of residence. However, if more than 20 percent of the entity's (or permanent establishment's) income is passive or more than 50 percent of the entity's (or permanent establishment's) income is passive or from services provided to related parties, the controlled foreign company rules will apply unless the taxpayer demonstrates that the location of the foreign entity (or permanent establishment) is not based solely on tax considerations. If the foreign entity (or permanent establishment) is located in a country identified as a noncooperative state or territory, the burden to prove that the entity (or permanent establishment) is principally engaged in commercial or industrial economic activities in its country of residence shifts from the tax authorities to the taxpayer.

4. Gain or Loss on the Sale of Foreign Subsidiary Stock

A 95-percent participation exemption applies to capital gains on dispositions of certain shareholdings by a French resident company. To qualify for the exemption, (1) the shareholding disposed of must be eligible for the dividend participation exemption regime described above, and (2) the seller generally must have held the shareholding for at least two years prior to disposal. Sellers may not utilize capital losses realized with respect to shareholdings eligible for this participation exemption.

A French resident company that realizes a capital gain on any other sale of a foreign subsidiary's stock generally must include the gain in its French taxable income. If a capital loss is realized, the loss is deductible.

5. Foreign Branches

Subject to the controlled foreign company rules described above, income a French resident company earns from foreign business operations, including from a branch, generally is exempt from French tax. Importantly, this exemption does not extend to income from passive foreign sources (for example, royalties, interest, and dividends that do not qualify for the participation exemption) that is not connected to the foreign business operations.

A French resident company generally cannot utilize losses from its foreign business operations for French tax purposes.

6. Intangible Property Income

No special tax treatment applies to royalties. When received by French resident companies, they are included in income and taxed in the same manner as other income, although the long-term capital gain rate of 15 percent applies to certain proceeds derived from intellectual property.

D. Germany[37]

1. In General

Dividends received by a German resident corporation from a foreign corporation are 95 percent exempt from German income taxation. This 95-percent exemption is generally the same as the exemption that applies to dividends received from German corporations.

The 95-percent exemption is available for dividends received in respect of both portfolio (less than 10 percent) holdings and substantial shareholdings. There is also no requirement that stock in respect of which exempt dividends are received be held for a certain minimum period.

If a German corporation directly receives foreign-source non-dividend income such as interest or royalties, that income is taxable in Germany under the generally applicable corporate tax rules.

2. Expenses

Deductions for expenses that support exempt foreign dividends generally are allowed. The five-percent portion of a dividend that is taxable is intended to be a proxy for rules that would disallow a deduction for expenses related to exempt foreign income.

Although deductions for expenses related to exempt dividends are generally allowed, deductions for interest expense are limited under rules that took effect in 2008. Broadly, unless one of three possible exceptions applies, a company's excess of interest expense over interest income ("interest surplus") is deductible only up to 30 percent of the company's taxable income before interest, taxes, and depreciation and amortization. The rules apply irrespective of where the ultimate shareholders of the company are residents of Germany.

The restriction on the deductibility of interest surplus generally does not apply if a company's interest surplus is less than €3 million. A company also is not generally subject to the limitation if it is not part of a group of companies. A company is considered part of a group of companies if it is or could be part of a consolidated group for German accounting purposes. This exception is not available if interest on loans from 25-percent-or-greater shareholders or certain related parties exceeds 10 percent of the interest surplus. If the company is part of a group of companies, the interest limitation rules nonetheless generally do not apply if the German resident company that is part of the group is not more thinly capitalized than the overall group under a measure of equity in relation to total balance sheet assets.

3. Controlled Foreign Company Rules

A German resident corporation or individual is subject to annual German income tax on the resident's share of certain items of passive income derived by a controlled foreign corporation in which the resident owns stock.

A controlled foreign corporation under German law is a nonresident corporation more than 50 percent of the stock (by vote) of which is owned directly or indirectly, and actually or constructively, by German resident taxpayers. Any German domestic corporation or resident individual that owns stock in a controlled foreign corporation is subject to the controlled foreign corporation rules regardless of the size of the stock ownership.

German law provides a list of items of income that are considered active and are therefore not subject to the controlled foreign corporation rules. Items of income of a controlled foreign corporation that are not on the active list are considered passive and are taxed on a current basis to the controlled foreign corporation's German shareholders unless either the tax rate test or European Union requirements described below are satisfied. Active income includes, with various exceptions, manufacturing, sales, and services income; certain banking, insurance, and financing income; limited categories of rental and royalty income; and most dividend income. Principal categories of passive income are interest and many royalties.

Passive income is not attributed to a controlled foreign corporation's German shareholders if the income is subject to income tax at a rate of at least 25 percent. The 25 percent rate threshold is an effective tax rate calculated under German tax law principles.

The controlled foreign corporation rules do not apply to a corporation organized in another European Union or European Free Trade Association member state if the corporation engages in meaningful industrial or commercial activity in its country of residence.

Under special rules, a German resident who owns at least one percent of a foreign company that mostly derives income of a passive investment character is subject to annual German income tax on the resident's attributable share of the foreign company's income. For these passive investment companies, the attribution rules apply even if German residents in the aggregate own 50 percent or less of the companies.

4. Gain or Loss on the Sale of Foreign Subsidiary Stock

With limited exceptions, a German corporation's gain from the sale of stock of another corporation, whether domestic or foreign, is generally 95-percent exempt from German income taxation. The five-percent taxable portion of gain is intended to represent financing costs associated with owning the stock of the other corporation.

A German corporate shareholder's loss from the sale of stock of another corporation generally is not allowed as a deduction.

5. Foreign Branches

German resident companies are taxable in Germany on income derived through foreign branch operations unless the terms of an income tax treaty exempt from German tax the income attributable to a permanent establishment that the German resident company maintains outside Germany. If a German company transfers property to a foreign branch the income of which is not exempt from German tax under a treaty, no taxable gain generally results from the transfer because income from the property will remain subject to German tax.

Subject to a number of limitations, foreign tax income tax paid in respect of income from foreign branch operations is allowed as a credit against German income tax.

6. Intangible Property Income

Germany has no special rules for the taxation of foreign-source royalty income. As described previously, German resident companies are subject to German corporate tax on royalties received from related and unrelated nonresident companies.

E. Japan[38]

1. In General

Until recently, Japan generally imposed corporate tax on worldwide income in a tax system generally similar to that of the United States. The corporate tax comprises three levies: an income tax imposed at the national level, an enterprise tax imposed by prefect authorities and an inhabitants tax imposed by prefect or municipal authorities. The national corporate income tax rates are graduated, with the highest marginal rate of 30 percent for years 1999 to 2010 for large companies, and lower rates for small and mid-sized companies (companies that have capital not in excess of ¥ 100 million ($1,228,780),[39] and that are not a subsidiary of a company with capital in excess of ¥ 500 million ($6,143,920). To the extent that income was subject to tax in both Japan and another jurisdiction, double taxation was relieved by operation of foreign tax credits or by operation of its various tax treaties. Earlier this year, it was announced that the national corporate income tax rates would be reduced by five percentage points, setting the new maximum rate at 25 percent.

In 2009, tax reforms moved the system towards a territorial regime. Introduced in an effort to encourage the repatriation of overseas earnings, the 2009 amendment to the tax laws introduced the foreign dividend exemption system. Under the foreign dividend exemption system, a company may omit 95 percent of qualifying distributions. To qualify, the dividends must be received from a foreign company in which the domestic corporation claiming the exemption has held at least 25 percent of the outstanding shares for a continuous period of at least six months. Foreign investment income, such as interest or royalties, is not exempted. In addition, gain from the transfer of shares in foreign subsidiaries does not qualify for the exemption.

2. Expenses

In general, all necessary and reasonable expenses, costs, and losses may be deducted from gross income in order to arrive at net income except where otherwise provided under the relevant laws. Japan does not have any rules that disallow a deduction for expenses of a Japanese resident corporation to the extent those expenses are attributable to exempt foreign dividends. However, Japan has thin capitalization rules designed to limit the ability of nonresidents of Japan to withdraw profits through deductible interest payments. No deduction is permitted for interest paid to a foreign controlling shareholder on indebtedness to the extent that the indebtedness causes the average balance of liabilities due (to either a foreign controlling shareholder or capital supplier) to the capital held by the foreign controlling shareholder to exceed a three-to-one ratio. Where a company maintains a less than three-to-one debt-to-equity ratio, it is not treated as thinly capitalized even if lending from a foreign controlling shareholder or capital supplier exceeds three times the foreign controlling shareholder or capital supplier's equity interest. In cases where the total average liabilities for a year of a company that may be subject to this rule do not exceed three times its own capital, the disallowance of the interest deduction does not apply.

A foreign controlling shareholder is a nonresident or foreign company that controls the domestic company by reason of majority capital ownership, whether directly or indirectly, or owns more than 50 percent of the domestic and foreign company's capital directly or indirectly, or has a special relationship with the company, such as one in which the domestic company's business is dependent on transactions with the foreign shareholder.

3. Controlled Foreign Company Rules

Japan has a set of rules under which the parent companies of specified foreign companies are considered to have received deemed dividends from the subsidiaries, in a manner similar to that of the CFC regime in the United States. The Japanese controlled foreign company regime is part of a set of anti-avoidance rules, including a general anti-avoidance rule for related corporations, to deter overly aggressive tax planning.

A controlled foreign company is a foreign corporation that is located in a low-tax country, is subject to an effective tax rate of less than 20 percent and is owned directly or indirectly by Japanese companies, resident individuals, or nonresidents who have a special relationship with residents, such as a family relationship, or are financially dependent on residents.

A portion of the income of a controlled foreign company is deemed to be income of the Japanese resident shareholder and is included in calculating the shareholder's gross income if a Japanese resident or corporation directly or indirectly holds 10 percent or more of the outstanding shares of the controlled foreign company; or a Japanese corporation belongs to a family shareholder group that directly or indirectly holds 10 percent or more of the outstanding shares of the controlled foreign company. Dividends paid by a controlled foreign company to a domestic corporation that are subject to the foreign dividends exemption rule are excluded from the taxable income of the domestic corporation.

Japanese shareholders who directly or indirectly own 10 percent or more of the shares of a controlled foreign company are subject to taxation on their share of taxable undistributed profits of the subsidiary.

A controlled foreign company's income is not deemed to be the income of the domestic corporation if the controlled foreign company is actually doing business in a low-tax country and satisfies the following requirements:

- The controlled foreign company maintains an office, store, factory or other fixed place of business necessary to conduct its business in the country where the head office of the controlled foreign company is located;
- The controlled foreign company actually controls and administers its business; and
- If the business of the controlled foreign company is a wholesale, banking, trust, securities, insurance, or ocean or air transport business, the controlled foreign company does business with parties that are regarded as unrelated for the purpose of the controlled foreign company regime; or
- If the business of the controlled foreign company is none of the above, the controlled foreign company does business mainly within the country where its head office is located.

A 2010 amendment to the Tax Special Measures Law created exceptions to the above exceptions.

A proportionate share of certain passive income of a controlled foreign company may be included in the domestic company's taxable income even in the above exceptions.

However, if the passive income of a controlled foreign company is less than ¥ 10 million (approximately $123,000) or less than five percent of a controlled foreign company's income, it is excluded.

Passive income taxable under the Special Measures Law includes the dividends received by a controlled foreign company from another company in which the controlled foreign company holds less than 10 percent of its shares; interest on bonds, gain from redemption or sale of bonds, capital gains from the sale of shares through financial instrument exchanges where the controlled foreign company holds less than 10 percent of the shares, royalties (unless the intellectual property was developed by the controlled foreign company) and income from the leasing of vessels or aircrafts.

4. Gain or Loss on the Sale of Foreign Subsidiary Stock

Capital gains from the sale or transfer of shares in foreign subsidiaries is not eligible for the foreign dividend exemption.

5. Foreign Branches

The tax treatment of income received by a Japanese corporation from a member organization in a foreign country depends upon how that member organization is regarded under Japanese tax law.

The juridical entities are entities that are themselves taxpayers under Japanese law include the kabushiki kaisi (the closest equivalent to a corporate entity) and yugen kaisha ("YK", a close counterpart to a limited liability partnership, authority for which was abolished in 2006, but existing YKs may continue to operate as tokurei yugen kaisha ("TYK")). For such entities, the profit allocated from the partnership is regarded as a dividend when it is actually sent to the domestic corporation and is eligible for the foreign dividend exemption. If the partnership is regarded as a kumiai (association) that is a flow-through, then each individual member is subject to tax for the share of profit under Japanese law. The profit so distributed is not eligible for the foreign dividend exemption. Branches are in the nature of unincorporated associations, and profits from the foreign branches of corporations are not eligible for the exemption.

6. Intangible Property Income

Income from intellectual property owned by a domestic company or a controlled foreign company is generally treated as passive income and is not eligible for the foreign exemption. There is no special set of rules applicable to income from intellectual property.

F. Netherlands[40]

1. In General

The Netherlands generally taxes resident companies on their worldwide profits, including foreign-source dividends, interest, and royalties, at a 25-percent rate, with relief from double taxation provided by way of a foreign tax credit. However, Dutch law applies the principles of territorial taxation by exempting certain qualifying distributions from corporate taxation under a participation exemption regime.

The participation exemption applies to both domestic and foreign shareholdings. In general, a shareholding is treated as an eligible participation under the participation exemption regime if the taxpayer (other than a Dutch qualified investment company that is subject to a corporate income tax rate of zero percent) holds at least five percent of the nominal paid-up capital of a company of which the capital is partially or wholly divided into shares.[41] A less than five percent direct shareholding may also be a qualifying participation if another company in the group owns a stake of at least five percent in the same subsidiary. However, an interest of five percent or more in a passive subsidiary (i.e., one that is largely investing or passively financing) is only considered a participation if the subsidiary complies with the subordination requirement (i.e., an effective tax burden of at least 10 percent). Additionally, the participation exemption does not apply if the Dutch taxpayer or the subsidiary is considered to be an investment institution. Notwithstanding the five-percent ownership requirement, if a participation is maintained for more than one year, the participation exemption will continue to apply for an additional three years even if the interest held by the Dutch resident falls below five percent.

2. Expenses

The Netherlands does not have rules that disallow a deduction for expenses of a Dutch resident company to the extent those expenses are attributable to income that is exempt under the participation exemption regime.[42] Nonetheless, costs and expenses incurred on the disposal of a participation (for example, lawyers' fees, stock-exchange duties, and notary fees) are not deductible.

In general, interest payments on loans, bonds, debentures, and other debts of the company are fully deductible as normal business expenses for Dutch corporate income tax purposes. However, the Netherlands has thin-capitalization rules designed to avoid the erosion of the Dutch tax base within corporate groups by providing that interest paid in respect of excessive debt is generally not deductible. Under these rules, interest expenses (and other costs) with respect to related-party loans (or deemed related-party loans[43]) may be partly or completely disallowed if the taxpayer is part of a group, as defined in the Dutch Civil Code. The maximum amount of interest disallowed under these rules is limited to the net related-party interest.

The rules provide two ratios to determine the amount of excess debt. Under the first ratio, which is a fixed ratio, the average fiscal debt may not exceed more than three times the company's average fiscal equity plus €500,000 ($666,965).[44] For purposes of determining this ratio, debt is defined as the balance of the company's loan receivables and loan payables. The balance sheet for tax purposes is used to determine the average debt and equity.

Alternatively, when the company files its corporate tax return, it may elect to apply for the group ratio. Under this alternative, the company may look at the commercial consolidated debt-to-equity ratio of the (international) group of which it is a member. If the company's commercial debt-to-equity ratio does not exceed the debt-to-equity ratio of the group, the entire tax deduction for interest on related-party loans is allowed.

If there is no excessive debt, then the thin capitalization provisions do not apply.

3. Controlled Foreign Company Rules

The Netherlands does not have a formal controlled foreign company regime but does have a regime that is intended to discourage tax deferral through the creation of low-taxed passive subsidiaries referred to as "low-taxed portfolio participations." While there is no strict definition of a "country of low taxation," a company's activities are assumed to be passive when the country does not levy an effective tax rate of at least 10 percent on the income of the company. In this situation, in cases in which the parent holds at least a 25-percent participation and at least 90 percent of the subsidiary's assets are passive (defined as "free portfolio investments" under Dutch tax law), the shares of the participation must be marked-to-market annually with any increase in value being included in the taxable profits of the Dutch parent. This annual revaluation is required instead of the approach often used by other jurisdictions of requiring an attribution of the underlying profits of the shareholding to the Dutch parent. Furthermore, it occurs regardless of whether any of the underlying profits are distributed.

In cases in which a subsidiary qualifies as a low-taxed portfolio investment, it is excluded from the participation exemption regime. Instead, a foreign tax credit system applies to provide relief from double taxation at the Dutch parent. Under this system, income derived from a low-taxed portfolio participation is generally grossed up and taxed at the standard Dutch corporate income tax rate, while allowing a credit for the underlying taxes.

4. Gain or Loss on the Sale of Foreign Subsidiary Stock

In cases in which a domestic or foreign shareholding meets the above requirements to be treated as an eligible participation, any gain on the disposition of such shares is exempt from Dutch corporate taxation. Likewise, any loss on the disposition of such shares is nondeductible.

5. Foreign Branches

The profits of a foreign branch of a Dutch resident company that meets the definition of a foreign permanent establishment[45] generally qualify for an exemption through a proportional tax reduction (also commonly referred to as "exemption with progression").[46] Under this exemption with progression approach (which also applies to certain employment income and foreign immovable property income), the Dutch resident company must first compute Dutch tax based on its worldwide income, including the income of the foreign permanent establishment. The amount of tax due is then reduced by the Dutch resident company's ratio of foreign income to worldwide income.

Foreign losses of a permanent establishment are deductible against worldwide income in computing taxable income of the Dutch resident company. However, foreign losses incurred in a preceding year will reduce the foreign profits otherwise eligible for relief in subsequent years so as to reduce the relief and prevent the double counting of losses. Furthermore, as profits and losses of foreign permanent establishments are taken into account on a per-country basis, foreign profits derived from one country are not offset by losses incurred in another country.

To the extent a foreign permanent establishment is converted into a subsidiary, the participation exemption does not apply until the losses sustained through the former permanent establishment in the years prior to the conversion are fully recaptured. In such a situation, dividends distributed by the subsidiary and capital gains on the disposal of shares in the subsidiary are generally taxed until such losses are fully recaptured, after which the participation exemption is applicable. In some circumstances, however (e.g., the shares in the company in which the participation is held are transferred to a non-resident related entity), losses incurred through a foreign permanent establishment converted into a foreign subsidiary must be recaptured immediately.

6. Intangible Property Income

When certain requirements are met, a taxpayer may elect to apply the Dutch Innovation Box regime. The purpose of this regime is to encourage innovation and investment in research and development.[47] Net income from qualifying property within the Innovation Box is effectively taxed at a rate of five percent. This is accomplished by only taking into account 5/25ths of the qualifying profits. The special five-percent rate applies only to the extent that the net earnings derived from the qualifying property exceed a threshold. This threshold is the total intangible development costs attributable to the qualifying property. Such intangible development costs are deductible when incurred at the regular corporate income tax rate (i.e., currently 25 percent). Although losses on the exploitation of the qualifying property are also still deductible at the 25-percent rate, these losses are subject to recapture through an increase in the threshold.

Intangible assets qualify for Innovation Box treatment only to the extent the assets were developed by the taxpayer itself or on account of the taxpayer. For the Innovation Box regime to apply with respect to a given intangible asset, the taxpayer must have been granted a patent, a plant breeder's right (this right is granted for newly invented seeds), or a research and development declaration from the Ministry of Economic Affairs with respect to that intangible asset. Trademarks, logos, and similar assets do not qualify. For the income to qualify for the special five-percent rate, more than 30 percent of the income must be allocable to the patent, breeder's right, or research and development declaration.

A Dutch taxpayer may selectively elect the Innovation Box regime (e.g., elect with respect to some intangible assets and not others). Furthermore, there is no limit on the amount of income from intangible assets that can be taxed at the reduced rate.

G. Spain[48]

1. In General

Resident corporations[49] are subject to tax in Spain on their worldwide income. To prevent double taxation, there are exemptions, deductions, and tax credits applicable to income derived from foreign sources. Spain has two methods for granting double tax relief, 1) a tax credit or deduction against Spanish tax for the actual corporate income tax paid abroad, and 2) an exemption from income for qualifying participations. Spain generally does not tax the income of foreign subsidiaries until it is distributed. Any available exemption, deduction, or credit is applicable when income is distributed.

Dividends and capital gains from foreign subsidiaries qualify for an exemption from the Spanish corporate tax if the resident corporation owns a participation of at least five percent of the foreign company and has held the participation for at least one year prior to the date on which the dividend is payable. In addition, certain anti-avoidance criteria must be met for the exemption to apply.

In order to qualify for the exemption, the income from the foreign subsidiary must have been subject to tax in the foreign country that is deemed equivalent to the Spanish corporate tax. The subsidiary must have been subject to and not exempt from such tax for the entire year in which the dividend is received. The tax in the foreign country is deemed to be equivalent to the Spanish corporate tax if the foreign subsidiary has a permanent establishment located in a country with which Spain has a tax treaty with an exchange of information clause. At least 85 percent of the foreign subsidiary's income out of which the dividend was paid must be derived from business activities carried on outside Spain. The exemption does not apply if the foreign subsidiary is located in a country that is considered a tax haven under Spanish regulations.[50]

The exemption is not available if the main purpose of the subsidiary is to benefit from the tax exemption,[51] or if losses of the subsidiary are deductible by way of depreciation of the relevant participation.[52]

2. Expenses

Spain does not have expense disallowance rules for expenses attributable to exempt dividends and capital gains.

Spain has thin capitalization rules that apply to related party debt unless the related party is a resident of another European Union country that is not considered a tax haven under Spanish law. If the net interest-bearing debt of an entity that is not a financial institution, made directly or indirectly, to one or more related individuals or entities that are not resident in Spain exceeds three times its capital, the interest attributable to the excess is considered a dividend and not as a deductible expense. The deemed dividend is subject to any applicable dividend withholding tax. With the permission of the Spanish tax administration, the taxpayer may be able to apply a different ratio, based on the financing that the entity would have been able to obtain under normal market conditions from unrelated parties, if the lender is not located in a listed tax haven.

3. Controlled Foreign Company Rules

Spain has controlled foreign company rules referred to as the "international tax transparency regime." Under this regime, a Spanish resident company is liable for corporate income tax on some passive income, such as interest, dividends, capital gains, and real estate losses, of non-European Union resident companies or of companies based in tax haven countries.[53]

These rules apply where the Spanish resident company owns at least 50 percent of the capital, equity, or voting rights, and where the controlled foreign company has "tainted income." Tainted income includes: (1) income from real estate or related rights, unless the real property is effectively connected to a business activity; (2) income derived from participating in the equity of any kind of entity or as a consequence of granting third parties the right to use the company's financial resources;[54] (3) income from banking, financial, insurance and service activities supplied directly or indirectly to resident individual or corporate related parties, if the related party is entitled to deduct the amount paid for Spanish income tax purposes;[55] and (4) capital gains from the transfer of these types of assets accrued by the controlled foreign company. If the controlled foreign company pays local corporate tax on the tainted income that is at least 75 percent of the tax the company would have paid under the Spanish tax regime, it is not subject to these rules.

Income derived from business activities, capital gains, and the transfer of rights of business assets is excluded from taxable income if it is derived from entities in which the resident taxpayer has a direct or indirect interest of more than five percent and the following prerequisites are met: (1) the nonresident company has the supervision and management of the participation through the appropriate organization of means and personnel; and (2) at least 85 percent of the income of the entities from which the income is obtained is created by carrying out business activities.

If the amount of passive income derived from the Spanish resident parent company is 15 percent or more of the net profits or four percent of the total turnover of the controlled foreign company, the Spanish resident company includes the proportionate share of income in its tax base.

4. Gain or Loss on the Sale of Foreign Subsidiary Stock

Capital gains from the sale of foreign subsidiary stock also qualify for an exemption from the Spanish corporate tax if the participation requirements, one-year holding period, and anti-avoidance criteria discussed above are met. The subsidiary must have been subject to an equivalent tax throughout the entire holding period for capital gains to be excluded.

5. Foreign Branches

Income derived from a foreign branch is exempt from Spanish corporate income tax if the foreign branch is considered a permanent establishment.[56] To be exempt, the income of the foreign permanent establishment must be derived from the carrying out of business activities. This condition is met if at least 85 percent of the income corresponds to income obtained abroad, and is not subject to the deduction under the Spanish income tax regime. Wholesale commerce, services, credit and financing, and insurance and reinsurance are activities which could be considered as deriving foreign income. Additionally, the income derived by the permanent establishment must be subject to tax with an equivalent tax to the Spanish income tax, and must not be located in a tax haven country.

The exemption for foreign branch income does not apply where losses from the branch were allowed in prior tax periods. The exemption applies to the income from the branch only after the losses are fully recaptured. Additionally, the exemption for foreign branch income does not apply where the permanent establishment was established abroad for the sole purpose of benefiting from this preferred tax treatment.

6. Intangible Property Income

Spain adopted a patent box regime in 2007 that reduces the rate of corporate income tax on income derived from intellectual property. Fifty percent of the income derived from the transfer of the right to use qualifying intellectual property is exempt from corporate tax in Spain. Intellectual property rights included in the incentive regime include patents, drawings or models, plans, secret formulas or procedures, and rights on information related to industrial, commercial, or scientific experiments. The patent box regime does not distinguish between intellectual property income from foreign and domestic sources.

In order to qualify for the reduced tax: (1) the intellectual property must have been created by the company transferring the right; (2) the recipient of the right must actually use the intellectual property for business activities; (3) if the recipient is a related company, the intellectual property cannot be used to generate a deductible expense for the transferring company; (4) the recipient company must not be located in a listed tax haven jurisdiction; (5) in the case where one intellectual property contract includes other services, the consideration related to the intellectual property must be clearly differentiated within the contract; and (6) the transferring taxpaying company must keep records of income and expenses pertinent to the intellectual property rights subject to the transfer.

H. Switzerland[57]

1. In General

Switzerland is a federation of 26 sovereign cantons (states). Corporate income taxes are levied at both the federal (at a flat 8.5-percent rate) and cantonal (at varied rates) levels, with cantonal taxes exceeding federal taxes in several cantons.[58] In addition, Switzerland's 2,600 municipalities are generally empowered to levy their own taxes.

Swiss resident companies, defined as those that are incorporated in Switzerland or are effectively managed or controlled from Switzerland, generally are taxed on a territorial basis. Income from foreign permanent establishments and foreign real property is exempt from Swiss taxation, but considered when determining tax rates.[59] In addition, tax relief is granted for dividends received from foreign and domestic participations at both the federal and cantonal level, and the cantons and municipalities generally exempt holding companies from cantonal and municipal income taxes.[60]

The tax relief granted for certain qualified dividends takes the form of a "participation deduction." Dividends qualify for a participation deduction if the parent company owns (i.e., "participates in") at least 10 percent of the total share capital of the subsidiary, or holds shares worth at least one million Swiss Francs (CHF) ($1.069 million).[61] Additionally, a parent company can receive the participation deduction if it is entitled to 10 percent of the profits of the subsidiary. A company does not need to have held its shares for any minimum period to qualify for the participation deduction. As described more fully below, a company also receives a deduction for capital gains from the sale of qualifying participations.

The tax relief equals a company's net income from qualifying participations over the company's worldwide taxable net income. The company's total corporate income tax is reduced by an amount equal to this percentage. The net income from qualifying participations equals gross dividends received from the participation less financing costs and administrative costs (which are presumed to equal five percent of the gross dividend received, as discussed further below).

2. Expenses

In general, a Swiss resident company may fully deduct expenses other than interest that are related to earning income that is exempt from tax (income from foreign permanent establishments and foreign real property) or the tax on which may be offset by the participation deduction. Switzerland requires a formulary allocation of interest expense to such income (using an asset ratio method that compares the tax book value of the investment that generated the income to total assets). The application of these rules has an effect similar to a disallowance of some interest expense deductions; however, these rules generally apply only to the extent that such interest is attributable to a foreign participation in a year in which the foreign participation distributes an exempt dividend to Switzerland. The amount of the participation deduction equals the gross dividend received from the participation less attributable financing costs and administrative costs. The administrative costs are presumed to equal five percent of the gross dividend received from the participation, although this presumption is rebuttable.

In general, there are no limitations on the deduction of interest expense to the extent the debt is owed to independent third parties (which are not collateralized by the debtor company's shareholders or parties related to the shareholders), other than the indirect disallowance discussed above. If debt is owed to related parties, financial companies may have a maximum debt-to-equity ratio of six-to-one. For other companies, a company may have debt equal to a percentage of its assets (the percentages vary from 50 percent of fixed assets to 100 percent of cash). A company may attempt to establish that debt exceeding these safe harbors is nevertheless arm's-length; if the company is successful, any interest paid with respect to that debt is fully deductible.

3. Controlled Foreign Company Rules

Switzerland does not have controlled foreign company rules.

4. Gain or Loss on the Sale of Foreign Subsidiary Stock

The participation deduction applies to capital gains on substantial participations sold by a Swiss resident company. To qualify for the deduction, (1) the participation sold must represent at least 10 percent of the total capital of the subsidiary or entitle the seller to at least 10 percent of the profits of the subsidiary, and (2) the seller must have held the participation for at least one year prior to the sale.

A Swiss resident company that realizes a capital gain on any other sale of a foreign subsidiary's stock generally must include the gain in its Swiss taxable income. If a capital loss is realized, the loss is deductible.

5. Foreign Branches

Income a Swiss resident company earns from a foreign permanent establishment, including a branch, is exempt from Swiss tax at the federal level.

A Swiss resident company may use losses of a foreign permanent establishment to offset profits realized in Switzerland to the extent those losses cannot be utilized at that time in the country in which the permanent establishment is located. If the losses are set off against profits of the permanent establishment in the country in which it is located within the next seven years, however, then an amount of income equal to the loss utilized in the permanent establishment's country of residence becomes taxable in Switzerland.

6. Intangible Property Income

No special tax treatment applies to royalties at the federal level. When received by Swiss resident companies, they are included in income and taxed in the same manner as other income.

Royalties may be exempt from cantonal income tax if received by a cantonal holding company. In addition, the canton of Nidwalden introduced the first license box system in Switzerland on January 1, 2011. Under this system, companies (or branches) in Nidwalden pay a flat tax of 1.2 percent on their net licensing income in lieu of any other cantonal or municipal income taxes that would otherwise apply to that income. Licensing income includes payments received for the use (or right to use) certain intellectual property, including copyrights, patents, trademarks, designs or models, plans, and secret formulas or processes. The license box system is available with respect to income from both existing and new intellectual property, as well as income from both self-developed intellectual property and intellectual property acquired from third parties. A company (branch) that desires to utilize the license box system must apply and get tax authority approval. In addition, the company (branch) must have substance in Nidwalden, such as owning office space, employing qualifying personnel, or exercising management functions in the canton.

I. United Kingdom[62]

1. In General

The United Kingdom generally taxes resident companies on all income and capital profits regardless of where they arise. Corporations pay tax at a rate of 27 percent on profits equal or exceeding £1.5 million ($2.3 million).[63] A small profits rate applies to small corporations with a graduated rate and phase-out structure in place. The United Kingdom is currently in the process of lowering its corporate rate, with the aim of reaching a flat rate, applicable to large corporations, of 24 percent.

The United Kingdom is also in the process of making significant changes in its tax system to move towards a more territorial tax system. In 2009, legislation was introduced that exempts 100 percent of dividends received by large- and medium-sized companies from United Kingdom taxation. Small companies (those employing less than 50 people and with annual turnover or balance of £10 million ($15.5 million) or less) are not eligible for the exemption unless the dividend paying company is located in a territory that has a double tax treaty with the United Kingdom containing a standard OECD nondiscrimination clause.

The exemption of foreign dividends was partly intended to remove the distinction between United Kingdom-source dividends and European Union-source dividends in order to comply with the principles of freedom of establishment and the free movement of capital provided for in the European Community Treaty. The exemption is broader than it would have to be under the treaty, as it does not distinguish between European Union and non-European Union member states, but applies to dividends from all countries outside the United Kingdom.

Dividends from the following categories are exempt: (1) the dividend is paid from a company controlled by the United Kingdom company;[64] (2) the dividend is paid in respect of non-redeemable ordinary shares; (3) the United Kingdom company is a portfolio shareholder;[65] (4) dividends are paid in respect of profits that do not reflect the results of a transaction or series of transactions which achieve a (non-negligible) reduction in United Kingdom taxation; or (5) if dividends are similar to interest, and the receiving company is not connected, the paying company is not an open-ended investment company, unit trust or offshore fund, and the shares are not held for an unallowed purpose (i.e., to obtain a tax advantage). The exemption from tax is broad, but companies may elect out.

Distributions from the following categories are not eligible for the exemption: (1) non-redeemable shares if there is a scheme to avoid taxation and rights are obtained equivalent to the rights of either a preferential shareholder or a shareholder of a redeemable share; (2) a portfolio shareholding where a larger shareholding is split between connected companies in order to meet the portfolio shareholding limitations; (3) part of an arrangement to yield a return that is economically equivalent to interest and part of a tax advantage scheme; (4) tax advantage schemes that include any deduction given under foreign tax law in respect of an amount calculated by reference to the distribution; (5) tax advantage schemes that involve recipients that make payments or give up income in order to receive a distribution; (6) tax advantage schemes that involve payments not at arm's length; and (7) distributions that have been artificially diverted from a company for which the distribution would have been a trade receipt.

2. Expenses

In general, the United Kingdom allows domestic tax deductions for expenses that are associated with foreign-source dividend income. The United Kingdom has had thin capitalization rules since April 1, 2004. These rules apply to both domestic and cross-border loan transactions. The thin capitalization test relies heavily on the arm's-length standard to regulate excessively leveraged financing structures. A United Kingdom company is thinly capitalized for tax purposes when it has more debt than it could and would have borrowed on its own resources, because it is borrowing either from or with the support of related parties. In this case, the transfer pricing rules generally disallow the deduction for interest expense that exceeds what it would have been in the absence of the special relationship between the borrower and the lender. Other anti-avoidance rules apply to limit interest in certain situations including where one of the main purposes for the loan arrangement is to secure a tax advantage.

The United Kingdom also introduced a limited interest restriction measure (the "worldwide debt cap"). The worldwide debt cap applies to medium- and large-sized companies and limits the deductibility of interest payments in certain instances. The limit is based on a formula derived from a comparison of the enterprise's internal debt with its external debt. This worldwide debt cap limitation restricts the deductibility of interest and other finance expense on intra-group debt of United Kingdom companies in cases in which the United Kingdom interest expense is excessive by reference to such expense in the worldwide group.[66]

3. Controlled Foreign Company Rules

The United Kingdom has controlled foreign company rules that provide for taxation of the controlled foreign company profits under certain conditions. The profits are taxable if (1) the company is resident outside the United Kingdom; (2) the company is controlled by persons resident in the United Kingdom;[67] and (3) the company is subject to a lower level of taxation in the territory in which it is resident. A lower level of taxation means, with respect to any accounting period, the taxation paid on the company's profits is less than three quarters of the corresponding United Kingdom taxation that would be chargeable on such profits if the company were resident in the United Kingdom.[68] If the controlled foreign company rules apply, then all of the company's income apportionable to the United Kingdom resident is subject to tax; no distinction is made between passive and active income.[69] There are certain exceptions to the controlled foreign company rules, including a de minimis exception if the chargeable profits for the relevant account period do not exceed £50,000 ($77,499), an exception for income sourced in certain excluded countries (including countries in the European Economic Area), and a motive test where the transaction giving rise to the controlled foreign company did not have as a purpose a reduction in United Kingdom tax by diverting profits from the United Kingdom.

The United Kingdom has proposed reforming the controlled foreign company rules. The 2011 budget proposal includes narrowing the controlled foreign company rules to target profits that are artificially diverted from the United Kingdom. The new rules include an exemption for intra-group activities where the activities have minimal connection to the United Kingdom, and for controlled foreign companies whose main business is the exploitation of intellectual property where the controlled foreign company and the intellectual property have minimal connection to the United Kingdom. Additionally, the de minimis exception is £200,000 ($309,996) under the 2011 proposed budget.

4. Gain or Loss on the Sale of Foreign Subsidiary Stock

The United Kingdom tax system provides for a participation exemption from capital gains tax for United Kingdom resident companies derived from a substantial shareholding. A substantial shareholding arises when a company holds no less than 10 percent of the company's share capital, is beneficially entitled to no less than 10 percent of the company's profits, or would be beneficially entitled to no less than 10 percent of the assets upon the winding-up of the company. Additionally, the company that is disposing of the assets must have owned the shares for a minimum of twelve consecutive months within a two-year period prior to disposal. There is also a requirement that the investing company and the company invested in must be a trading company or a member of a trading group. For these purposes, a "trading company" is a "company carrying on trading activities whose activities do not include to a substantial extent activities other than trading activities." In this context, the term "substantial" is interpreted to mean where non-trading income, activities, or expenses are more than 20 percent of the activities of the company.

5. Foreign Branches

The United Kingdom is considering an exemption for profits from foreign branches of United Kingdom companies. Currently, foreign branch income is taxable. The large majority of businesses in the United Kingdom do not utilize foreign branches. Branches tend to be used by larger companies in the oil and gas, banking, and insurance sectors.

Under the proposed exemption for foreign branches, companies may elect to exempt the profits from foreign branches if they are attributed to a permanent establishment in accordance with either a treaty or, where no such treaty exists, in accordance with the OECD model convention. If profits are exempt from corporate tax, then losses would also be excluded to the extent they arise from foreign permanent establishments. The election once made would be irrevocable. The exemption would exclude capital gains as well as investment income that is effectively connected to the branch.

Anti-avoidance rules similar to the controlled foreign company rules would apply to prevent abuse. Where the foreign tax liability of the foreign branch is less than three quarters of the corporate tax that would be payable on the same profits if they were taxable in the United Kingdom, then the branch must meet certain conditions (including the motive test) in order for the exemption to apply.

6. Intangible Property Income

The United Kingdom does not currently have special rules for treating foreign source intellectual property income differently from other categories of foreign-source income. The government plans to introduce a preferential tax regime for profits arising from patents.[70] The "patent box" rules would apply a 10 percent corporate tax on income from patents, including patent royalties and imbedded royalty income from the sales of patented products booked in the United Kingdom. The patent box regime will be elective beginning in April 2013, and will apply to patents for which the technology was first commercialized after November 29, 2010.

In late November 2010, the United Kingdom government published details of its corporate tax reform program proposal containing details of proposed changes to the United Kingdom's controlled foreign company regime with important implication for the taxation of foreign intellectual property profits. While the reforms are generally considered to be more favorable to taxpayer, the new rules are, nonetheless, intended to ensure that intellectual property profits artificially diverted to low tax jurisdictions remain taxable in the United Kingdom, but that the ways in which groups manage their commercial operations overseas are not distorted or inhibited. One of the reforms is a tax exemption for controlled foreign companies that have a main business of exploiting intellectual property where the intellectual property and the controlled foreign company have minimal connection with the United Kingdom.[71]

End Notes

[1] This document may be cited as follows: Joint Committee on Taxation, Background and Selected Issues Related to the U.S. International Tax System and Systems that Exempt Foreign Business Income, (JCX-33-11), May 20, 2011.

[2] Secs. 951-964. Unless otherwise specified, all section references are to the Internal Revenue Code of 1986, as amended (the "Code").

[3] Sec. 954.

[4] Secs. 953(e) and 954(h), (i). The temporary exceptions from the subpart F provisions for active financing income applied only for taxable years beginning in 1998 (Taxpayer Relief Act of 1997, Pub. L. No. 105-34). Those exceptions were modified and extended for one year, applicable only for taxable years beginning in 1999 (Tax and Trade Relief Extension Act of 1998, Pub. L. No. 105-277). The Tax Relief Extension Act of 1999 (Pub. L. No. 106- 170) clarified and extended the temporary exceptions for two years, applicable only for taxable years beginning after 1999 and before 2002. The Job Creation and Worker Assistance Act of 2002 (Pub. L. No. 107-147) modified and extended the temporary exceptions for five years, for taxable years beginning after 2001 and before 2007. The Tax Increase Prevention and Reconciliation Act of 2005 (Pub. L. No. 109-222) extended the temporary provisions for two years, for taxable years beginning after 2006 and before 2009. The Energy Improvement and Extension Act of 2008 (Pub. L. No. 110-343) extended the temporary provisions for one year, for taxable years beginning after 2008 and before 2010. The Tax Relief, Unemployment Insurance Reauthorization, and Job Creation Act of 2010 (Pub. L. No. 111-312) extended the temporary provisions for two years, for taxable years beginning after 2009 and before 2012.

[5] Sec. 954(c)(6). The temporary look-through rules applied only for taxable years of foreign corporations beginning after December 31, 2005 and before January 1, 2009, and to the taxable years of U.S.10-percent shareholders with or within which the specified tax years of such foreign corporations end. Sec. 954(c)(6)(B). The Energy Improvement and Extension Act of 2008 (Pub. L. No. 110-343) extended these temporary rules for one year, for taxable years beginning after 2008 and before 2010. The Tax Relief, Unemployment Insurance Reauthorization, and Job Creation Act of 2010 (Pub. L. No. 111-312) extended the temporary provisions for two years, for taxable years beginning after 2009 and before 2012.

[6] Sec. 1297(a).

[7] Sec. 1297(b).

[8] Secs. 901, 902, 960, 1295(f).

[9] Secs. 901, 904.

[10] Sec. 904(c).

[11] Treas. Reg. sec. 1.861-8(b) and Temp. Treas. Reg. sec. 1.861-8T(c).

[12] Temp. Treas. Reg. sec. 1.861-9T and Treas. Reg. sec. 1.861-17.

[13] Sec. 864(e)(1), (6); Temp. Treas. Reg. sec. 1.861-14T(e)(2).

[14] Secs. 864(e)(5), 1504.

[15] Sec. 1504(b)(3).

[16] Pub. L. No. 108-357, sec. 401.

[17] Hiring Incentives to Restore Employment Act, Pub. L. No. 111-147, sec. 551(a) (2010).

[18] Sec. 904(d). AJCA generally reduced the number of income categories from nine to two, effective for tax years beginning in 2006. Before AJCA, the foreign tax credit limitation was applied separately to the following categories of income: (1) passive income, (2) high withholding tax interest, (3) financial services income, (4) shipping income, (5) certain dividends received from noncontrolled section 902 foreign corporations (also known as "10/50 companies"), (6) certain dividends from a domestic international sales corporation or former domestic international sales corporation, (7) taxable income attributable to certain foreign trade income, (8) certain distributions from a foreign sales corporation or former foreign sales corporation, and (9) any other income not described in items (1) through (8) (so-called "general basket" income). A number of other provisions of the Code, including several enacted in 2010 as part of Pub. L. No. 111-226, create additional separate categories in specific circumstances or limit the availability of the foreign tax credit in other ways. See, e.g., secs. 865(h), 901(j), 904(d)(6), 904(h)(10).

[19] Sec. 904(d)(3).

[20] Sec. 904(d)(4).

[21] For a detailed description of the U.S. transfer pricing rules, see Joint Committee on Taxation, Present Law and Background Related to Possible Income Shifting and Transfer Pricing (JCX-37-10), July 20, 2010, pp. 18- 50.

[22] The term "related" as used herein refers to relationships described in section 482, which applies to "two or more organizations, trades or businesses (whether or not incorporated, whether or not organized in the United States, and whether or not affiliated) owned or controlled directly or indirectly by the same interests."

[23] Proposals have been made for the adoption of a territorial system in the United States, including National Commission on Fiscal Responsibility and Reform, The Moment of Truth (December 2010), pp. 28-35; The President's Economic Advisory Board, The Report on Tax Reform Options: Simplification, Compliance, and Corporate Taxation, August 2010, pp. 89-91; U.S. Department of the Treasury, Approaches to Improve the Competitiveness of the U.S. Business Tax System for the 21st Century, December 20, 2007; President's Advisory Panel on Federal Tax Reform, Simple, Fair and Pro-Growth: Proposals to Fix America's Tax System (November 2005); Joint Committee on Taxation, Options to Improve Tax Compliance and Reform Tax Expenditures (JCS-02- 05), January 27, 2005, pp. 186-97.

[24] Sec. 163(j).

[25] For analysis of two recent proposals, see Joint Committee on Taxation, Description of Revenue Provisions Contained in the President's Fiscal Year 2011 Budget Proposal (JCS-2-10), August 16, 2010, pp. 241-85.

[26] Sec. 965.

[27] This description of Australian law relies largely on information found on the Australian Tax Office website, www.ATO.gov.au, and Law Library of Congress, Taxation of Foreign Source Income of Resident Corporations, Report for Congress (April 2011). This description and the descriptions of the tax rules of the eight other countries that follow are intended to serve as general overviews. Many details have been omitted and simplifying generalizations have been made for ease of exposition.

[28] U.S. dollar equivalents were calculated using the currency rate for January 1, 2011, according to OANDA's FX Converter, available at http://www.oanda.com.

[29] The Australian government recently proposed draft legislation that would reform the foreign source attribution rules. To review the draft and explanatory materials, see The Treasury, "Exposure Draft--Reform of the Foreign Source Income Deferral Rules," www.treasury.gov.au/contentitem.asp?NavId=37&contentID=1930 (as of May 17, 2011).

[30] This description of Canadian law relies largely on Patrick Marley & Richard Tremblay, Business Operations in Canada, BNA Tax Management Portfolio No. 955-4th; International Bureau of Fiscal Documentation ("IBFD") Canada Taxation and Investment; and Law Library of Congress, Taxation of Foreign Source Income of Resident Corporations, Report for Congress (April 2011).

[31] This includes a reduction to the Canadian federal rate that relates to a 10-percent rebate that applies to income that has been earned in a Canadian province or territory and an additional 10-percent rate reduction to the extent the income does not currently benefit from other preferential tax treatment.

[32] Advisory Panel on Canada's System of International Taxation, Final Report: Enhancing Canada's International Tax Advantage (December 2008), available at http://www.apcsit-gcrcfi.ca/index-eng.html (hereinafter December 2008 Advisory Panel Report).

[33] Although the 2007 Budget proposed restricting interest deductibility on debt used to acquire foreign corporation shares paying exempt dividends, this rule was withdrawn as part of the 2009 Budget.

[34] The information in this section is based in large part on Edouard Milhac & Annabelle BailleulMirabaud, Business Operations in France, Tax Management Portfolio No. 961-4th; Eric Robert, International Bureau of Fiscal Documentation, IBFD European Taxation Database, France, available at http://checkpoint.riag.com (last accessed May 16, 2011); and Law Library of Congress, Taxation of Foreign Source Income of Resident Corporations, Report for Congress (2011).

[35] Most tax treaties, however, provide a tax credit for withholding taxes paid on passive income.

[36] Small and medium-sized enterprises are taxed at a reduced rate of 15 percent on the first €38,120 ($50,849) of profits. Except where otherwise indicated, the quoted tax rates and threshold amounts apply in 2011. U.S. dollar equivalents were calculated using the currency rate for January 1, 2011, according to OANDA's FX Converter, available at http://www.oanda.com.

[37] This description of German law relies largely on Dirk Pohl, Business Operations in Germany, BNA Tax Management Portfolio, 962-3rd; International Bureau of Fiscal Documentation ("IBFD") European Tax Surveys, Germany – Corporate Taxation; and Law Library of Congress, Taxation of Foreign Source Income of Resident Corporations, Report for Congress (April 2011).

[38] This description of Japanese law relies largely on IBFD Asia-Pacific Taxation, Japan Country Analysis: Corporate Taxation and Law Library of Congress, "Taxation of Foreign Source Income of Resident Corporations, Report for Congress" (April 2011).

[39] U.S. dollar equivalents were calculated using the currency rate for January 1, 2011, according to OANDA's FX Converter, available at http://www.oanda.com.

[40] This description of Dutch law relies largely on Kees van Raad (as updated by Maarten van der Weijden), Business Operations in The Netherlands, BNA Tax Management Portfolio, 973-2nd; International Bureau of Fiscal Documentation ("IBFD") European Tax Surveys, Netherlands – Corporate Taxation; Law Library of Congress, Taxation of Controlled Foreign Corporations in Selected OECD Countries, Report for Congress (October 2009); and Ernst & Young, The 2010 Worldwide Corporate Tax Guide - Netherlands (April 2010).

[41] Where under the terms of a tax treaty with another European Union member state the dividend tax is reduced according to a voting rights criterion (as, for example, under the treaties with Germany, Ireland, and the United Kingdom), a participating interest also qualifies if the Dutch taxpayer controls at least five percent of the voting rights of the company located in the other member state.

[42] Prior to 2004, expenses incurred with respect to qualifying foreign participations, such as interest expenses, were not deductible for Dutch corporate income tax purposes, unless the expenses were instrumental in generating Dutch taxable income. In the Bosal case, the European Court of Justice ruled that this measure was incompatible with European Union law and, consequently, was not applicable to expenses related to qualifying European Union participations. Case C-168/01, Bosal Holding BV v. Staatssecretaris van Financien, 2003 E.C.R. I9409. As a result, the Netherlands changed this rule with respect to both qualifying European Union and non- European Union participations.

[43] Deductions for interest on third-party debt is generally allowed; however, in cases in which such debt is formally granted by a third party but is, in substance, actually owed to a related party, the thin-capitalization rules apply.

[44] U.S. dollar equivalents were calculated using the currency rate for January 1, 2011, according to OANDA's FX Converter available at http://www.oanda.com.

[45] The Dutch definition of permanent establishment is similar to that which is found in the OECD Model Convention. The OECD Model Convention defines a permanent establishment as a fixed place of business through which the business of an enterprise is wholly or partially carried on. Organisation for Economic Cooperation and Development, Model Tax Convention on Income and on Capital, article 5(1) (2010).

[46] Income from certain foreign finance activities carried on through a foreign permanent establishment does not qualify for this exemption. Instead, relief from double taxation is accomplished by way of a foreign tax credit.

[47] The Innovation Box succeeded the Patent Box regime, which was effective from January 1, 2007, until it was replaced by the Innovation Box as of January 1, 2010.

[48] This description of Spanish law relies largely on Baker & McKenzie Madrid S.L., "Business Operations in Spain," BNA Tax Management Portfolio, 989-5th; Law Library of Congress, Taxation of Foreign Source Income of Resident Corporations, Report for Congress (April 2011); and IBFD European Tax Surveys, "Spain – Corporate Taxation."

[49] A company is resident in Spain if it has its statutory seat or place of effective management in Spain. Spanish residence can be presumed by the tax administration when a corporation is located in a tax haven or a no-tax jurisdiction and its principal assets are in Spain or its main business is located in Spain, unless the taxpayer can prove that the corporation is managed in the tax haven jurisdiction and that there are valid economic reasons for it to be established there.

[50] Spanish regulations list 48 countries as tax havens, including Hong Kong, Cayman Islands, Bermuda, Malta, the Isle of Man, Lichtenstein, Macao, Luxembourg (with respect to income from certain entities), and Singapore. For the complete list of countries deemed to be tax havens under Spanish law, see, Real Decreto 1080/1991 of July 5, 1991, as amended by Real Decreto 116/2003, available at http://www.boe.es/boe/dias/1991 /07/13/pdfs /A23371-23371.pdf.

[51] This is deemed to be the main purposes of a subsidiary when the subsidiary carries on the same activities in the same market that were previously carried out by a Spanish entity within the same group.

[52] Spanish law generally allows for depreciation of the shares of the subsidiary when a dividend is paid. However, the Spanish resident corporation cannot both exempt the income and take a deduction for the depreciation in shares.

[53] A controlled foreign company that is resident in a tax haven jurisdiction is deemed to have tainted income of 15 percent of the Spanish shareholder's cost of acquiring the tax haven company, unless the Spanish shareholder

provides evidence of contrary income amounts, or includes the tax haven company in its consolidated balance sheet.

[54] This category includes all kinds of financial income derived from equity or debt instruments and includes many exemptions including an exemption for income from credit activities that can be characterized as business activities.

[55] This type of income will not be tainted income if more than 50 percent of the controlled foreign company's income from such activities arises from transactions with unrelated parties.

[56] An entity is considered to be doing business through a permanent establishment if it has any permanent facilities or workplaces abroad where it carries out its business activities in whole or in part. If the activities are located in a country with which Spain has a tax treaty, the provisions of the treaty apply to determine if there is a permanent establishment.

[57] The information in this section is based in large part on Peter R. Altenburger et al., Business Operations in Switzerland, Tax Management Portfolio No. 986-3rd, Roger M. Cadosch, International Bureau of Fiscal Documentation, IBFD European Taxation Database, Switzerland, available at http://checkpoint.riag.com (last accessed May 2, 2011), and Law Library of Congress, Taxation of Foreign Source Income of Resident Corporations, Report for Congress (2011).

[58] The discussion that follows describes the tax treatment at the federal level. Cantonal tax treatment generally is similar to federal tax treatment, except as otherwise noted.

[59] This feature of the Swiss tax system has no effect on a company's federal taxes, but is often significant in determining cantonal taxes as many cantons have progressive corporate tax rates.

[60] The exemption from cantonal and municipal income taxes is available to a holding company if (1) the main purpose of the company is to hold and manage long-term investments in affiliated companies, (2) the company does not carry on an active trade or business in Switzerland, and (3) at least two-thirds of the company's total assets consist of qualifying investments or two-thirds of the company's total income is derived from qualifying investments.

[61] Except where otherwise indicated, the quoted tax rates and threshold amounts apply in 2011. U.S. dollar equivalents were calculated using the currency rate for January 1, 2011, according to OANDA's FX Converter, available at http://www.oanda.com. Prior to 2011, the required participation levels were 20 percent of the total share capital or CHF two million ($2.137 million).

[62] This description of United Kingdom law relies largely on Peter Nias, James Ross, Lee Khvat, and Clare Morison, "Business Operations in the United Kingdom," BNA Tax Management Portfolio, 989-5th; Law Library of Congress, Taxation of Foreign Source Income of Resident Corporations, Report for Congress (April 2011); IBFD European Tax Surveys, "United Kingdom – Corporate Taxation;" and information found on the HM Treasury website at http://www.hm-treasury.gov.uk/.

[63] U.S. dollar equivalents were calculated using the currency rate for January 1, 2011, according to OANDA's FX Converter, available at http://www.oanda.com.

[64] Dividends could also qualify under this class, subject to certain conditions, if the United Kingdom company is one of two persons who, taken together, control the dividend paying company.

[65] A portfolio shareholder holds less than 10 percent of the issue share capital and is entitled to less than 10 percent of the profits of the paying company.

[66] Under these rules, a Gateway Test is applied to determine if net debt of the United Kingdom taxpayer is greater than three quarters of the gross debt of the worldwide group. If the net debt exceeds this threshold, the United Kingdom company must apply more detailed rules to determine the portion of related party interest expense that is disallowed. These rules, however, do not apply to certain qualifying financial services groups. Susan Bell, "Section 11 and Schedule 5 Worldwide Debt Cap," British Tax Review, Issue 1 (2011).

[67] Control for these purposes means the power of a person to secure either by holding shares or voting power or by powers conferred by the articles of association or other document that the affairs of the company are conducted in accordance with his wishes. A company may also meet the control test if two persons together control it and, broadly, a United Kingdom resident person has at least a 40 percent interest and another person has at least a 40 percent interest an no greater than a 55-percent interest.

[68] There are anti-avoidance provisions targeted at "designer rate" tax regimes which set aside the lower level of taxation condition where the tax payable is determined under provisions the HMRC has determined to be designed to enable companies to exercise significant control over the amount of tax that they pay. The regulations identify specific provisions in specific locations as designer-rate tax regimes.

[69] In response to the 2006 European Court of Justice ruling in Cadbury Schweppes (Case C-196/04), a reduction is allowed for profits that are not wholly artificial arrangements where the subsidiary is engaged in genuine economic activity in another member state.

[70] The government will issue a consultation document on the patent box measure in May 2011, with legislation proposed for the Finance Bill 2012. See HM Treasury, Overview of Tax Legislation and Rates, (March 23, 2011) p. 22, available at http://cdn.hm-treasury.gov.uk/2011budget_taxation_overview.pdf.

[71] HM Treasury's 2010 report explained that the rules would be designed to target high-risk areas including: (1) circumstances where intellectual property has been developed in the United Kingdom and transferred to a low-tax jurisdiction; (2) where intellectual property is held offshore and effectively managed in the United Kingdom (an example would be where 90 percent of the activity takes place in the United Kingdom but most of the profits arise in a low-tax jurisdiction); and (3) United Kingdom funds are used to invest in intellectual property that is held offshore, but the United Kingdome does not receive a return on that investment.

In: Taxing U.S. Multinational Corporations
Editor: Angelique Gilder
ISBN: 978-1-62618-145-8

Chapter 4

INTERNATIONAL CORPORATE TAX RATE COMPARISONS AND POLICY IMPLICATIONS*

Jane G. Gravelle

SUMMARY

Advocates of cutting corporate tax rates frequently make their argument based on the higher statutory rate in the United States as compared with the rest of the world; they argue that cutting corporate taxes would induce large investment flows into the United States, which would create jobs or expand the taxable income base enough to raise revenue. President Barack Obama has supported a rate cut if the revenue loss can be offset with corporate base broadening. Others have urged on one hand, a revenue raising reform, and, on the other, setting deficit concerns aside.

Is the U.S. tax rate higher than the rest of the world, and what does that difference imply for tax policy? The answer depends, in part, on which tax rates are being compared. Although the U.S. statutory tax rate is higher, the average effective rate is about the same, and the marginal rate on new investment is only slightly higher. The statutory rate differential is relevant for international profit shifting; effective rates are more relevant for firms' investment levels. The 13.7 percentage point differential in statutory rates (a 39.2% rate for the United States compared with 25.5% in other countries), narrows to about 9 percentage points when tax rates in the rest of the world are weighted to reflect the size of countries' economies. (The OECD rates fell by slightly over1/2 of a percentage point between 2010 and 2012).

Regardless of tax differentials, could a U.S. rate cut lead to significant economic gains and revenue feedbacks? Because of the factors that constrain capital flows, estimates for a rate cut from 35% to 25% suggest a modest positive effect on wages and output: an eventual one-time increase of less than two-tenths of 1% of output. Most of this output gain is not an increase in national income because returns to capital imported from abroad belong to foreigners and the returns to U.S. investment abroad that comes back to the United States are already owned by U.S. firms.

The revenue cost of such a rate cut is estimated at between $1.2 trillion and $1.5 trillion over the next 10 years. Revenue feedback effects from increased investment

* This is an edited, reformatted and augmented version of Congressional Research Service, Publication No. R41743, dated December 28, 2012.

inflows are estimated to reduce those revenue costs by 5%-6%. Reductions in profit shifting could have larger effects, but even if profit shifting disappeared entirely, it would not likely offset revenue losses. It seems unlikely that a rate cut to 25% would significantly reduce profit shifting given these transactions are relatively costless and largely constrained by laws, enforcement, and court decisions.

Both output gains and revenue offsets would be reduced if other countries responded to a U.S. rate cut by reducing their own taxes. Evidence suggests that the U.S. rate cut in the Tax Reform Act of 1986 triggered rate cuts in other countries.

It is difficult, although not impossible, to design a reform to lower the corporate tax rate by 10 percentage points that is revenue neutral in the long run. Standard tax expenditures do not appear adequate for this purpose. Eliminating one of the largest provisions, accelerated depreciation, gains much more revenue in the short run than in the long run, and a long-run revenue-neutral change would increase the cost of capital. Other revisions, such as restricting foreign tax credits and interest deductibility or increasing shareholder level taxes, may be required.

This report focuses on the global issues relating to tax rate differentials between the United States and other countries. It provides tax rate comparisons; discusses policy implications, including the effect of a corporate rate cut on revenue, output, and national welfare; and discusses the outlook for and consequences of a revenue neutral corporate tax reform.

Advocates of cutting corporate tax rates frequently make their argument based on the higher statutory rate observed in the United States as compared with the rest of the world.[1] Sometimes the higher rate alone is used as an argument, and in other cases the arguments include claims that cutting corporate taxes would induce large investment flows into the United States, which would create jobs or expand the base enough to raise revenue.

President Barack Obama has supported a rate cut if the revenue loss can be offset with corporate base broadening, while the Citizens for Tax Justice has urged a revenue raising reform and business leaders have urged setting deficit concerns aside.[2] House Majority Leader Eric Cantor has also proposed a 25% corporate rate in the context of tax reform and Ways and Means Chairman Dave Camp has proposed a 25% combined with a move to a territorial tax system. [3]

Many issues arise regarding the corporate tax outside of the global perspective that are addressed in other reports.[4] This report focuses on the global issue relating to tax rate differentials between the United States and other countries. The first section provides tax rate comparisons. The second section discusses policy implications, including the effect of a corporate rate cut on revenue, output, and national welfare; the possibility that a rate cut may induce reactions from other countries; and the outlook for and consequences of a revenue-neutral corporate tax reform.

Effective Tax Rate Comparisons

Several important features affect the interpretation of the comparative tax rates: the type of rate, what taxes are included, and the use of weighted measures to adjust for size differences. A number of tax rate comparisons follow the discussion of these features.

Types of Tax Rates

Three basic types of tax rates are reported: the statutory rate, the effective rate, and the marginal effective rate. The statutory rate is the rate in the tax statute; in the case of the United States, it is the top marginal corporate tax rate of 35%. The effective rate is determined by the ratio of taxes paid divided by profits. The effective rate captures the tax benefits that reduce the taxable income base relative to financial profits. The marginal tax rate is calculated from a projected investment project: it estimates the share of the pre-tax return that is paid in taxes.

Each type of tax rate has its advantages and disadvantages, and is useful for considering certain types of behavior. For example, the statutory rate would potentially affect firms' attempts to shift profits by altering the source of borrowing or transferring assets or products at prices that are not arm's length.[5] Even the statutory rate, however, needs some adjustments for this purpose. For example, most multinational firms in the United States are eligible for the production activities deduction, which reduces the U.S. statutory tax rate by 9%, from 35% to 31.85%.

The effective tax rate is taxes paid divided by profits. The effective tax rate captures some of the tax benefits and subsidies, reducing the tax paid per dollar of profit. This measure can make a country with a high statutory rate but narrow base more comparable to a country with a low tax rate and broad base. It is probably more suited to assessing the true relative burdens on investment than the statutory tax rate. However, these types of tax rates may not capture timing effects (such as accelerated depreciation) very well and generally depend on accounting measures of profit that may vary across countries.

The marginal effective tax rate is, in theory, the appropriate measure for determining the effects of tax rate differentials on investment. However, in some cases marginal tax rates do not include all of the components of investment; frequently, they are restricted to investment in fixed assets or fixed assets and inventory. This report estimates an overall marginal effective tax rate that includes inventories and intangibles as well as buildings and equipment. Marginal tax rates also depend on estimates of economic depreciation, expected inflation, and rates of return.

Also briefly discussed is a measure referred to as the effective average tax rate. The implications of this tax rate, which combines statutory and marginal effective rates, are not clear.

Types of Taxes Included

Most tax measures reflect the effect of both national and sub-national corporate income taxes. Of the 31 Organisation for Economic Co-operation and Development (OECD) countries, 8 countries (Canada, Germany, Japan, South Korea, Luxembourg, Portugal, Switzerland, and the United States) have sub-national corporate taxes. In some cases, these sub-national taxes are more significant than those in the United States. In the case of the United States, these corporate income taxes imposed by the state increase the statutory rate (without the production activities deduction) to 39.2%. With the production activities deduction, the combined rate is 36.3%.[6]

Countries can also have other taxes that impose a burden on capital. In the United States, these taxes are imposed by the states and localities, and they include property taxes, franchise taxes, and retail sales taxes that apply to capital goods. These taxes are much more difficult to measure and are generally not included in comparative tax rate measures, although one study (discussed below) includes franchise, and transfer and sales taxes, but not property or wealth taxes.

Simple (Unweighted) versus Weighted Averages of Tax Rates

Another issue that affects the comparisons between U.S. and worldwide tax rates is whether tax rates are simple (unweighted) averages or whether they are weighted in some fashion to indicate their relative importance. If tax rates are not weighted, then a small economy, such as Iceland, can have the same effect on the average of international rates as a large economy, such as Germany or Japan. In general, smaller countries tend to have lower tax rates and thus unweighted averages are lower than weighted averages in most cases. In the results presented in this report, both weighted and unweighted averages are reported, but weighted averages are more relevant to making comparisons of measures of the tax burden on capital deployed around the world.

Tax Rate Comparisons: United States Compared with OECD and Large Economies

Table 1 reports the three measures of effective tax rates, with marginal rates restricted to equipment and structures separately, for the United States and the OECD excluding the United States. The statutory rate is reported with and without the production activities deduction.

The overall statutory rates are slightly lower, although similar, for 2012, with the rate in the OECD excluding the United States falling a little over a half a percentage point. The U.S. rate is estimated at 39.1%, while the OECD weighted average is 28.9% and the unweighted average is 24.9%.[7]

The marginal tax rates do not reflect the effect of the production activities deduction that likely applies to most multinational corporations and would decrease these tax rates by 2-3 percentage points as of 2010. (The deduction was 3% in 2005-2006 and 6% for 2007-2009.) Thus while the difference between the statutory rate and the simple average—a difference of 13.7 percentage points—is frequently reported, a difference of about half that much—or 6.6 percentage points— occurs when the adjusted statutory rate of 36.2% is compared with the weighted average of 29.6%. ‘

The effective tax rate (which would automatically capture the production activities deduction and other provisions) is about the same. The marginal effective rate rates are also about the same when adjusted. Thus the tax rate most relevant for the purpose of incentives to invest is similar for the United States and the rest of the OECD with respect to equipment and structures investment.

Table 1. Corporate Tax Rates, United States and Rest of the OECD

Tax Rate Measure and Year	United States	OECD Excluding United States, GDP Weighted Average	OECD Excluding United States, Unweighted Average
Statutory (2010)	39.2	29.6	25.5
Statutory (2010) with Production	36.3	29.6	25.5
Activities Deduction			
Effective (2008)	27.1	27.7	23.3
Marginal Effective Equipment (2010)	23.6	21.2	17.3
Marginal Effective Equipment (2005)	23.0	21.1	18.7
Marginal Effective Buildings (2005)	29.0	26.4	23.4

Source: Statutory tax rates and gross domestic product (GDP), Organisation for Economic Co-operation and Development (OECD), http://www.oecd.org /dataoecd/26/56/33717459.xls and http://stats.oecd.org/Index.aspx? Dataset Code=SNA_TABLE1. Effective tax rate from Price WaterhouseCoopers, *Global Effective Tax Rate Comparisons—Methodology and Results*. Marginal tax rates, 2005, Institute for Fiscal Studies, http://www.ifs.org.uk/ publications/3210. Marginal tax rates 2010, Arparna Mathur and Kevin Hassett, *Report Card on Effective Corporate Tax Rates*, American Enterprise Institute, http://www.aei.org /outlook/101024. PriceWaterhouseCoopers reports similar effective tax rate data in their study Global Effective Tax Rates, April 14, 2011, at http://businessroundtable.org/uploads/studies-reports/downloads/Effective_Tax_ Rate_Study.pdf.

The marginal tax rates do not reflect the temporary bonus depreciation in effect for 2008-2010 in the United States, which allowed 50% of the cost of equipment to be deducted. A provision allowing 100% of the cost to be deducted is in place for 2011. Because these are temporary provisions, it seems appropriate to exclude them. Whether these measures are captured in the effective tax rate depends on the treatment of deferred taxes, but measures from different years appear similar.

The OECD excludes some large countries, such as China and Brazil. Table 2 provides the statutory and effective tax rate comparisons for the 15 largest countries, which account for three-quarters of world gross domestic product (GDP). The results are similar to those in Table 1 with the weighted average about 1 percentage point higher. With the production activities deduction the rates differ by 5.6 percentage points. The effective rate is the same.

Table 2. Corporate Tax Rates in the 15 Largest Countries

Tax Rate Measure and Year	United States	Remaining 14 Large Countries, GDP Weighted Average	Remaining 14 Large Countries, Unweighted Average
Statutory (2010)	39.2	30.7	29.8
Statutory (2010) Including	36.3	30.7	29.8
Production Activities Deduction			
Effective (2008)	27.1	27.2	25.3

Source: Statutory tax rates are at http://www.worldwide-tax.com/#partthree; effective tax rates are from same source as Table 1. GDP is from the World Bank http://siteresources.worldbank.org/DATA STATISTICS/ Resources/GDP.pdf.

Table 3, Table 4, and Table 5 provide results for effective tax rates from other studies. Table 3 reports the Markle and Shackleford study that estimates the effective tax rate of domestic firms in different countries. Because a smaller number of countries are examined, Table 3 compares the U.S. rate with that of the six large countries.

Table 3. Effective Corporate Tax Rates, United States Compared with Six Countries

Tax Rate Measure	United States	Six Large Countries, GDP Weighted Average	Six Large Countries, Unweighted Average
Effective (2005-2009)	23.0	24.5	26.2

Source: Kevin S. Markle and Douglas A. Shackleford, "Cross-Country Comparisons of Corporate Income Taxes," working paper, February 2011.

Note: The six countries are Canada, France, Germany, India, Japan, and United Kingdom.

Table 4 and Table 5 report the Swenson and Lee study that estimated effective rates for firms headquartered in various countries for 2006 and 2007. The tables report for 2006 pre-dated the start of the recession and do not include years with bonus depreciation. Both results confirm the findings of other studies: effective tax rates in the United States and in other countries are similar.

Table 4. Effective Tax Rates, United States and OECD

Tax Rate Measure	United States	OECD Excluding United States, GDP Weighted Average	OECD Excluding United States, Unweighted Average
Effective (2006)	29.5	28.4	23.7

Source: Charles Swenson and Namryoung Lee, "The Jury Is In: U.S. Companies are Overtaxed Relative to Their International Competitors," AICPA, July 17, 2008, at http://www.cpa2 biz.com/Content/media/ PRODUCER_CONTENT/Newsletters /Articles_2008/Tax/juryin.jsp. Rate table at https://media.cpa2biz.com/ newsletter /2008/Tax/july/juryin_table.htm.

Table 5. Effective Tax Rates in the 15 Largest Countries

Tax Rate Measure	United States	Remaining 14 Large Countries, GDP Weighted Average	Remaining 14 Large Countries, Unweighted Average
Effective (2006)	29.5	28.7	27.3

Source: Charles Swenson and Namryoung Lee, "The Jury Is In: U.S. Companies are Overtaxed Relative to Their International Competitors, AICPA, July 17, 2008, at http://www.cpa2biz.com /Content/media/PRODUCER_CONTENT/Newsletters/Articles_2008/Tax/juryin.jsp. Rate table at https://media.cpa2biz.com/ newsletter /2008/Tax/july/juryin_table.htm.

Table 6 returns to the estimates of marginal effective tax rates, and expands the marginal rate analysis to reflect the other categories of assets, inventories, and intangibles. It provides a weighted average of these tax rates, using data on capital stock shares from the United States but applying the same shares to other countries. Note that intangibles are generally taxed at negative tax rates both in the United States and abroad. Expenditures on research, advertising, and human capital investment are generally deducted when incurred, which leads to a zero effective tax rate, and most countries (including the United States) have additional subsidies or credits for research expenditures.

Table 6. Marginal Effective Tax Rates, United States and Weighted OECD

	U.S. Without Production Activities Deduction	U.S. With Production Activities Deduction	OECD Excluding United States, OECD, GDP Weighted	OECD Excluding United States, GDP Weighted, Adjusted by Statutory Rate Changes
Equipment	23.0	21.2	21.1	18.9
Structures	29.0	26.7	26.4	23.6
Inventories	39.2	36.2	29.6	29.6
Intangibles	-4.7	-4.7	-9.7	-9.7
Total	22.2	20.2	18.3	16.4

Source: Tax rates on equipment and structures from Table 1, Inventories taxed at statutory rates. Tax rates on intangibles, Department of Finance, Canada, *Tax Expenditures and Evaluations 2009 : Part 2, An International Comparison of Tax Assistance for Investment in Research and Development*, http://www.fin.gc.ca /taxexp-depfisc/2009/ taxexp0902-eng.asp. Weights are 24.2% equipment, 39.6% structures, 9.7% inventories, and 26.5% intangibles. For intangibles, 49% arise from R&D, which is taxed at rates of -10.1% in the U.S, -22.2% in the weighted OECD average, and -54.2% in the simple OECD average. The remaining intangibles arising from human capital investment and advertising are taxed at a 0 rate. Data on corporate equipment, structures, and inventories for 2003 from Flow of Funds Accounts 1995-2004, p. 96, http://www.federalreserve.gov /Releases/Z1/Current/ annuals/a1995-2004.pdf. Estimates of intangibles from Carol Corrado, Charles Hulten, and Daniel Sichel, *Intangible Capital and Economic Growth*, Finance and Economic Discussion Series, Division of Research and Statistics Federal Reserve Board, 2006-4, http://www.federalreserve.gov /releases/z1/20050921/z1.pdf.

As Table 6 indicates, the overall marginal effective tax rates for the United States accounting for the production activities deduction and for the OECD countries weighted by GDP are similar, 20% and 18%. The differences are larger if the OECD rate is adjusted by average statutory rate changes that have occurred in these OECD countries since 2005, although base broadening could offset that reduction.[8] Marginal tax rates are also significantly lower than the statutory rates: the U.S. rate is about half the statutory rate and the weighted OECD rate is about 60% of the statutory rate. The next measure is another marginal tax rate measure (Chen and Mintz). This measure has a number of differences from those in Table 1 and Table 4. It includes equipment, structures, inventories, and land, but not intangibles. It also includes the effects of transfer taxes that fall on capital and debt finance. In the United States, these taxes are primarily state and local retail sales taxes that apply to capital goods purchases or inputs into construction and are quite large. It also includes franchise taxes. It does not, however, include wealth, capital stock, or property taxes. The measure also allows for debt finance and uses capital stock weights for Canada. Table 7 reports these estimates for the OECD. Based on comments made in a previous analysis, indicating the size of these additional state and local taxes, the table reports a number with these additional taxes subtracted out to allow more comparability to other results. As compared with the numbers in Table 6, the discrepancy in the weighted OECD and the United

States is larger. If the adjusted rates in Table 6 are recomputed to exclude intangibles, they would be 28.7% for the United States and 23% for the OECD (weighted). This differential of 5.7 points shrinks to 3.8 points when intangibles are included. The only other differential is that these rates should be lowered to reflect the effects of debt finance. Normally, higher statutory tax rates result in a larger negative tax rate on debt, so the United States rate should fall more for this reason (although this effect can vary with inflation). The differential between the United State and the OECD as reported in the original study is 16.2 percentage points (34.6% minus 18.4%). Out of that differential, 5.2 points are due to using an unweighted average, 5.0 points are due to including transfer taxes, 1.9 points are due to excluding intangibles, and the remaining 4.1 points are similar to the difference found in Table 6.

Table 7. Marginal Tax Rates Including Transfer and Franchise Taxes, United States Compared with the OECD

Tax Rate Measure	United States	OECD Excluding United States, GDP Weighted Average	OECD Excluding United States, Unweighted Average
Average Marginal Tax Rate 2010	34.6	23.6	18.4
Average Marginal Tax Rate Correcting for Additional Taxes	27.6	21.6	16.4

Source: Duanjie Chen and Jack Mintz, "New Estimates of Effective Corporate Tax Rates on Business Investment," CATO Institute Tax and Budget Bulletin, No. 64, February 2011, http://www.cato.org/pubs/tbb/ tbb_64.pdf. Indications that transfer taxes added 7 points for the United States and 2 points for other countries on average is from the previous year's tax rates, "U.S. Effective Corporate Tax Rate on New Investments: Highest in the OECD," May 2010.

An updated study for 2012 shows similar relationships. The United States tax rate was 35.6%, the OECD excluding the United States was 24.0% weighted and 19.6% unweighted.[9]

Table 8 reports the comparative rates for the 15 largest countries. These rates are closer together, and quite close when adjusted for transfer taxes.

The Chen and Mintz study makes an important point, namely that other taxes outside of the corporate tax can affect the relative burden of tax in a way that could affect investment. (These types of taxes would not be relevant for profit shifting.) The main reservation about this finding is that the inclusion of these other capital taxes is partial. The other main capital tax in the United States is the property tax, which probably adds another 3 percentage points to the rate, but other countries also have property taxes as well as wealth taxes.[10]

Table 9 reports a fourth type of tax rate measure, which is named by its developers the "effective average tax rate." Estimates using this method differentiate between a normal (or riskless) return, which is taxed at an effective rate that reflects the various tax benefits such as accelerated depreciation, and the excess return, which is taxed at the statutory rate. Thus, it is a mix of marginal tax rates and statutory tax rates. This measure is reported because it is available and cited by some researchers. Some evidence suggests that it is a better predictor of location than other measures.[11] It shows U.S. taxes to be significantly higher than OECD rates, but the implications of such a measure for economic behavior are not clear.

Table 8. Marginal Effective Tax Rates Including Transfer Taxes, 15 Largest Countries

Tax Rate Measure	United States	Remaining Large 14 Countries, GDP Weighted Average	Remaining Large 14 Countries Excluding U.S. – Unweighted Average
Average Marginal Tax Rate 2010	34.6	26.3	27.0
Average Marginal Tax Rate	27.6	24.3	25.0
Correcting for Additional State and			
Local Taxes			

Source: Duanjie Chen and Jack Mintz, "New Estimates of Effective Corporate Tax Rates on Business Investment," CATO Institute Tax and Budget Bulletin, No. 64 ,February 2011, http://www.cato.org/pubs/tbb/tbb_64.pdf. Indications that transfer taxes added 7 points for the United States and 2 points for other countries on average is from the previous year's tax rates, "U.S. Effective Corporate Tax Rate on New Investments: Highest in the OECD," May 2010.

Economists sometimes, when examining investment subsidies, differentiate between the normal and excess return. The normal return's tax burden is affected by items such as accelerated depreciation and investment subsidies, whereas the excess profit is subject to the statutory rate. In these views, however, it is the tax on normal return that would, in any case, affect economic behavior. The excess return is generally seen as bearing little or no tax burden because the reduction in expected return due to tax is offset by the reduction in variance of after tax return (i.e., the tax reduces gains and losses).

One reason that a combination of statutory and effective marginal rates might have an effect on location is that firms may locate some physical activity in a country to facilitate profit shifting associated with setting up subsidiaries to exploit developed intangibles.[12]

Table 9. "Effective Average Tax Rate," United States and OECD

Tax Rate Measure	United States	Most OECD Excluding United States, GDP Weighted Average	Most OECD Excluding United States, Unweighted Average
Effective Average (2009)	37.4	29.8	24.3

Source: Michael P. Devereux, Christina Elschner, Dieter Endres, and Christoph Spengel, "Effective Tax Rates Using the Devereux-Griffith Methodlogy," ZEW Center for European Economic Research, October 2009, http://ec.europa.eu/taxation_customs/resources/documents /common /publications/studies/etr_company_tax.pdf. This research was focused on the European Union and selected additional countries; it excludes Australia, Chile, Iceland, New Zealand, Mexico, and Korea.

Summing up

This comparison suggests some important precautions in comparing tax rates. First, it is important when forming a composite rate for the rest of the world to weight the tax rates by output or some other measure of economic importance. Because small countries tend to have lower rates than large ones, comparing rates using simple averages across countries exaggerates the differential between the United States and tax burdens elsewhere in the world. Second, weighted statutory tax rates differ but effective tax rates do not. Marginal effective tax rates have small differences. Third, in comparing the differences in statutory rates, the effect of the production activities deduction narrows the differential by close to half. Finally, although the role of subnational taxes outside of the corporate tax appears to be important for investment decisions, a full comparison has yet to be made. This analysis suggests that reform of state and local sales taxes could contribute to a more efficient system.

ECONOMIC EFFECTS OF A U.S. RATE CUT

The previous analysis has shown that U.S. statutory corporate tax rates are about 10 percentage points higher than a weighted average of the OECD or the large countries that account for most of output (7 percentage points when including the production activities deduction). Effective tax rates are about the same, and marginal effective tax rates are only slightly larger in the United States. The effects of including other capital taxes have not yet been explored on a comprehensive basis, although U.S. retail sales taxes on capital goods and franchise taxes are estimated to create an additional 5 percentage point differential.

This section explores the effects of a U.S. rate cut on the United States. The first subsection examines the effects on revenue, output, and national income for a corporate rate cut in isolation, only looking at capital flows. The second subsection discusses potential implications for profit shifting. The third subsection considers the possibility that other countries would react to a U.S. rate cut by cutting their rates as well. Finally, discussions of outlook for and consequences of a revenue neutral corporate tax reform are presented.

Effects on Revenue, Output, and National Welfare, Assuming No Tax Rate Changes by Other Countries or Offsetting Base Broadening in the United States

This section examines the effects of a corporate rate cut from 35% to 25% on revenues and international capital flows, and their effects on the U.S. economy (including feedback effects on revenues and effects on national welfare). It focuses on issues specific to global economy considerations of the corporate tax, not the traditional corporate tax issues that would also occur in a closed economy.

Revenues

The Congressional Budget Office (CBO) projects a 10-year corporate revenue of $4,360 billion from FY2013 to FY20221.[13] If this number were multiplied by 10/35 to estimate the revenue loss, the result would be $1,245 billion per year, on average.[14] The loss, however, is likely to be larger because net tax liability is the tax rate times taxable income, minus credits. Rate changes would not normally affect credits, and, if not, the revenue loss would be projected based on tax liability before credits. According to Internal Revenue Service (IRS) data, corporate tax before credits is 134% of corporate tax after credits.[15]

One of the major credits, the foreign tax credit, would be affected, in some cases, by a rate cut. The foreign tax credit is limited to the U.S. tax because of foreign source income, so as the U.S. rate falls, the limit on credits also falls. In some cases, the credit would not be affected, or not affected proportionally, because the foreign tax credits are less than the limit and a change in the limit would not necessarily change foreign tax credits. (These firms are termed excess limit firms.) In other cases, firms have creditable taxes above the limit; with credits equal to the limit, a reduction in the limit would reduce foreign tax credits proportionally. (These firms are termed excess credit firms.)

Tax liability after the foreign tax credit but before other credits (general business credits and the alternative minimum tax credit) is 105.7% of tax liability after all credits. If foreign tax credits are reduced proportionally, the average loss is almost $132 billion. If foreign tax credits are not affected at all, the average loss per year is $168 billion.[16]

These estimates suggest that over the 10-year period, $1.3 trillion to $1.7 trillion would be lost in revenues due to the proposed rate cut. This number does not include any behavioral feedback effects, which could reduce the cost, but also does not include debt service or crowding out of private capital, which would increase the cost.

Estimates implied by this calculation are larger than projections based on a percentage point rate increase contained in CBO's Budget Options which, applying the percentage loss to the new baseline suggests revenue losses of about $1,113 trillion.[17] Some part of the discrepancy may reflect the fact that liabilities lag collections and that the first full year does not apply because estimates are based on fiscal years. In addition, to the extent that firms have unused foreign credits, a rate increase would raise less than reduction of the same size would cost. Other behavioral effects may occur as well.

Regardless of the precise estimate, a revenue loss in excess of $1 trillion and in excess of $100 billion a year would be expected over the next ten years.

Effects on U.S. Output and Wages

What about the effects on the U.S. economy? The discussion sometimes focuses on job creation. Job creation is an important issue for the government to address during cyclical downturns. Standard economic theory suggests such policies should be temporary; in contrast, advocates of corporate rate cuts are proposing permanent cuts. In any case, temporary or permanent corporate rate cuts are unlikely to be very effective stimulus policies.[18]

Economic theory suggests that there is no reason to view general job creation as a long-run objective of government policies. The economy can generate the jobs needed by the natural process of growth and market adjustment. In 1961 and 1991, the unemployment rate was the same, 6.7%. Employment, however, rose from 66 million to 117 million. Employment tends to grow steadily; the unemployment rate fluctuates. Long-term jobs policies, according to economic theory, therefore, should not be aimed at increasing jobs, although they can be designed to reduce structural or frictional unemployment (such as improving the skills of disadvantaged workers).[19]

Rather, the capital flows induced by a corporate rate cut generally have effects on the level of output and on wage levels, rather than the number of workers. Despite the claimed effects of cutting the corporate tax on encouraging the flow of foreign-owned capital into the country from abroad (inbound capital) or discouraging the flow of U.S. capital to other countries (outbound capital), there are many forces that constrain the movement of capital. As capital flows into a country, its greater abundance coupled with a fixed amount of labor drives the wage rate up and the rate of return down, so that the pre-tax return to capital falls. If the economy is large enough to affect the rest of the world's returns, the proportional flow of capital is lessened further, because shift of capital from abroad (with no change in taxes) raises the after tax return abroad and draws some of the capital back. Capital flows are further reduced if there are significant non-corporate sectors (because a rate cut would draw capital from the unincorporated sectors of the economy as well as from abroad). Finally, the flow of capital would be further limited if capital is not perfectly mobile or products are not perfect substitutes.

A study by Gravelle and Smetters used a general equilibrium model to capture the effects of imposing a 35% tax, allowing for four sectors in the U.S. economy and a mirror foreign economy.[20] The estimated change in the capital stock, assuming the conditions most conducive to capital inflows, was 4.5%. (This scenario assumes that individuals and firms view investments in different locations as perfect substitutes and consumers view foreign and domestic products as perfect substitutes; these are referred to as the portfolio and product substitution elasticities and are set, effectively, at infinity.)[21] This effect implies a 4.7% increase from eliminating the tax (4.5/(1-4.5)). To convert a percentage change in the capital stock to a percentage change in output, multiply by the capital share of income, which was 0.29, to get a 1.36% increase in output. Because a partial change is proposed, multiply by 10/35 to obtain an estimated percentage change in output of 0.39%. With constant factor shares, which are assumed in this model, wages will also increase by this percentage.[22]

A similar magnitude of effects can be obtained by examining revenue reductions and incidence estimates for this same perfectly mobile case. CBO projects the corporate tax at 2% of GDP.[23] This revenue is as a percentage of gross output (which includes output that replaces capital and thus is not a part of an income concept). To convert it to a percentage of net of depreciation output (which is 82% of gross output[24]), divide by 0.82, for corporate revenues that are 2.27% of domestically generated income. To capture the effect of reducing the tax by 10 percentage points, multiply by 10/35, to obtain a tax cut of 0.65% of income. Incidence studies indicate that about 73% of the burden of the corporate tax falls on labor under this perfectly mobile assumption,[25] so this number is multiplied by 0.73 to obtain an increase in labor income of 0.47% of total income. Based on national income accounts, the share of labor income is 76%,[26] so dividing 0.47 by 0.76 yields a 0.62% increase in output and in wages.

Both estimates suggest a relatively small effect on output, of around 0.5%, but this estimate is too large. Perfect product substitution is not possible in a multi-good economy.[27] Moreover, empirical evidence suggests elasticities that are smaller. Gravelle and Smetters propose as a more reasonable case a model with portfolio and product substitution elasticities of 3. This assumption yields a 1.6% change in the capital stock. Following the methodology outlined above, the effect on output and wages is 0.13%, rather than 0.4%. These elasticities reduce the share of the burden borne by labor to 21% and, again, following the same methodology would cause an output and wage effect of about 0.18% rather than 0.62%.[28]

Two other aspects might make these effects even lower or perhaps reverse the sign. First, the effect of debt capital is not incorporated into any of these models. Because about a third of the capital stock is financed by debt, the magnitude of the first set of estimates (using capital stock estimates) should be reduced by about one-third to account for the presence of debt.

This would be the expected outcome if returns to debt-financed investment were taxed at a zero rate, as would be the case if there were no inflation and no accelerated depreciation. However, since both of these conditions exist in the U.S. tax code, debt is subsidized at the corporate level because inflation is generally positive and the effective marginal tax rate is below the statutory rate. Lowering the statutory rate reduces these subsidies and discourages debt. This effect may be desirable for issues such as the debt-equity distortion, but can actually discourage capital inflows, as suggested in one study.[29]

Second, the estimates of capital stock assume that the United States has a territorial tax (i.e., the only tax due is on domestic profits). Although a relatively small share of foreign source income is taxed, the U.S. system is not fully territorial, but rather defers the tax until income is repatriated (except for branch income and some passive income that is easily shifted).[30] Under the U.S. system, the tax on income that is repatriated or currently taxed can be partially or fully offset by credits for foreign taxes paid. Most foreign source income is not taxed either because it is not repatriated or because credits are used to offset the tax; in addition to credits for tax paid in a country, unused credits from countries with higher taxes than the United States can be used to offset tax on income repatriated from low tax countries (called cross crediting).[31]

Effects on National Income and National Welfare

Even though output (or domestically generated income) increases by small amounts, that output gain does not represent a gain in U.S.-worldwide income. The gains that labor experiences are offset by the losses in the pre-tax return by the existing domestic capital, reducing the benefits of these firms. For example, in the case where labor income increases by 21% of the tax, existing capital, which absent capital flows would have had income increase by 100% of the tax cut, now has that increase offset roughly by 21% of the tax due to the lower pretax return. Although labor and capital both have higher after tax income, there is a transfer between the government and individuals, which must be offset by other tax increases or reduced spending either now or in the future.

Although there will be some gains in national welfare, they are likely to be only a small fraction of the revenue change. They would arise from income that transfers from foreigners to U.S. persons.[32] For thinking about this effect, consider separately inbound capital (capital owned by foreigners and invested in the United States) and outbound capital (capital owned by U.S. persons and invested abroad). The increase in inbound capital generates returns, but those returns are the income of the foreign investors. Thus, the only gain for the United States is the change in taxes, and the lower pre-tax rate of return on inbound investment. For outbound capital, the returns already belong to U.S. firms, and the gain is from moving capital back into the United States where taxes formerly paid to foreign governments are paid to the United States.

A recent study examined these effects, using data on foreign and domestic tax rates from a 2008 GAO study and estimates of inbound and outbound capital from the National Income and Product Accounts and found modest effects.[33] The estimated output effects in this study were larger than those calculated above because the study used a partial equilibrium framework with a simplified single sector model designed to distinguish between outbound and inbound capital flows. The purpose, however, was to consider the general magnitude of welfare effects. The estimates found that there was a slight *loss* (3% of the additional output) for inbound capital because the reduction in the tax rate on existing capital inflows was less than fully offset by taxes on induced capital flows and the small reduction in pre-tax returns. For outbound capital, the main source of increased capital, there was a gain of 12% of output because taxes on this capital were paid to the United States rather than foreign governments. Overall, only about 9% of the output increase was a benefit to the United States which, for the magnitude of effects calculated, is less than two-hundredth of 1% of output and less than 3% of revenue.

These findings are quite consistent with optimal tax theories. For inbound capital, the optimal tax rate should be 1/(1+e) where e is the elasticity of the flow of inbound capital.[34] Because the study used an estimated effective tax rate of 25% and the optimal tax rate is 25% when e is 3, a negligible effect on welfare would be expected. For outbound capital, the optimality rule is to tax foreign source income net of foreign taxes for a small country, with a slightly higher rate on outbound capital returns for a large country.[35] Because current tax rules impose taxes much smaller than this rate and cause too much capital to be allocated abroad, cutting the U.S. tax rate improves welfare. However, the effects are small compared with either the U.S. economy or revenue.[36]

Revenue Feedback Effects

A final issue is the magnitude of revenue feedbacks from the output increase. Recall that the corporate tax cut discussed is about 0.65% of net output.

This increase in output is taxed with a mix of both labor and capital taxes. The marginal tax rate on labor income is estimated by CBO at 28.4% and the capital income tax rate is estimated at 11.5%.[37] The 11.5% is further reduced by 2 percentage points to account for the reduction in the corporate rate, to 9.5%. The overall marginal tax rate is 23.7%. Multiplying the 0.13% and the 0.18% increases in output by 23.7% yields an offset of 4.7% to 6.6%. (If infinite elasticities were assumed and the output effects of 0.4% and 0.62% were considered the feedback effects would be from 14% to 23% of revenue.)

There are three reasons this feedback effect is probably too large (aside from the reservations about output effects due to debt finance discussed above). First, this tax on labor income does not account for the expectation that increases in labor income might be partially received through tax exempt employee fringe benefits or partially spent on tax favored purchases (such as charitable contributions). Second, absent other changes the share of individual taxes collected as payroll taxes would eventually lead to increased outlays for Social Security. Finally, the transition to the new capital stock will not be immediate.

In all the scenarios, these revenue offsets from behavioral changes would likely be smaller than the increase in revenue due to debt service, which is estimated at 25% on average over the 10- year period. In addition, if the increase in the debt displaces the capital stock, output would be reduced by 2021 enough to reduce revenues by 15% to 23% of the static cost. If revenues are not offset, and the increased debt crowds out the U.S. capital stock, output would be reduced about, 0.4% by 2021, an effect more than twice as large as the effects estimated from international capital inflows.[38]

Profit Shifting and Revenue Effects

Another aspect of behavior that is of concern for revenue is the possibility of profit shifting. It is more difficult to judge this effect. Because the evidence discussed above suggests that the revenue offset from corporate rate changes due to investment flows is likely in the neighborhood of 5%, real output effects do not appear large enough to make a corporate rate cut pay for itself in increased revenues, as some advocates claim.

Before examining profit shifting directly, consider the evidence cited to support the argument that there is a significant revenue shift. First, proponents point to studies that indicate a "Laffer curve" with a revenue maximizing tax rate of around 30%, using cross country panel data. These four studies were reviewed in a CRS report that found, due to both interpretation of the studies by proponents and statistical problems, these studies did not appear to support a gain in revenue from a cut in the U.S. tax rate.[39]

Proponents also make the general argument that the United States collects a smaller share of revenue relative to GDP than other countries, even though its rate is higher. For example, Hassett points out that the U.S. corporate revenue is 2% of GDP whereas the revenue of most other countries is 3%, and that the share has grown in some countries as rates have decreased.[40] Two factors other than profit shifting affect corporate revenues and their changes as a percent of GDP, the size of the base and the share of business income (and income in general) that is corporate source. Data shown earlier indicates that although the statutory rate is higher in the United States, the effective rate is not. Revenues patterns over time will reflect a combination of rate changes and base changes, and some countries financed some or all of their recent rate reductions with base broadening.[41] In addition, the size of the corporate sector will be affected by the ability of firms to operate in noncorporate form. A 2007 study by the U.S. Department of Treasury indicates that the U.S. rules allowing large firms to operate in noncorporate form are more generous than those of other countries. It also documented that the share of business income received by corporations in the United States had declined from 80% to 50% as more generous limits of the number of shareholders small corporations could have to elect taxation as unincorporated businesses were adopted and special forms of business such a limited liability corporations, taxed as partnerships, grew.[42] A recent OECD study indicated that corporate tax revenues, in addition to offsetting base changes, were increased by incentives to operate firms in corporate form and additional compliance measures.[43]

It is possible to consider the effect of profit shifting by examining direct estimates of the cost of profit shifting. These estimates of profit shifting suggest that they amount to 14% to 20% of total corporate tax revenue, which would not be enough to offset the revenue loss even if profit shifting disappeared entirely.[44] How much of a reduction in profit shifting might reasonably be expected? Because the profit shifting clearly occurs to the very low tax rate countries,[45] even a cut to 25% would leave a large benefit to profit shifting (it would lead to a combined federal and state rate of 29.8%, and 27.7% for eligible firms if the production activities deduction were retained). Recent discussions of a plan referred to as the double-Irish, Dutch sandwich showed two companies that, having moved profits to Ireland (with a 12.5% rate), took further steps to shift profits to Bermuda (with a 0% rate).[46] Because the cost in most cases is small, most firms would probably continue to shift profits to the limit currently allowed by law as interpreted by the courts, and probably considerably less than proportionally to the tax rate change.

As discussed below, reforms to the tax treatment of foreign source income, by eliminating deferral and by restricting the foreign tax credit, or by focusing on limiting profit shifting techniques, might reduce the ability or benefits of profit-shifting and raise revenues.

Other Countries' Reactions to a U.S. Rate Reduction

An important policy issue for the United States is whether other countries might react to a U.S. rate reduction. Evidence shows that the initial cut in corporate tax rates around the world may have been triggered by the cut in the U.S. corporate tax rate from 48% to 35% from 1986 to 1988 as a result of the Tax Reform Act of 1986. Figure 1 shows the statutory tax rates, beginning in 1981, for the United States and for the remainder of the OECD. The U.S. combined state and federal tax rate was about 50% and fell to just below 40% over those two years. Except for a slight rise in 1993, the tax rate has remained constant ever since. Two OECD numbers are provided: the unweighted numbers varying with the admission of new OECD members as well as tax rates and the GDP weighted tax rates of the OECD nations (outside the United States) in 1981. (Tax rates are shown in the Appendix, and they also indicate that the weighted average holding member country constant is about a percentage point higher.) The tax rates for 2012 are similar to those for 2010: the unweighted average fell slightly from 25.5 to 24.9, but the weighted average was slightly higher, 29.8 compared to 29.6. The U.S. rate fell from 39.2% to 39.1%.[47] While the simple (unweighted) average, which includes new entrants to the OECD, suggests a relatively continuous decline in rates, the weighted average indicates a more discrete pattern of tax cuts. As indicated by the graph, tax rates on average were close together before 1987 but rates of other countries began dropping in the next few years. For the weighted OECD average, the first drop followed the U.S. tax cut, but subsequently, rates were relatively constant over the next several years (and still slightly above U.S. rates). Tax rates then fell again, but stabilized around 2002 and were relatively unchanged until 2007, when Germany began cutting its tax rate. The fall beginning in the late 1990s may have been associated with the lower tax rates of the emerging former eastern bloc countries. If one country cuts its tax rate, it attracts capital from other countries, which benefits labor and possibly overall national welfare, at the expense of other countries, as discussed above. However, if all countries cut their tax rates, none will gain capital but all will lose revenue. The observation of rate cuts in the rest of the world in the wake of the U.S. tax cut is not proof that countries will cut their rates again if the United States does, but it does provide some support for that expectation.

It is also possible that a smaller rate cut that does not move the United States to rates below those of other large countries would be less likely to trigger a response. For 2010, statutory tax rates for the next two largest countries in the remaining OECD, Japan and Germany, were 39.54% and 30.18% respectively, although Japan is proposing a 5 percentage point rate cut. The United Kingdom and France are respectively 28% and 34.4%, although the United Kingdom is planning further cuts to 24%. If the United States cut its federal rate to 25% its rate would be 29.8%; with the production activities deduction it would be 27.7%. A rate cut to 30% would result in a 34.5% rate (32% with the production activities deduction).[48] That rate would be similar to the rates in France, Japan, and Germany.

Revenue-Neutral Rate Reduction and Corporate Reform

If revenue concerns require offsetting corporate base broadening, what changes might be made and what are the consequences for international capital flows and profit shifting? This section discusses base broadening options, focusing on the largest corporate tax expenditures.

The base broadening provisions are listed in Table 10, along with the reduction in the corporate rate the revenue change would allow for. Note that while each proposal is stated in terms of the rate reduction its revision would permit, the rate reductions for several provisions taken together are slightly smaller than the sum of their individual rate reductions because the progressively lower rates make base broadening less valuable.

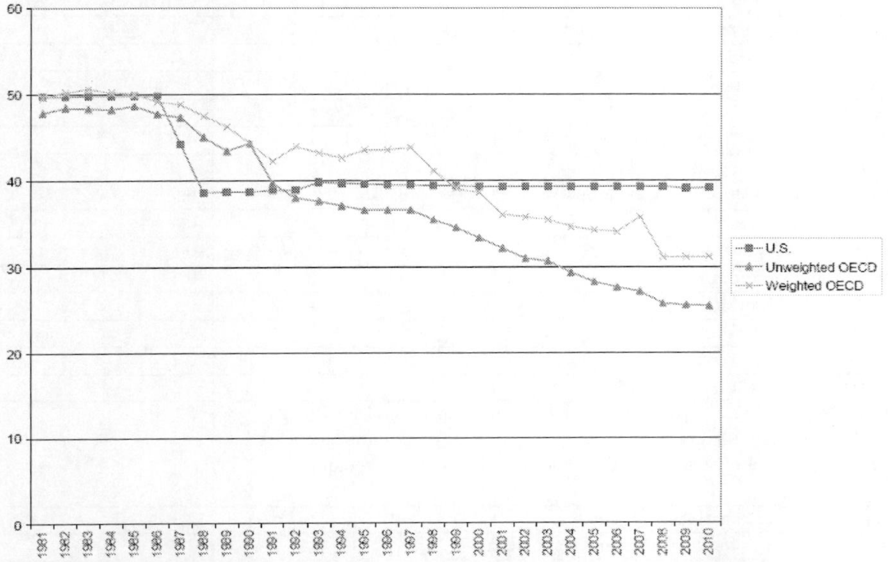

Source: CRS calculations based on tax rate data and GDP from the Organisation for Economic Co-operation and Development.

Notes: The weighted OECD measure provides for a constant set of initial countries, although this measure is only slightly different from that which covers all OECD countries with information available at any time. The unweighted measure includes the OECD countries in that year.

Figure 1. Statutory Tax Rates, United States and OECD (Excluding United States), 1981-2010.

Accelerated Depreciation

Of the items listed among corporate tax expenditures, the single largest provision is accelerated depreciation for equipment which, abstracting from the effect of temporary bonus depreciation, costs a little more than 6% of revenue and would allow a rate reduction of about 2 percentage points.[49] This measure is based on an alternative depreciation system. (Much more revenue would be raised in the short run, but revenue neutrality based on a 10-year budget window would lead to a long-run loss, because slowing depreciation leads to much larger revenue gains in the short run compared with the long run.) Equipment, in particular, is taxed at rates well below the statutory rate, at least at current inflation rates. Nevertheless, the desirability of restricting depreciation is unclear. A revenue neutral revision that cuts the rate in exchange for higher taxation of new investment would raise the marginal effective tax rate, because the rate reduction would apply to the return to existing capital. Moreover, estimates suggest that the value of depreciation under the alternative system would be too small and would tax investments at effective rates in excess of the statutory rates.[50] This provision would also raise revenues on unincorporated businesses, equivalent to about 30% of the corporate loss, which would permit a larger corporate rate reduction, by 3.3 percentage points. In addition, there is some accelerated depreciation for buildings, primarily rental housing, but the revenue losses are largely for unincorporated businesses.

Table 10. Rate Reduction Permitted by Certain Options

Possible Change in Provision	Percentage Point Reduction in Corporate Tax Rate
Eliminate Accelerated Depreciation for Equipment (steady state)	3.3
Repeal Production Activities Deduction	1.2
Taxation of Foreign Source Income	
—End Deferral	0.8
—End Deferral Plus Per Country Foreign Tax Credit Limit	4.0
—President Obama's Proposals	1.0
—Territorial Tax with Deduction Allocation	0.5
Repeal Title Passage Rule	0.4
Repeal LIFO Inventory Accounting	0.8
Eliminate Subsidies for Fossil Fuels	0.3
Eliminate Graduated Rates for Corporations	0.3
Eliminate Insurance Subsidies	0.1
Eliminate Credit Union Exemption	0.1
Eliminate Deduction for Inflation Portion of Interest	2.5
Eliminate all Corporate Tax Expenditures (foreign source provisions other than deferral and disallowing interest deductions not part of tax expenditures; includes other tax expenditures not listed, does not include benefits to unincorporated businesses)	5.6
Shifting Into Corporate Forma (see table notes)	2.3
Rolling Back 2003 Rates for Dividends and Capital Gainsb	4.0

Source: CRS calculations, see text.

Notes: These provisions are all estimated beginning at a 35% corporate rate and the sum would be larger than the combined effect. If evaluated at the lower rate the reduction would fall proportionally for most base broadening provisions, so the reduction would be 86% as large (.30/.35) if evaluated at a 30% rate.

a Assumes income distributed as in the early 1980s, a starting corporate rate of 30% and an individual rate of 30%. See text for other calculations.

b Assumes a lower realization elasticity consistent with more recent evidence. With elasticity currently in use by the Treasury Department, the reduction would be 2.3 percentage points.

Production Activities Deduction

The next largest tax expenditure is the production activities deduction, which allows a deduction of 9% of taxable income for domestic production for certain industries, primarily manufacturing, electricity and natural gas production, and construction. This provision has been estimated at $163.1 billion[51] over 10 years, which would allow a corporate tax rate reduction of 1.2 percentage points. This provision has been criticized as distorting the tax treatment of different industries by granting differential tax rates. In addition, it creates administrative and compliance problems in both distinguishing domestic content and identifying eligible activities. About a quarter of the cost benefits unincorporated businesses and these revenues are included in the above estimate; without those revenues the reduction would be under a percentage point.[52]

The only reservation about this deduction is that it is more likely to apply to multinationals because of the industry restrictions and a revenue neutral substitution could raise the true statutory rate. For example, a 1.2 percentage point reduction in the federal rate would allow, after interacting with state taxes, a reduction from 39.2% to 38.1%, whereas firms with the production activities deduction have a rate of 36.3%. One option would be to tailor the provision more closely to the characteristics of multinationals, including disallowing the deduction for unincorporated businesses and further restricting the eligible activities (e.g., disallow electricity production as a qualified activity), and use those revenues to cut the rate, while retaining the deduction. If restricted to corporate manufacturing most than half of revenues would be recouped.[53]

Tax Treatment of Foreign Source Income

The next largest tax expenditure after accelerated depreciation for equipment and the production activity deduction is the deferral of tax on foreign source income, which is projected at $114.2 billion over 10 years,[54] and it would permit a corporate tax rate reduction of 0.8 percentage points. This move toward worldwide tax would also, independently, increase the amount of capital in the United States by discouraging outbound capital and would reduce the benefit of profit shifting mechanisms, perhaps significantly. A much larger reduction would be possible, by about 4 percentage points rather than 0.8 percentage points, if the foreign tax credit were limited to offsetting tax only on income earned in that country as was proposed in S. 3018, 111th Congress.[55] This change would eliminate most cross-crediting and raise significantly more revenue; it would also be projected to gain a similar amount in welfare gain to the rate cut itself.[56]

Other revenue raising alternatives affecting taxation of foreign source income have been proposed. President Obama has proposed a set of revisions that is estimated to raise $129.2 billion over 10 years: the major proposals are disallowing interest and certain other deductions of the parent company to the extent income abroad is not taxed currently ($37.7 billion), limiting foreign tax credits that can offset income to the same share as the share of income repatriated ($51.4 billion), a provision to tax excess returns of intangibles ($20.8 billion), and limiting foreign tax credits for certain extractive companies ($10.8 billion). These provisions would allow a rate cut of about a percentage point.[57] An alternative would be to move to an actual territorial tax that exempts all active income earned abroad but disallows part of overhead expenses of parent companies, which is estimated to raise $76.2 billion[58] and allow a rate cut of 0.5 percentage points. There are many other revisions to the treatment of foreign source income that would raise varying amounts of revenue.[59]

Revenue offsets that increase the taxation of foreign source income can be significant and reinforce the capital flow and welfare effects of a rate cut in a global economy. Whether revenue increases from the treatment of foreign source income can be used as revenue offsets is unclear. Most proponents of rate reductions are also strong opponents of increasing the tax on foreign source income, and indeed favor lowering that tax burden, perhaps by moving to a territorial system without cost allocation, which would likely lose a small amount of revenue.[60] Such a change would reduce capital investment in the United States, although probably slightly, and offset the capital flow and welfare gains of a rate cut.

Title Passage Rule

The next largest tax expenditure is the sales source rule exception or the title passage rule. This provision is essentially an export subsidy, but, because of its design it is only available to multinational firms that have foreign operations and excess foreign tax credits. The provision allows half of income from sales of items to be allocated to the country in which the title passes for purposes of the foreign tax credit, which increases the limit on the foreign tax credit and the tax credits available for firms with excess credits.

It is difficult to justify this provision; the revenue gain from eliminating this provision of $53.7 billion over 10 years[61] would permit a reduction in the corporate tax rate of 0.4 percentage points.

LIFO Inventory Accounting

Another option is the repeal of LIFO (last in, first out) accounting, which allows firms to treat goods sold as the latest acquired; eliminating this provision would raise $97.5 billion over 10 years[62] and allow a 0.8 percentage point reduction in the corporate rate. Most firms do not use LIFO because they must conform tax and book methods.[63] There is, however, a justification for LIFO, in that, on average, it eliminates the tax on inflationary gains.[64]

Other Tax Expenditures and Base Broadening Provisions

There are several remaining tax expenditures but most are either small or would be questionable as offsets for a variety of reasons.[65] If every corporate tax expenditure were repealed, including those mentioned previously, the corporate rate could be cut by 5.6 percentage points, to 29.4%, assuming no behavioral responses.[66] (In the category addressing the treatment of foreign source income, only the deferral provision is a tax expenditure.)

Larger cuts could occur if the repeal of benefits for unincorporated businesses were used to cut corporate rates. Without revenue from the repeal of deferral, the rate would fall by approximately 0.8 percentage points less, or to 30.2%

The Joint Committee on Taxation estimates a rate of 28% for repeal of corporate preferences excluding deferral, but this estimate allows for higher gains from depreciation during the budget horizon. (They note this rate would not be revenue neutral in the long run).

The incentives for research and development, which taken together are larger[67] than the cost of the title passage rule, are popular provisions that have some economic justification, and, in the case of expensing, would be extremely difficult to administer. The research credit is temporary and the President's 2012 budget proposals would make it permanent. Special provisions for insurance companies are almost the size of the title passage rule, and would be an option as would the relatively smaller provisions for fossil fuels. The President's budget proposals would restrict insurance company provisions for a $14 billion gain (0.1 percentage point) and benefits for fossil fuels for a $43.6 billion gain (0.3 percentage points).[68] Provisions such as tax-exempt bonds or the low-income housing credit are, however, designed to benefit others (state and local governments or low-income tenants) and if the corporate benefit were removed, these activities would largely migrate to the unincorporated sector.

Lower rates for small corporations would allow a 0.3 percentage point reduction. Taxing income of credit unions would allow less than 0.1 percentage points. There are a number of energy subsidies that are directed at conservation whose repeal is not generally considered, as is the case for corporate charitable deductions.

In addition, there are also some tax expenditures that are not in the tax expenditure budget. For example, a tax reform bill introduced by then-Chairman of the Ways and Means Committee Rangel in the 110th Congress (H.R. 3970) included a provision extending the write period for acquired intangibles that raised $20 billion over 10 years.[69]

Limits on Interest Deductions

Restricting the deduction of interest would permit a significant reduction in rates. Although the benefits vary with expected inflation, disallowing the deduction for the inflation portion of interest is estimated to allow a reduction of the tax rate in the neighborhood of 2.5 percentage points and, in a closed economy, would be an efficient reform.[70] It might also reduce the use of debt as a method of profit shifting (by borrowing in high tax countries). There is, however, a reservation about this change when considering international capital flows: a revenue neutral change could decrease the net inflow of capital if debt is more mobile than equity.

Shifts between Individual and Corporate Taxes: Restrictions on Using the Non-Corporate Form, and Shifting Tax Burdens to the Shareholder Level

According to a Treasury study, the share of business income that is in corporate form has declined from 80% to 50% since the early 1980s, primarily through the increase in the number of shareholders for small corporations that are allowed to elect partnership treatment (Subchapter S corporations) and the growth in new organizational forms such as limited liability corporations that are taxed as partnerships.[71] Using the tax rates currently in effect, if all business owners moving to this form are in the top 35% tax bracket, and if dividends and capital gains are distributed and realized based on economy wide averages as well as being subject to the current 15% rate, returning to the early 1980s share would allow a rate cut of 3 percentage points without altering overall individual and corporate revenue.[72] Note, however, that the contribution to rate reduction declines rapidly as the corporate rate is cut. For example, a base broadener, such as those discussed above, that allowed a 3 percentage point rate cut starting at a 35% rate would allow a 2.6 percentage point reduction applying to a 30% rate and a 2.3 percentage point reduction starting at a 25% rate. The effect of moving operations to corporate form depends on the differential between the individual and corporate tax, and would reduce the rate by 1.3 percentage points starting at a 30% corporate rate, and actually raise the corporate rate if starting at a 25% rate. This potential rate reduction is larger, however, if the individual rate is lower. According to estimates, the average tax rate for all partnership and Subchapter S income is 30%.[73] In that case, the percentage point reductions are 5, 2.3, and 1.5, respectively, beginning at a 35%, 30%, and 25% corporate tax rate. Because these shifts into the noncorporate sector are driven by new forms of large companies, it is likely that the tax rate is higher than average for partnership and Subchapter S income (many partnerships, for example, are no different from proprietorships except they have two owners instead of one), but probably lower than the top rate. In a global economy, it is better to allow tax cuts within the corporate sector at the corporate rather than the individual level. One option is rolling back the 2003 cuts in dividends and capital gains, which would allow a rate cut of about 2.5 percentage points, and perhaps as much as 4 percentage points.[74] These increases in rates are scheduled to occur after 2012 when the Bush tax cuts expire, however, and whether they can be counted as revenue raisers depends on scoring options. The last two options interact, however. The more taxes are collected at the individual level by raising taxes on dividends and capital gains, the larger a rate reduction from shifting income into the corporate sectors. If dividends were taxed at full rates and capital gains at 20%, then at a 30% individual tax rate and a 35% corporate rate, the reduction is 6.5 percentage points. These effects depend as well, of course, on how the individual tax rate on ordinary income develops, which is currently scheduled to rise.

Summing up

This section has identified enough provisions to allow the corporate tax rate to be reduced to 25% without losing revenue over the long run (i.e., that do not depend on large short-run gains, such as those from reducing accelerated depreciation), but that would require going beyond corporate tax expenditures (which would account for only 5 percentage points) to business preferences associated with unincorporated businesses, foreign tax credit restrictions, or more fundamental reforms.

APPENDIX. STATUTORY TAX RATES, 1981-2010

Table A-1. Statutory Tax Rates in the United States and the Rest of the OECD Countries, 1981-2020

Year	United States	OECD Unweighted	OECD Weighted	OECD Weighted Fixed Countries
1981	49.7	47.8	49.6	49.6
1982	49.7	48.4	50.1	50.2
1983	49.8	48.3	50.5	50.6
1984	49.8	48.2	50.2	50.2
1985	49.8	48.6	50.0	50.0
1986	49.8	47.7	49.0	49.1
1987	44.2	47.3	48.7	48.8
1988	38.6	45.0	47.4	47.5
1989	38.7	43.4	46.2	46.2
1990	38.7	44.3	43.2	44.3
1991	38.9	39.7	44.1	42.2
1992	38.9	38.0	43.8	43.9
1993	39.8	37.6	43.1	43.2
1994	39.7	37.1	42.4	42.6
1995	39.6	36.6	43.1	43.5
1996	39.5	36.6	43.1	43.5
1997	39.5	36.6	43.3	43.8
1998	39.4	35.5	40.8	41.1
1999	39.4	34.6	38.8	39.1
2000	39.3	33.4	37.6	38.6
2001	39.3	32.2	35.5	36.1
2002	39.3	31.0	35	35.8
2003	39.3	30.7	34.6	35.5
2004	39.3	29.4	33.8	34.7
2005	39.3	28.3	33.1	34.3
2006	39.3	27.7	32.5	34.1
2007	39.3	27.2	32.0	35.8
2008	39.3	25.8	29.8	31.2
2009	39.1	25.6	29.6	31.2
2010	39.2	25.5	29.6	31.2

Source: Statutory tax rates and GDP, Organisation for Economic Co-operation and Development (OECD), http://www.oecd.org/dataoecd/26/56/33717459.xls and http://stats.oecd.org/Index.aspx?DatasetCode= SNA_TABLE1.

Note: The table provides the data incorporated into Figure 1; the OECD weighted line in that figure uses fixed countries.

End Notes

[1] These advocates include several economists. For example, see Kevin Hassett, "Let's Cut Corporate Taxes to Create More Jobs," *Bloomberg*, January 9, 2006, http://www. bloomberg.com/apps/news?pid= newsarchive&cid=hassett&sid= aZDVcYUY1j2c and "Laffer Curve Pays Billions If Obama Just Asks," *Bloomberg Business Week*, February, 13, 2011, http://www.businessweek.com/news/2011-02-13/laffer-curve-pays-billions-if-obama-just-asks-kevin-hassett.html; Robert Carroll, "Comparing International Corporate Tax Rates: U.S. Corporate Tax Rate Increasingly Out of Line by Various Measures," Tax Foundation, *Fiscal Facts*, No. 143, August 28, 2008, http://www.taxfoundation.org/ publications/show/23561.html; Duanjie Chen and Jack Mintz, "New Estimates of Effective Corporate Tax Rates on Business Investment," *CATO Institute Tax and Budget Bulletin*, No. 64, February 24, 2011, http://www.cato.org/pubs/ tbb/tbb_64.pdf, and Curtis Dubay, "Corporate Tax Reform Should Focus on Rate Reduction,"The Heritage Foundation, February 11, 2011, http://www.heritage. org/Research/ Reports/2011/02/Corporate-Tax-Reform-ShouldFocus-on-Rate-Reduction.

[2] See "Obama Backs Corporate Tax Cut If Won't Raise Deficit," *Bloomberg*, January 25, 2011, http://www.bloomberg.com/news/2011-01-26/obama-backs-cut-in-u-s-corporate-tax-rate-only-if-it-won-t-affectdeficit.html.

[3] See "Leader Cantor Unveils Pro-Growth Economic Plan at Stanford University," press release, March 21, 2011, http://majorityleader.house.gov/newsroom/2011/03/embargoed-leader-cantor-unveils-pro-growth-economic-plan-atstanford-university.html. See CRS Report R42624, *Moving to a Territorial Income Tax: Options and Challenges*, by Jane G. Gravelle, for a discussion of the Camp proposal.

[4] See CRS Report RL34229, *Corporate Tax Reform: Issues for Congress*, by Jane G. Gravelle and Thomas L. Hungerford, for a more general discussion of corporate tax issues. In general, the corporate tax contributes revenue and progressivity to the tax system as well as protecting the individual income tax base by preventing or limiting the use of the corporation as a tax shelter. It imposes costs in distortions in the allocation of capital between the corporate and noncorporate sector, the use of debt versus equity finance, and savings behavior. Although the tax creates a savings distortion, it probably has a limited effect on the size of the domestic capital stock, because of income and substitution effects.

[5] An arm's length price is the price that would occur for sales or asset transfers between unrelated firms.

[6] The combined rate without the production activities deduction is 0.392 which implies a state tax rate of 0.0646 (solving the equation 0.35+x(1-.0.35) = 0.392). With the production activities deduction the U.S. rate is 0.3185 and the combined rate is .3185+.0646*(1-.3185) = 0.363, or 36.3%.

[7] Calculated from OECD data. Corporate rates at: http://www.oecd.org/ctp/taxpolicyanalysis /oecdtaxdatabase.htm#C_CorporateCaptial; GDP at http://stats.oecd.org/Index.aspx?D ataSetCode=SNA_ TABLE1.

[8] Rate changes between 2005 and 2010 largely reflect the reduction in the German tax rate, although the U.K. rate also fell. However, these measures do not reflect changes in the base, which apparently provided some offsetting revenue. See Simon Kennedy, "Tax Cut War Widens in Europe," *New York Times*, May 28, 2997, http://www.nytimes.com/ 2007/05/28/business/worldbusiness/28iht-tax.4.5899993.html?_r=1.

[9] Calculated from data in Duanjie Chen and Jack Mintz, Corporate Tax Competitiveness Rankings for 2012, CATO Institute, Tax and Budget Bulletin, No. 65, September 2012, http://www.cato.org/sites/cato.org/files /pubs/pdf/tbb_65.pdf.

[10] According to Jennifer Gravelle, "Empirical Essays on the Causes and Consequences of Tax Policy: A Look at Families, Labor, and Property" (Ph.D. diss., George Washington University, January 2008), the effective property tax rate, which applies almost solely to buildings, is 1.59%. Multiplying this rate by the share of buildings in the capital stock (39.6%) and by one minus the tax rate of 36.2%, because these taxes are deductible, results in an overall rate of 0.4%. Assuming a pre-tax equity return of 12%, it adds about 3 percentage points to the rate. For information on property and wealth taxes in the European Union, which can be quite significant in some countries, see the documents at http://ec.europa.eu/taxation_customs/taxation /gen_info/economic_analysis/tax_structures/index_en.htm.

[11] Michael Devereux and Rachel Griffith, "Taxes and the Location of Production: Evidence from a Panel of US Multinationals," *Journal of Public Economics*, vol. 68, June 1998, pp. 335-367.

[12] For example, newspaper reports have indicated that Google and Forest Labs set up sales and production facilities in Ireland as part of a measure that ultimately caused profits to be realized in Bermuda. See Jesse Drucker, "Google 2.4% Rate Shows How $60 Billion Lost to Tax Loopholes," *Bloomberg*, October 21, 2010, at http://www.bloomberg.com/ news/2010-10-21/google-2-4-rate-shows-how-60-billion-u-s-revenue-lost-to-tax-

loopholes.html and Jesse Drucker, "U.S. Companies Dodge $60 Billion in Taxes in Global Odyssey," *Bloomberg*, May 13, 2010, at http://www.bloomberg.com/news/2010-05-13/american-companies-dodge-60-billion-in-taxes-even-tea-party-wouldcondemn.htm.

[13] See Congressional Budget Office, *The Budget and Economic Outlook, Fiscal Years 2013-FY2022*, January 2013, p. 85, at: http://www.cbo.gov/sites/default/files/cbofiles/attachments /01-31-2012_Outlook.pdf.

[14] For a roughly flat tax rate, the percentage reduction in revenues would be the same as the percentage reduction in rate, so multiplying by the ratio of the percentage point reduction, 10 percentage points, to the original rate, 35, provides an estimate of the revenue loss.

[15] Internal Revenue Service, Statistics of Income, Corporate Income Tax Returns for 2007, http://www.irs.gov/taxstats/ article/0,,id=170726,00.html.

[16] The lower number multiplies $125 billion by 1.057 and the higher number multiplies $125 billion by 1.34.

[17] See Congressional Budget Office, Reducing the Deficit: Spending and Revenue Options, p. 173 at: http://www.cbo.gov/sites/default/files/cbofiles/ftpdocs/120xx/doc12085/03-10-reducingthedeficit.pdf. The estimate for 2012-2021 was $100.6 billion while the baseline was $3.923 billion.

[18] Corporate rate cuts are not likely to be effective as a short-run stimulus. Several CRS Reports discuss the effectiveness of alternative tax provisions. See CRS Report R40104, *Economic Stimulus: Issues and Policies*, by Jane G. Gravelle, Thomas L. Hungerford, and Marc Labonte; CRS Report RS21136, *Government Spending or Tax Reduction: Which Might Add More Stimulus to the Economy?*, by Marc Labonte; CRS Report R41034, *Business Investment and Employment Tax Incentives to Stimulate the Economy*, by Thomas L. Hungerford and Jane G. Gravelle; CRS Report RS21126, *Tax Cuts and Economic Stimulus: How Effective Are the Alternatives?*, by Jane G. Gravelle; and CRS Report R41006, *Unemployment: Issues and Policies*, by Jane G. Gravelle, Thomas L. Hungerford, and Marc Labonte.

[19] If labor supply were responsive to wage increases, increased wages induced by capital flows could increase the size of the labor force, but evidence suggests that labor supply is relatively inelastic. See CRS Report RL31949, *Issues in Dynamic Revenue Estimating*, by Jane G. Gravelle, for a review of labor supply elasticity research.

[20] Jane G. Gravelle and Kent A. Smetters, "Does the Open Economy Assumption Really Mean That Labor Bears the Burden of a Capital Income Tax?" *Advances in Economic Analysis and Policy*, vol. 6, iss. 1, 2006, pp. 1-40. Results of simulations are on p. 25.

[21] An elasticity is the percentage change in quantity divided by percentage change in price and a substitution elasticity is the percentage change in the ratio of two quantities divided by the percentage change in the ratios of their prices. For the portfolio elasticity the ratio is between domestic and foreign assets relating to their relative after tax returns, while for the product substitution elasticity it is the ratio of the domestic and imported traded good as it relates to the relative prices. Other elasticities also appear in the model, which are generally set at 1; these include substitution between factors of production and products produced by the different sectors.

[22] This correlation requires a Cobb-Douglas production function, which has a unitary factor substitution elasticity.

[23] Congressional Budget Office, *The Budget and Economic Outlook, Fiscal Years 2012-FY2021*, January 2011, p. 87. http://www.cbo.gov/ftpdocs/120xx/doc12039/01-26_FY2011Outlook. pdf.

[24] *Economic Report of the President*, February 2010, p. 360, data are for 2006, the year before the recession began.

[25] This finding was reported by William Randolph, *International Burdens of the Corporate Income Tax*, Congressional Budget Office, Working Paper 2006-09, August 2006, http://www.cbo.gov/ftpdocs/75xx /doc7503/2006-09.pdf as well as by Jane G. Gravelle and Kent A. Smetters, "Does the Open Economy Assumption Really Mean That Labor Bears the Burden of a Capital Income Tax?" *Advances in Economic Analysis and Policy*, vol. 6, iss. 1, pp. 1-40. An earlier general equilibrium study found 84% of the burden fell on labor under these circumstances: John Mutti and Harry Grubert, "The Taxation of Capital Income in an Open Economy: The Importance of Resident-Nonresident Tax Treatment," *Journal of Public Economics* 27 (August 1985): 291-309. Their study assumes a production function with a much lower elasticity, so that the change in wage rate would be much larger than the change in overall output. This type of function allows a smaller percentage change in the capital stock to have a larger effect on labor income. Although their effects on wages are larger, their effects on capital inflows and total output are smaller. Another study sometimes mentioned is Arnold C. Harberger. Harberger's paper, "Corporate Tax Incidence: Reflections on What is Known, Unknown, and Unknowable," in John W. Diamond and George R. Zodrow, eds., *Fundamental Tax Reform: Issues, Choices, and Implications* (Cambridge, Mass.: MIT Press, 2008). That paper reports 130% of the tax falling on labor income, but the analysis is not really a model of the U.S. economy calibrated to observed values, but an illustration. The illustration assumes a much higher capital intensity in the corporate

traded sector relative to the economy as whole than evidence suggests. For a discussion of these four models and their underlying differences, see Jennifer Gravelle, *Corporate Tax Incidence: Review of General Equilibrium Estimates and Analysis*, Congressional Budget Office, Working Paper 2010-03, May 2010, http://www.cbo. gov/ftpdocs/115xx/doc11519/05-2010-Working_Paper-Corp_Tax_Incidence-Review_of_Gen_Eq_Estimates.pdf.

26 *Economic Report of the President*, February 2010, p. 362, data are for 2006, the year before the recession began. The share is calculated as the sum of compensation of employees plus 75% of proprietor's income, divided by the sum of compensation of employees, proprietor's income, corporate profits, rental income and interest income.

27 In economics parlance, the result would be a corner solution where a country produces only one, or a few traded goods.

28 The only other study that examines lower elasticities is that of John Mutti and Harry Grubert, "The Taxation of Capital Income in an Open Economy: The Importance of Resident-Nonresident Tax Treatment," *Journal of Public Economics* 27 (August 1985): 291-309. Their study still finds a large share of the burden falling on labor, but assumes a very low factor substitution elasticity that dominates the outcome and also makes it not possible to generalize about output effects from their incidence results. For a discussion of the role of the factor substitution elasticity as well as a review of the literature on elasticities, see Jennifer Gravelle, *Corporate Tax Incidence: Review of General Equilibrium Estimates and Analysis*, Congressional Budget Office, Working Paper 2010-03, May 2010, http://www.cbo.gov/ftpdocs/115xx/doc11519/05-2010-Working_Paper-Corp_Tax_ Incidence-Review_of_Gen_Eq_Estimates.pdf. This paper finds the portfolio and product substitution elasticities of 3 to be consistent with the evidence but suggests that the factor substitution elasticity should be somewhat lower, leading to a share of the tax falling on labor of around 40% but a smaller capital flow and a smaller total change in output.

29 Harry Grubert and John Mutti. (1994), "International Aspects of Corporate Tax Integration: The Role of Debt and Equity Flows," *National Tax Journal*, vol. 47, March, 1994, pp. 111–133.

30 If dividends are eventually to be taxed, then there is no obvious benefit to deferral because the income will either be taxed currently or taxed with interest in the future (and the present value of the tax will be the same). However, some income can be indefinitely deferred in the steady state to allow for growth, firms have developed techniques for repatriating without paying tax, and firms can use excess foreign tax credits from high tax countries to shield income from tax.

31 The residual tax rate on foreign subsidiaries of U.S. parents is 4%. See U.S. Government Accountability Office, *U.S. Multinational Corporations: Effective Tax Rates are Correlated With Where Income is Reported*, GAO-08-950, 2008.

32 To the extent that taxes in the United States are higher than elsewhere, there could be efficiency gains as well, although Gravelle and Smetters find these to be small. They find an efficiency gain of 3% of revenue for eliminating the tax entirely. Because the excess burden rises with the square of the tax rate, about half the gain, 1.5% of revenue, would occur with the first 10 percentage points. However, this gain accrues to the world (and the United States would presumably get only a share equal to its share of world GDP, or about one-half of a percent of revenue) and is measured assuming there are no other taxes. Given other countries have similar tax rates, the effect could disappear entirely or be negative. But in any case, it is small enough to be disregarded.

33 Jane G. Gravelle, "International Tax Policy: Are We Heading in the Right Direction?" December 2010, Forthcoming in the Proceedings of the National Tax Association.

34 This result is derived by maximizing the benefit to inbound capital K: $F(K) - r(1-t)K$ with respect to t, the U.S. tax rate, where $F(K)$ is a production function and recognizing that r and K are functions of t and r is the marginal product of capital.

35 This optimality rule maximizes the benefit to outbound capital, K, with respect to the foreign tax rate $(F(K) + r(1-tf)K$, where tf is the foreign tax rate.

36 As mentioned earlier, this study focuses on the income effects of international capital flows. Reductions in the corporate tax rate could produce welfare gains, largely through reduction in the debt-equity distortion and changes in the composition of consumption, effects that would occur in a closed economy. In CRS Report RL34229, *Corporate Tax Reform: Issues for Congress*, by Jane G. Gravelle and Thomas L. Hungerford, these costs are estimated at about 10% to 15% of the corporate tax. Based on revenues of 2% of GDP and the rule of thumb that the excess burden rises with the square of the tax rate, the gain would be 0.1% to 0.15% of output from ten percentage point rate reduction. These welfare tradeoffs do not rely on global economy considerations, and would largely not be experienced by an increase in income, but rather a decrease in risk and a more optimal composition of consumption.

[37] The rates are for 2009, which better reflect current tax rates. See Congressional Budget Office, *Analysis of the President's Budget*, March 2010, Tables 2.2 and 2.3, at http://www.cbo.gov /ftpdocs/112xx/doc11280/03-24-APB.pdf.

[38] This calculation uses the 2021 GDP of $24 trillion projected by 2021 and assumes capital is 3.5 times output, for a total capital stock of $84 trillion. The cumulative revenue loss of $1.2 trillion is 1.4% of this capital stock, and multiplied by 0.3 would reduce output by 0.42%. Multiplied by the tax rates of 0.237 and divided by the static loss of 0.65% indicates an increase in the revenue loss of 15%. Using the $1.5 trillion estimate, the calculation yields an additional revenue loss of 20% and adding debt service net of the feedback effects from capital inflows yields 23%. Projected GDP is from CBO data at http://www.cbo.gov /ftpdocs/120xx/doc12039 /Year-by-YearForecast_110125.xls.

[39] See CRS Report RL34229, *Corporate Tax Reform: Issues for Congress*, by Jane G. Gravelle and Thomas L. Hungerford. All of the studies were had methodological deficiencies due to lack of country fixed effects. One study did not find statistically significant effects in any case. The most sophisticated study actually found a much higher rate of 57% for a country like the United States. That study and another study were re-estimated using fixed effects and the statistical significant disappeared. This final study had an extremely short panel.

[40] See Kevin Hassett, "Laffer Curve Pays Billions If Obama Just Asks," *Bloomberg Business Week*, February, 13, 2011, http://www.businessweek.com/news/2011-02-13/laffer-curve-pays-billions-if-obama-just-asks-kevin-hassett.html.

[41] See Steven Matthews, "Tax Reform: An International Perspective," Power Point presentation at the American Enterprise Institute, February 25, 2011, http://www.aei.org/docLib /MatthewsTaxReform.pdf.

42 United States Department of the Treasury, "Treasury Tax Conference on Business Taxation and Global Competitiveness: Background Paper," July 30, 2007, at http://www.ustreas.gov /press/releases/hp500.htm.

[43] OECD, *Tax Policy Reform and Economic Growt*h, OECD Publishing., 2010, http://dx.doi.org/10.1787/ 9789264091085-en.

[44] For reviews of profit shifting, see CRS Report R40623, *Tax Havens: International Tax Avoidance and Evasion*, by Jane G. Gravelle. The estimates used include those of Christian and Schultz of $30 billion compared with corporate revenues of $151 billion in 2001, those of Sullivan of $26 billion compared with revenues of $187 billion, and those of Clausing and Avi-Yonah of $60 billion compared with revenues of $370 billion. Corporate revenue numbers are from CBO, http://www.cbo.gov/ftpdocs/120xx/doc12039 /Historical Tables[1].pdf. Because the rate cut reduces revenues by 31% to 38%, the offset is less than 100% even if all profit shifting ended. A more recent estimate by Clausing indicates a loss of 20% to 30% depending on the method used. See Kimberly A. Clausing, "The Revenue Effects of Multinational Firm Income Shifting," *Tax Notes*, March 28, 20011, pp. 1581-1586.

[45] See, for example, Government Accountability Office, *U.S. Multinational Corporations: Effective Tax Rates are Correlated With Where Income is Reported*, GAO-08-950, August 2008. Other evidence is discussed in CRS Report R40623, *Tax Havens: International Tax Avoidance and Evasion*, by Jane G. Gravelle.

[46] See Jesse Drucker, "Google 2.4% Rate Shows How $60 Billion Lost to Tax Loopholes," *Bloomberg*, October 21, 2010, at http://www.bloomberg.com/news/2010-10-21/google-2-4-rate-shows-how-60-billion-u-s-revenue-lost-to-taxloopholes.html and Jesse Drucker, "U.S. Companies Dodge $60 Billion in Taxes in Global Odyssey," *Bloomberg*, May 13, 2010, at http://www.bloomberg.com/news/2010-05-13/american-companies-dodge-60-billion-in-taxes-even-teaparty-would-condemn.htm.

[47] Calculated from OECD data. Corporate rates at: http://www.oecd.org/ctp/taxpolicyanalysis /oecdtaxdatabase.htm#C_CorporateCaptial; GDP at http://stats.oecd.org/Index.aspx? DataSetCode=SNA_ TABLE1.

[48] Calculations are made by dividing revenues by an estimate of corporate taxes adjusting for the credits, so the revenue base of $3,293 billion for FY2012-FY2021 is increased to $4,728 billion. This number divides corporate revenues by the ratio of $112 billion to $135 billion per year, which relates the estimate of the rate cut without considering the effects of credits to the midpoint between allowing foreign tax credits and not allowing them (recall those estimates were $120 billion and $150 billion on average).

[49] Estimates of depreciation as a percentage of revenues are from Jane G. Gravelle, "Practical Tax Reform for a More Efficient System, *Virginia Tax Review*," vol. 30, fall 2010, pp. 389-406.

[50] See Jane G. Gravelle, "Reducing Depreciation Allowances to Finance a Lower Corporate Tax Rate," National Tax Journal, vol. 64, December 2011, pp. 1039-1053; "Practical Tax Reform for a More Efficient System, *Virginia Tax Review*," vol. 30, fall 2010 , pp. 389-406;. Statement Before the Senate Committee on Finance, Tax Reform Options: Incentives for Capital Investment and Manufacturing, March 6, 2012, at: http://www.finance.senate. gov/imo /media/doc/Testimony%20of%20Jane%20Gravelle.pdf

[51] Estimates by the Joint Committee on Taxation as reported in Congressional Budget Office *Reducing the Deficit: Spending and Revenue Options*, March 10, 2011, http://www.cbo.gov/ftpdocs/120xx/doc12085/03-10-ReducingTheDeficit.pdf.

[52] Based on data in Joint Committee on Taxation, *Estimates of Tax Expenditures for Fiscal Years 2010-2014*, JCS-3-10, December 21, 2010, http://www.jct.gov/publications.html?func= startdown&id=3717. See also CRS Report R41988, *The Section 199 Production Activities Deduction: Background and Analysis*, by Molly F. Sherlock, and Jane G. Gravelle Statement Before the Senate Committee on Finance, Tax Reform Options: Incentives for Capital Investment and Manufacturing, March 6, 2012, at: http://www.finance.senate.gov /imo/media/doc/Testimony%20of%20Jane%20Gravelle.pdf.

[53] Jane G. Gravelle Statement Before the Senate Committee on Finance, Tax Reform Options: Incentives for Capital Investment and Manufacturing, March 6, 2012, at: http://www.finance.senate.gov/imo/media/doc /Testimony%20of%20Jane%20Gravelle.pdf.

[54] Estimates by the Joint Committee on Taxation as reported in Congressional Budget Office, *Reducing the Deficit: Spending and Revenue Options*, March 10, 2011, http://www.cbo.gov/ftpdocs/120xx/doc12085/03-10-ReducingTheDeficit.pdf.

[55] Estimate provided by Senator Ron Wyden, based on Joint Committee on Taxation scoring of S. 3018, 111th Congress.

[56] For revenue estimates and analysis of this provisions, see Jane G. Gravelle, "International Tax Policy: Are We Heading in the Right Direction?" December 2010, Forthcoming in the Proceedings of the National Tax Association. This provision should raise about $60 billion of revenue a year, much more than eliminating deferral alone. Note that further measures might need to be taken to prevent corporations from inverting (moving their headquarters abroad), although current rules are already in place that appear to have been effective in preventing these inversions.

[57] *General Explanations of the Administration's Fiscal Year 2012 Revenue Proposals*, U.S, Department of Treasury, February 2011.

[58] Estimates by the Joint Committee on Taxation as reported in Congressional Budget Office, *Reducing the Deficit: Spending and Revenue Options*, March 10, 2011, http://www.cbo.gov/ftpdocs/120xx/doc12085/03-10-ReducingTheDeficit.pdf.

[59] See CRS Report R40623, *Tax Havens: International Tax Avoidance and Evasion*, by Jane G. Gravelle, for a discussion. Other options include eliminating deferral and limiting tax credits for tax haven or low tax countries, requiring a share of foreign income to be repatriated, and formula apportionment.

[60] See "Obama Backs Corporate Tax Cut If Won't Raise Deficit," *Bloomberg*, January 25, 2011, http://www.newsmax.com/Newsfront/ALLTOP-BB-BNALL-BNSTAFF/2011/01/25/id/383906.

[61] Estimates by the Joint Committee on Taxation as reported in Congressional Budget Office, *Reducing the Deficit: Spending and Revenue Options,* March 10, 2011, http://www.cbo.gov /ftpdocs/120xx/doc12085/03-10-ReducingTheDeficit.pdf.

[62] Ibid.

[63] Ibid.

[64] This proposal would also repeal another method, the lower of cost or market, which is more difficult to justify.

[65] Most of these are discussed in Jane G. Gravelle, "Practical Tax Reform for a More Efficient System, *Virginia Tax Review*," vol. 30, fall 2010, pp. 389-406.

[66] Based on sums for FY2012-FY2014, reported in U.S. Committee on the Budget, *Tax Expenditures: Compendium of Background Material on Individual Provisions*, December 2010, compared with revenue projections as adjusted, for the same years. See http://www.gpo.gov/fdsys/pkg/CPRT-111SPRT62799/pdf/CPRT-111SPRT62799.pdf. Using these years avoids the effects of bonus depreciation.

[67] Joint Committee on Taxation, Letter from Thomas A. Barthold, October 27, 2011.

[68] *General Explanations of the Administration's Fiscal Year 2012 Revenue Proposals*, U.S. Department of Treasury, February 2011.

[69] See CRS Report RL34229, *Corporate Tax Reform: Issues for Congress*, by Jane G. Gravelle and Thomas L. Hungerford, for a list of provisions in H.R. 3970.

[70] See CRS Report RL34229, *Corporate Tax Reform: Issues for Congress*, by Jane G. Gravelle and Thomas L. Hungerford.

[71] United States Department of the Treasury, "Treasury Tax Conference on Business Taxation and Global Competitiveness: Background Paper," July 30, 2007, at http://www.ustreas.gov /press/releases/hp500.htm.

[72] To be revenue neutral, the new corporate tax plus the tax on after tax earnings of shareholders, which is $t(B+dB) +ts(1-t)dB$, where t is the corporate tax, ts is the tax at the shareholder level, B is the base and dB is the change

in the base, must be equal to the current corporate tax less the individual tax on the change in base. The calculations assume that four-seventh of the corporate steady state return is paid in dividends, that half of capital gains is realized and that none of the earnings are in tax exempt forms such as IRAs, 401(k)s or pension funds.

[73] Weighted marginal tax rate based on data by the Tax Policy Center, Table T10-0211, http://www.taxpolicycenter.org/numbers/displayatab.cfm?DocID=2787.

[74] Based on estimates provided in the FY2011 budget proposals, indicating a revenue gain of $344.4 billion, $233.3 billion for dividends and $111.1 billion for capital gains. See "General Explanations of the Administration's Fiscal 2011 Revenue Proposals," February 2010, at http://www.treasury.gov/resource-center/tax-olicy/Documents/ greenbk10.pdf. Because these changes do not affect the corporate base and interact with the corporate rate change, the estimate is the percentage of revenue times the tax rate. This estimate was for a year earlier, so was increased by 5% to reflect economic growth. These estimates assume a large realizations elasticity, and would be considerably higher if that elasticity were reduced to levels consistent with recent empirical research. Based on data in CRS Report R41364, *Capital Gains Tax Options: Behavioral Responses and Revenues*, by Jane G. Gravelle, Table 2, the capital gains revenue would increase from $13.9 billion in 2019 to $33.1 billion, if lower elasticties are used. That implies the $111.1 billion would be higher and would permit a reduction of 3.6 percentage points.

INDEX

A

B

C

F

G

H

I

R

S

Y